On the Brink

On the Brink

The Great Lakes in the 21st Century

DAVE DEMPSEY

Michigan State University Press
East Lansing

green press INITIATIVE

Michigan State University Press is a member of the Green Press Initiative and is committed to developing and encouraging ecologically responsible publishing practices. For more information about the Green Press Initiative and the use of recycled paper in book publishing, please visit www.greenpressinitiative.org. This title was printed on New Leaf EcoOffset 100 (100% post-consumer waste, processed chlorine free).

∞ The paper used in this publication meets the minimum requirements of ANSI/NISO Z39.48–1992 (R 1997) (Permanence of Paper).

Michigan State University Press
East Lansing, Michigan 48823–5245
Printed and bound in the United States of America.
10 09 08 07 06 05 04 1 2 3 4 5 6 7 8 9 10
LIBRARY OF CONGRESS CATALOGING-IN-PUBLICATION DATA

Dempsey, Dave, 1957–
On the brink : the Great Lakes in the 21st century / Dave Dempsey.
p. cm.
Includes bibliographical references and index.
ISBN 0-87013-705-0 (pbk. : alk. paper)
1. Lake ecology--Great Lakes. 2. Great Lakes—Environmental conditions.
I. Title.
QH104.5.G7D46 2004
333.95′28′0977—dc22

2004000271

Cover design by Erin Kirk New
Book design by Sans Serif Inc.

Cover photo (front): The industrial riches made possible by the convenient water route and adjacent mineral, timber, and other natural resources of the Great Lakes have also threatened the health of the ecosystem. In the 21st Century, the challenge for Great Lakes Basin residents and governments is whether they can learn from the past to assure that ecosystem health—the basis for prosperity—is central to policies and actions, not an afterthought. Photo courtesy of Great Lakes Sea Grant/University of Minnesota.

Cover photo (back): More than 30 years after its creation, Sleeping Bear Dunes National Lakeshore is considered a tourism asset as well as a reservoir of biological diversity important to the future of the ecoregion. Photo courtesy of Elizabeth Harris.

Visit Michigan State University Press on the World Wide Web at:
www.msupress.msu.edu

To my grandmother and grandfather,
and to my mother and father,
who first showed me the lakes,
and how to love them well—
who also introduced me to
politics and government,
and taught me how important
these are to saving our most cherished places.

Contents

Acknowledgments

No book is the product of one person's inspiration or perspiration. Others, though they may not know it, contribute all along the way in the years that it takes to conceive, research, and write a book. Several uncommon souls helped bring this book forward.

Lana Pollack, president of the Michigan Environmental Council, suggested to me the idea of a book about the Great Lakes and was instrumental in pruning some of the excess growth from this one. As she did throughout her career in the State Senate of Michigan, she somehow manages every day to juggle a thousand thoughts and projects without losing sight of the ultimate objectives—a cleaner, healthier environment and a more humane and just society.

Dr. Henry Regier, the former University of Toronto professor and Great Lakes fishery commissioner, helped guide my research and thinking in several important ways. While he bears no responsibility for my mistakes of fact or interpretation, he deserves the respect of all residents of the Great Lakes region for his career of intellectual and spiritual integrity in the service of ecosystem restoration.

Patrick Diehl, a longtime colleague at the Michigan Environmental Council, read every line of the manuscript and offered many useful suggestions to improve, and especially to shorten, the verbiage. A gifted writer himself, Pat is a stickler for proper usage and is fighting a (so far) successful battle in defense of the English language at MEC. My other MEC colleagues, too numerous to name here, are also examples of principle, intelligence, and passion in pursuit of environmental quality.

Professionals and advocates who contributed answers to specific questions and their helpful judgments included Michael Penskar, a botanist with the Michigan Natural Features Inventory; Sharon Hanshue and Kevin Kincare of the Michigan Departments of Environmental Quality and Natural Resources; Dr. J. R. "Jack" Vallentyne, retired from the Canadian Department of Fisheries and Oceans; Stephanie Burns, historian and active citizen; Lee Botts, a force of nature in the battle to protect the Great Lakes since the 1960s; and Margaret Dochoda, fishery biologist at the Great Lakes Fishery Commission.

The continuing example of advocates standing up for their piece of the Great Lakes ecosystem, or the vision of a unified and healthy whole, also inspired me. Some of these include Cameron Davis, executive director of the Lake Michigan Federation; Greg Reisig, tireless champion of valuable isolated wetlands in the Grand Traverse region of Michigan; Terry Swier, fighter of the Nestle/Perrier bottled water project in Michigan; Daryl Smith, information officer for the Ontario Ministry of Natural Resources, for providing information and photographs relating to the history of Rondeau Park; and Margaret Wooster, former executive director of Great Lakes United in Buffalo. I also want to thank the Joyce Foundation of Chicago, Illinois, not only for supporting research related to this book on Great Lakes governance issues, but also for that institution's longtime support of Great Lakes ecosystem protection.

Thanks also to the W. K. Kellogg Foundation of Battle Creek, Michigan for supporting research related to this manuscript.

My gratitude is owed also to Julie Loehr and Martha Bates of the Michigan State University Press, who believed in the manuscript and smoothed the way to publication.

I want to thank bighearted friends Derwin Rushing, Lois Debacker, Tom Vance, Joe VanderMeulen, Lisa Reed, Kathleen Aterno, Libby Harris, Marlene Fluharty, Carol Misseldine, Leslie Brogan, and Margaret Schulte. Finally, thanks to my brothers, Jack and Tom, who shared my first views of the Great Lakes from the back of a station wagon sometime in the early 1960s; to my sister-in-law, Suzzanne, who has enhanced the environment wherever she has lived; and to my nephew, Michael, and niece, Anna, both of whom inspire my supreme confidence in the possibilities of the twenty-first century.

Introduction

People don't experience public policies—just the results of them. They experience foul beaches, declining stocks of contaminated fish, tainted drinking water, skies yellowed by smog, wetlands smothered in concrete, plummeting Great Lakes water levels. Or, if the policies are shaped a different way, they enjoy honey-gold beaches, abundant fish that are safe to eat, clean drinking water, skies as blue as Lake Superior, wetlands that please the eye with vegetation and waterfowl, and Great Lakes levels that cycle in a predictable and mostly natural pattern.

In fact, people in recent times have experienced both.

Over the last century and a half, the inhabitants of the Great Lakes Basin, both Canadian and U.S. citizens, have contended with the results of laws and programs that have swung in a cycle of neglect and care following political laws more fathomable than those of the lake levels themselves.

Great Lakes fish stocks collapsed and their connecting channels clogged with human and industrial waste. The enactment of new laws and the spending of billions of dollars replenished the fish and perceptibly improved the quality of the water.

Wetlands bordering the lakes and their tributaries gave way to roads, factories, stores, and homes. The passage of wetland protection laws and the creation of wetland restoration programs helped retard the loss of wetlands and in a few locations began to restore them.

As industrial, resort, and second-home development galloped up and down the shores of the lakes, governments moved boldly to purchase some of the most spectacular and naturally valuable remaining places, preserving these crown jewels for all time.

Did this happen because of enlightened public leadership—because of visionaries in high places who thought long and hard about their obligations to serve future generations? In most cases, no. Instead, after decades of accepting or succumbing to the pressures of corporate and social elites who profited from the abuse and neglect of the Great Lakes, elected and appointed officials responded to an increasing public indignation about deteriorating conditions and a clamor for reform.

At least for a while.

Sometime in the 1980s, as Great Lakes conditions visibly improved and a new political fashion swept both sides of the border, the clamor died away. A struggling regional economy elevated economic development over the apparently less urgent problems of the lakes. As elected officials pounded away at the ineffectiveness, inefficiency, and evil of government, doubts about the ability of public institutions to work in the public's interest thwarted laws and programs. The number of two-income households increased, reducing the time many adults could devote to civic participation. The armies of deregulation and public disinvestment were freed to march in the dark.

But the disease of the Great Lakes Basin, it turns out, was *not* cured. Invasions of exotic species attracted the dismayed attention of scientists—and citizens, who crunched the shells of a 1988 arrival, the zebra mussel, while trudging on Great Lakes beaches. Dozens of people died and four hundred thousand were sickened when contaminants fouled the drinking water supply of Milwaukee in 1993. Seven people died and more than twenty-three hundred took ill in Walkerton, Ontario, in May 2000 after pathogens entered their drinking water supply. Its protection was undermined by government budget cuts and corner-cutting by the water utility. Great Lakes water levels fell to near historic lows in the late 1990s, prompting worry from shoreline property owners and all basin residents anxious about the future of the lakes.

All of these trends were related, in some way, to decisions made by public officials in Ottawa, Washington, D.C., Toronto, eight state capitals, and several thousand municipalities. The fact that these decisions are made in so many places—that what amounts to a single vast, international river basin is fragmented among a dozen large governments and thousands of smaller ones—is only part of the problem. The relatively small portion of the public engaged in debates over the Great Lakes is another. The most gallant, frustrated, or worried citizens in the lakes spoke out, questioned, organized, or proposed solutions to deal with the problems of the 1990s. But they were a precious few.

While the multiplying problems of the last decade can be traced in great measure to a growing gulf between citizens and their governments, there is nothing unique in kind about this period. A close look at the history of the Great Lakes since the mid 1800s reveals that the same governments have always done only what the public permitted, or pressured, them to do. When exploiting the lakes for immediate riches seemed the wisest course, when the struggle for survival distracted the public, or when the faith of the electorate flagged in the ability of governments to solve the problems of individuals as well as the collective, the lakes frequently deteriorated. But when the full-throated voice of the citizen rang true, both individually and in great numbers, the lakes recovered.

Unfortunately, the pattern of the past cannot hold in the new century. The new problems facing the lakes are not simply or easily cured. More than clean water acts and wetland protection laws will be necessary to combat the risks imposed by climate change, population growth, energy waste, and an economy that continues to reward, even subsidize, actions that sicken the lakes.

Another part of the pattern has changed. The relationship between the people and their governments is itself diseased. Cynicism about the motives of elected officials and the responsiveness of government to the problems of people is near all-time highs. The increasing dominance of government decision making by interests that benefit financially from exploitation of the Great Lakes system frustrates the public will. Time available in busy lives for concerned citizens to articulate and participate in the decision-making processes of their governments is scarce.

Finally, and perhaps most importantly, the vital connection between the daily lives of millions of Great Lakes inhabitants and the water system in which they live has been sundered. The busy worker who drives alone in a low-mileage sport utility vehicle fifty miles one-way to work may not connect the greenhouse gases he or she generates with long-term forecasts of significant declines in Great Lakes levels resulting from climate change. The homeowner who leaves a dripping faucet unattended for weeks and waters his or her lawn during the heat of the summer day might be surprised to realize that these actions increase the risk that Great Lakes water might one day be exported to other regions or continents. And the concerned but busy citizen who sits down once a year and writes a generous check to an environmental group seeking to protect the lakes may calm his or her conscience and in so doing lessen the chance for a true citizen uprising that will assure the Great Lakes will be protected in an enduring way.

While hard-won new laws and new programs will be helpful in protecting the future of the Great Lakes system, the ultimate protection of the lakes will not begin there. It will begin in the appreciation of millions of individuals who fondly call the lakes home or who visit and revere this singularly spectacular spot on the globe.

It will ripen with the cultivation of an ethic of place.

No one who has grown up among or visited the Great Lakes can fail to appreciate them. In winter they heave in fierce cold winds and groan under the restraint of crackling ice. In summer, to the hiker atop a Superior bluff or a swimmer standing on the shores of a Toronto or Chicago beach, they glimmer deep and seemingly infinite blue.

The widespread public appreciation of the lakes that is taken for granted today has developed over generations. In the early stages of European settlement, particularly after the mass immigration of American and Canadian citizens in the first half of the nineteenth century, the impulse to exploit, channel, dam, and dump into the lakes was at least as strong as the impulse to conserve, protect, and defend them. The balance of exploitation and appreciation has shifted in our day. But it is still possible to say that wherever the Great Lakes and the lands that drain into them have turned their face of beauty, they have inspired—and still inspire—both loving reverence and the will to manipulate and master.

A lasting Great Lakes ethic will mature in a respect for the fragility and complexity as well as the majesty of the world's largest freshwater system. When this respect comes to pass, the basin's inhabitants and visitors can collectively enact a reform more sweeping than any statute.

Saving the Great Lakes is not something to be left to others. It is not an overstatement to say that the Great Lakes are too important to be trusted to government. In fact, the Great Lakes are too important to be trusted to environmentalists. The boisterous, messy, entertaining, complicated, and hopeful history of the lakes teaches us that individuals have been the source of their cyclical comebacks. And the source, in turn, of their passion to make change happen has been a personal link to the lakes. To the fish. To the lighthouses. To the passing freighters and sunken shipwrecks. To the dunes. To the rookeries. To startling horizons and the great skies that reflect the waters below. To the wonder these things inspire.

This book traces the history of individuals and societies in the United States and Canada over the last one hundred fifty years coming to terms with the significance of the Great Lakes and the opportunity they represent for another kind of greatness. It looks forward to their most challenging century, in which that opportunity can at last be met.

But a straight narrative path, as out of place as a concrete sidewalk through a marsh, is not the best way to tell that story. The path winds. Like a trail along one of the great national or state parks overlooking Great Lakes vistas, it passes through high and low country, hugs the water's edge, and strays far from it.

Prepare to take the first step.

When I was a real little girl, my parents used to take me to the shores of Lake Michigan and up to Sleeping Bear Dunes. I have pictures of me in a blue pleated bathing suit with reddish blonde hair playing in the sand. I remember skipping stones. Dad taught me how to do it and it took a lot of practice and I remember getting up the following day and I couldn't move my arm because it was so sore.

—Stacey McDaniel

As teenagers [in Ontario's Niagara region] we paddled canoes, trying not to come in contact with the water itself, in the reservoir near the mouth of Twelve Mile Creek. These waters were subsequently developed as the course for the Henley Regatta. In the 1940s it was a huge cesspool into which raw industrial and domestic wastes from St. Catherines and Thorold were loaded. It was then almost completely deserted except for a few foolish teen-agers. . . . One summer in the early 1950s I was an electrician's helper in the General Motors Plant on the banks of Twelve Mile Creek. Dismantling old electrical equipment while innocent about any risks associated with unknown chemical contaminants, we washed our oily hands with PCB-laden fluid; some that we spilled undoubtedly still persists in the Creek's sediment.

—Henry Regier

Prologue

A Day at the Shore

It is a weekend summer day fifty years in the future, roughly as close to the present as the second year of the U.S. Eisenhower administration and the sixth year of the Canadian Liberal government of Louis St. Laurent. Fifty years ago, the U.S. Supreme Court ruled school segregation unconstitutional in *Brown v. Board of Education* and Senator Joseph McCarthy betrayed his recklessness and began his descent in congressional hearings televised throughout the United States. The movie *Rear Window,* directed by Alfred Hitchcock and starring Grace Kelly and James Stewart, was a smash hit. Toronto began operating its first subway line along Yonge Street. Montreal Canadiens hockey player Maurice Richard made $15,000 for his starring efforts on the ice, scoring thirty-eight goals. And work began on the Great Lakes–St. Lawrence Seaway, which would ultimately require the moving of 192.5 million cubic meters of earth, the building of 72 kilometers of dikes, and the digging of 110 kilometers of channels to permit oceangoing vessels entry to the heart of the North American continent.

It is a weekend summer day fifty years in the future, and a young Michigan family of four heads to the Historic District of Port Huron. They depart on an ultra-high-speed train from the north central zone of the District of Southeast Michigan, a sprawling metropolis of eleven million that comprises the former city of Detroit and dozens of its onetime suburbs. Having only one day for this vacation, the father and mother, Emilio and Katherine, have chosen a nearby destination. Port Huron has been an oasis for members of Katherine's family since the 1950s, when her great-grandfather and great-grandmother honeymooned in a motel along the St. Clair River. Through the generations, they passed down memories of sitting during the evening with a bottle of wine and two glasses in a second-floor balcony facing the river, contentedly watching freighters glide both north and south on their way to distant Great Lakes and ocean ports.

Although much about the river and the Great Lakes has changed, the family tradition persists. The freighters alone were not the source of family lore; Katherine's forebears remarked on the beauty and intrigue of gazing out over the water at a friendly foreign nation, Canada, only a few hundred yards distant. Even more compelling, they said, was the thought that almost all of the water draining from three of the world's largest lakes—Superior, Michigan, and Huron—was flowing through this narrow neck on its way to a faraway sea. Fifty years in the future, Canada is still there, and water still flows through the channel of what was once known as the St. Clair River. It is now, officially, the St. Clair International Goodwill Channel Project.

But both Emilio and Katherine anticipate dramatic differences in some conditions from those her twentieth century ancestors knew. For one thing, Canada is now not so foreign a country, not in the way Katherine's great-grandparents thought of it, anyway. Instead, Canada is a signatory to a goodwill agreement with the two-hundred-seventy-eight-year-old United States. Under the agreement, Canada provides ready and economic access to raw materials such as water and timber while the United States provides to its neighbor, at no other cost, defense from both foreign and internal security risks. While controversial since its inception, the pact has had its defenders. Both nations derive security: one the security of armed protection, the other the security of resources needed for its prosperity in a world facing natural resource scarcity. In turn, the United States has offered strictly regulated amounts of Great Lakes and other surface water to strategic allies in Asia and Africa to strengthen cooperative ties and for humanitarian purposes.

But these changes are geopolitical. They are not readily apparent to a touring family. There are more obvious changes, and the first sign of them comes when the train rises off what was formerly the boundary of Lake St. Clair, near the old city of St. Clair Shores. Instead of traversing open water, the twenty-mile train trestle offers a view to its passengers of scattered, manicured canals and wetlands, interspersed with state-of-the-art, multilevel housing built on platforms raised ten feet above dry patches in the former lake bed. Katherine murmurs something, and Emilio leans forward to ask what she said.

"There was some kind of fight over those houses," she tells her husband. "I know there were some Greens who thought the lake bed should be a public park."

"But what can you do when there are so many people?" Emilio says. They both nod.

After entertaining their daughter and son with electronic coloring books that feature extinct Great Lakes birds and animals for a few minutes, they look up to see the train nearing what was once the far shore of the former lake. From there it is easy to see, off to the right, the deep channel blasted and dug by the International Corps of Engineers. As water levels plummeted below the historic range in the Great Lakes beginning in 2016, responding to both climate change and growing water uses, governments and shipping industry leaders huddled, plotting solutions to preserve the commercial navigation industry. In addition to tens of billions of dollars needed to dig deep basins in many of the historic ports of the region, the corps and its supporters successfully recommended spending $40 billion in U.S. money to lower the bed of the St. Clair River, Detroit River, and Welland Canal by ten feet. Now a deep canal runs diagonally from northeast to southwest across former Lake St. Clair.

Another canal is barely visible from the train. It winds through a marshy area to the east, across the border, its water nourishing the marshes and waterways among the Walpole Island First Nation. Exercising its sovereign powers, this aboriginal community has successfully staved off repeated legal assaults on its claim to the water needed to sustain its ancient lifeways.

Some say the deep engineered channel slashing across the St. Clair lakebed lacks the grandeur of the open waters, while others point to the stirring symbol of ships continuing to pass undaunted from the upper to lower lakes. Is there not a beauty in this demonstration of human ingenuity? Katherine, however, briefly imagines a vanished time when pleasure boats scattered themselves across Lake St. Clair's one hundred sixty-four square miles, and even this small connecting lake offered a blue horizon to those looking west from Ontario or east from Michigan. Canada is now so close you can almost touch it, but this intimacy is too new to seem natural.

The ultra begins to slow, and the scenery begins to creep rather than race by. Katherine and Emilio alert their children to prepare to disembark from the train. If they miss this Port Huron stop, they warn, the family will be forced to ride all the way to the Zone of Toronto, another twenty minutes along the line. Given the time required to wait for a train heading the other way and the transit itself, that will waste much of their vacation day.

Raquel, their nine-year-old daughter, registers deep anxiety. Scrambling to assemble her electronic toys, she knocks one into the aisle of the train, where it is almost trampled by a passenger hurrying to the door. "I'm sorry. I'm sorry," she repeats, as her mother reassures her and Emilio deftly scoops up the toys. Jason, their seven-year-old son, looks on worriedly.

"It's all right," Emilio says as the train stops. "The driver will wait for us to get off." Sending a signal to the driver, he pushes a button in a tiny electronic assistant that he wears as previous generations wore wristwatches. But even if the message is received, they will have only an additional ten seconds to escape the train. Emilio and Katherine nudge their children forward, quickly overtaking the other disembarking passengers. The train stops. The door opens with a quiet hiss. All of the Port Huron–bound passengers step out.

As the children gawk in excited confusion at the cavernous station with its comforting facsimile sunlight, the parents clutch them by the shoulder and turn them toward the electric taxis waiting patiently in a row just a few strides below the train platform. Choosing the second taxi, they clamber inside and lower the composite plastic bubble over their heads. Emilio inserts a government-issued token, punches a computer code into a console directing the taxi to their destination, and the four sit back for another brief, exhilarating ride. Knowing exactly where to take them, the taxi flees the station, emerging into a yellowish day that would be scalding were the family not cooled by the gentle air purification devices in the taxi's walls.

A few seconds out of the station, as the family travels at a brisk sixty-two miles per hour, Jason says, "Are we there yet?"

Emilio leans over and admonishes him gently. “It’ll only be another half minute or so.”

The ride is in fact brief. Darting in and out of thick taxi and truck traffic with a deftness that would have been startling to twentieth-century automobile drivers who contended with daunting city congestion, the taxi leaves the old historic city behind and deposits the family at the base of the former Lake Huron. The bubble retracts and the four step out. The ninety-seven-degree air is, to the parents’ gratitude, low in humidity. A few other traveling families are scattered over the plaza, some sitting in a row of pods watching videos of the area’s history, others waiting for a return taxi.

Briefly disoriented, Katherine looks about before spotting a monitor that will have the answers she needs. “Over there,” she says, pointing to the monitor mounted in a steel pillar between advertisements for life extension surgery and advanced college placement for ten- to twelve-year-old children. She leads the family to the monitor and begins keying in her questions.

“Where is the site of the old Lake Breeze Motel?”

“How far is it to the Uncovered Shipwrecks?”

“Where did the Battle of Sarnia and Port Huron take place?”

The questions are scarcely entered before the answers are supplied both on the screen and on a small recycled and recyclable piece of paper that the machine coughs up. Scanning it, Katherine turns to face her waiting family. “Over there,” she says, pointing to a small square of elevated earth only a hundred yards away. “That’s where my great-grandmother and -grandfather spent their honeymoon. That’s where the motel was. Imagine watching the freighters go by from there.”

Emilio nods thoughtfully, Raquel scrutinizes the patch of soil for meaning, and Jason shifts impatiently. Following their father’s example, the children turn as he pivots to look out over the deep gorge that was once the river. As Katherine holds back, reading the paper again, the other three step to the base of a glass elevator. "Go ahead," she calls, and after Emilio taps a button, the door opens, the father, son, and daughter step inside, and they quickly rise fifty feet, where they have an impressive view of the canal. It is more like a great ditch than a river now. Continuing a channel also deeply dug out in the old lake bed to the north, it flows southward between thirty-foot concrete-reinforced walls. A single fifteen-hundred-foot freighter is riding the current toward Detroit and Windsor. Raquel raises her hand to wave at the vessel, but there is no one on deck to respond. The entire crew of three is stationed inside the pilothouse, adjusting computer controls to assure a swift, safe, fifteen-knot passage through the narrow gorge.

"What's inside that ship?" Jason asks of his father.

"Corn and wheat from northern Wisconsin and Minnesota and Ontario," Emilio says. "They feed the world with what's grown there. Crops grow a lot better there than they used to, before it got warmer."

Raquel takes an interest in the conversation. "Why'd it get warmer?"

Gesturing toward the stained sky, Emilio says, "Too many people, too much pollution. It kept the warmth from getting back out into space."

"Is it ever going to get cool again?" his daughter asks. Emilio can see the wondering look in her eyes; she is imagining the past and future.

He says thoughtfully, "I don't know. There are some people who want things to go back to the way they were, but there are some good things about the way we have it now. People don't die of the cold, and the blizzards don't come often to this part of the world, and it's easier to grow things."

"What do you think?" Raquel says.

Looking out to the north, toward the shrunken lake, Emilio says, "I think it's really sad that things have changed so much, but I don't know what we can do about it."

Pushing a button, Emilio sends the three of them back to ground level. Greeting them, Katherine says, "I'd like to look at the shipwreck." Her husband nods and the family walks to the far side of the plaza. This time their taxi will have a human driver. Special training and a license are required of those who transport tourists past the boundaries of the historic lake. Looking up hopefully from the tiny video screen he is clutching in his hand, the young surrey driver they approach says, "Need a lift?"

Katherine explains the destination and Bill, the African-American driver, nods. The four climb into an electronic surrey. It is make-believe, of course, but as they enclose themselves in the cab the driver switches on a program that displays an animated picture of a visored horse tugging a surrey of the nineteenth century. The program also jiggles the cab as though the horse was pulling them over cobblestones. Jason exclaims and his parents smile. "I've read about this in school," he says. Emilio takes a moment to tap a button on his assistant and scans the forty-odd messages whose summaries flit across the tiny screen.

The surrey takes only eight minutes to cover the nine miles north and slightly east of old Port Huron. The cab opens. The driver waits beside it, offering an assisting hand to the children and to Katherine. Intent on getting out, they do not look up until they stand on the elevated platform overlooking the Uncovered Shipwreck. But it is hard to know they are at their destination. The transition from present to past has been seamless. They look all around to see blue waters that are troubled only slightly by a breeze that induces whitecaps. The horizon is the flat blue of water, except for a thin black strip to the west. The sun shines benignly over them.

"Is this what it was like?" Katherine says, slightly embarrassed to sound like a child herself. But she cannot conceal her wonder.

The driver nods proudly. "Isn't the effect amazing? If you were in a boat at this spot at the turn of the century, you would have seen this all around you."

Katherine has been so entranced by the scene that she is startled when she hears a low moan from her son. "What is it?" she says, turning in alarm.

She finds her husband and daughter comforting her son, whose eyes have ballooned with fear. "It's scary. There's so much—space."

Stepping over to Jason, Katherine puts her arms around his shoulders. "It's all right. It's going to be all right. It's make-believe." She tries to coax him. "Look around a little more. It's really beautiful. It's peaceful out here, or it was."

Jason's anxiety slowly subsides, and the family steps forward at the driver's gentle beckoning. "If you'll come this way, I'll show you the wreck," he says.

They walk along the platform, escaping the lake scene by passing through a doorway. Again they are experiencing the genuine day. Taking a moment for their eyes to adjust, they are soon squinting in astonishment at the steel hulk of a vessel such as they have not seen except in history videos. Sitting below them in a barren sand trench, the wreck has been faithfully preserved as it was when uncovered by the receding Lake Huron waters fifteen years before.

"When did it sink?" Jason asks, fascinated.

The guide, eager to entertain the child, steps forward to answer. "In 1913, in one of the worst gales that ever blew up here in this lake. It was a November storm that took everyone by surprise. One minute it was warm, almost summerlike, but the next a wind- and snowstorm blew out of nowhere. The captain of this ship thought it was indestructible because it was one of the new modern steel ships, carrying iron ore. Like so many captains in that storm, he fought bravely to keep his ship afloat and get it to shore, but the *Charles* was too far out. It went down in the night. All twenty-nine hands were lost."

Both children exclaim. Emilio is proud that they each have a vivid imagination, a capacity for imagining distant times both past and future. "When the water went down, were there any bodies?" Jason asks eagerly.

"Jason," his older sister scolds.

"Oh no," the guide says. "It was over one hundred years before the ship became visible again. It was mostly this, the hull, with some holes in it."

All five are silent for a moment. Ignoring the arrival of another taxi, they contemplate the scene, trying to envision the night so long ago that twenty-nine men lost their lives. A reach of the spirit is required; a still-broad river lake lies just to the east, but the tamed blue surface of the remnant Lake Huron appears to pose few dangers. There have been no shipwrecks in over seventy-five years—and, Emilio and Katherine reflect, that is a good thing, after all.

Emilio checks his personal assistant and is saddened to see that they must return to Port Huron soon if they wish to keep their late lunch reservation and then return home in time for evening plans. "We have to head back now," he says to his family. Jason moans but his wife and daughter seem resigned and say nothing. Ushering them back toward the surrey, the guide asks whether they have any questions.

"Can you tell us about the Battle of Sarnia and Port Huron?" Katherine says.

"Yes, yes, tell us about that," Jason urges.

The driver agrees to do so, as soon as they are seated in the cab. Closing the dome over them, he assumes his driver's seat outside it but is able to communicate through invisible speakers installed in the walls. He explains that in the summer of 2039, as the permanency of lowered Great Lakes levels sunk in, property owners along the former shoreline of Lake Huron had angrily rebelled. They exploded with anger when an international scientific commission ruled that a full lake restoration program would be impractical and prohibitively expensive. The riches needed to reverse climate conditions, to pump stored groundwater from the land into the lakes, and to engineer higher lake levels with dams and gates were not available. Further, the deepening of the shipping channels by the two governments had already hastened the outflow of Great Lakes water and could not be corrected without huge cost.

"The Great Lakes will never be as they were," said the panel's final report. "They have always been dynamic and always will be."

Interpreting this as the ultimate rejection of their demands for the lakefront vistas their families had enjoyed for a century or more, the property owners blockaded the International Goodwill Bridge linking Port Huron and Sarnia and threatened to explode it. They insisted on construction of a dam below the bridge and the redirection of Arctic-flowing rivers into Lake Superior, feeding the entire Great Lakes system.

"It looked terrible for a while," the driver says. "The armed forces of both nations marshaled themselves to break the blockade. Many observers thought thousands of lives would be lost. There were dozens of cars and trucks on the bridge, and they and all the people were going to fall with it, people thought. But it was a blessing that a peacemaker emerged."

The children listen wide-eyed as the guide tells them of Ontarian William Harris, the premier who walked bravely up the span to meet with the armed, hostile property owners. Negotiating with the protesters for nearly twenty-four hours, he produced the compensation program that prevented bloodshed. "And so it ended well. The protesters got new homes in Pictured Rocks and Pukaskwa National Parks on the Lake Superior shore. They adapted. We have to adapt in a time of change."

The ride is over. It is time for a quick lunch at the Edison Café, where the kids can be entertained by holographic shows illustrating the same human ingenuity that Thomas Edison, once of Port Huron, so famously exhibited. Then will come the return trip home on the ultra. Climbing out of the surrey, Emilio hands the driver a computerized token, handsomely tipping him for the smooth ride and reassuring storytelling. "I wish we could stay and hear more from you," Emilio says.

"Come back," the young man says.

Emilio starts to follow his family as it heads to the restaurant on the far side of the platform but hesitates and turns back to the guide. "Is it really possible to see the ancient waterfall and rapids on the Canadian side of the lake?"

The guide smiles and nods. "Yes, that's why the lower lake is really a good thing. There's so much more to see."

Not sure he agrees but trying to draw heart where he can, Emilio thanks the guide again and hurries to overtake his family. The meal goes swiftly, Jason and Raquel barely touching their sandwiches of grilled Canadian wheat bread and cheese as they gape at the projected figures of athletes, musicians, and astronauts moving all around them.

After lunch, the family returns to the platform to take the ultra. They have to shoulder their way onto the train. It will be a crowded ride back to town, as so many workers are ending their one- or two-day vacations. But there is a note of grace. An older couple that has been occupying a private, glass-walled compartment spots them, emerges, and encourages them to take their place. Katherine tries to dissuade them, but they won't hear of it.

So the four enter the compartment and compare thoughts behind the closed doors.

"It was neat," Jason says.

"But I wish I'd lived two hundred years ago," Raquel proclaims. "I would have liked to see the lake the way it was then."

"We can rent a program," Emilio says, referring to the animation they could electronically download from their local public electronic library. It is said to create a vivid full-room panorama of a freighter ride on the Great Lakes, circa 1970.

But Raquel shakes her head impatiently. "No," she says. "I want it like it was then—now."

Emilio looks sad, and Katherine starts to say something but stops. What can you really say to such an impossible dream? she wonders.

For the remainder of the twenty-minute ride to their station, the family, even Jason, is quiet. They are seeing and brooding over things no one else in the train can see, ghosts of the past and doubts about the future. For some reason, they were born with a rare restlessness.

I grew up in the State of New York, within sight of Lake Ontario. If you'd have said to us, go fishing in Lake Ontario, we'd have said, are you crazy?

The harbor, if you called it a harbor, had about 20 or 30 slips, but it was never filled. To fish you had to go out beyond the dead alewives. By mid-May, you weren't thinking about going out on the water with all the algae. What did people think about these conditions? "That's the price of progress, that's the way it is."

When I grew up, the Great Lakes meant nothing to most people. You could come to our high school and get money to save whales. We'd never seen a whale. You couldn't have gotten a cent to help the Great Lakes. The personal value of the Lakes was near zero to most people.

I could have thrown a rock from the front door of our house and hit the lake, if I threw it hard. But my parents built a heated, inground swimming pool for us. It was another technological fix. Instead of fixing the lake, we got a pool.

One of the most amazing changes in my lifetime has been the comeback of the Great Lakes.

—William Taylor

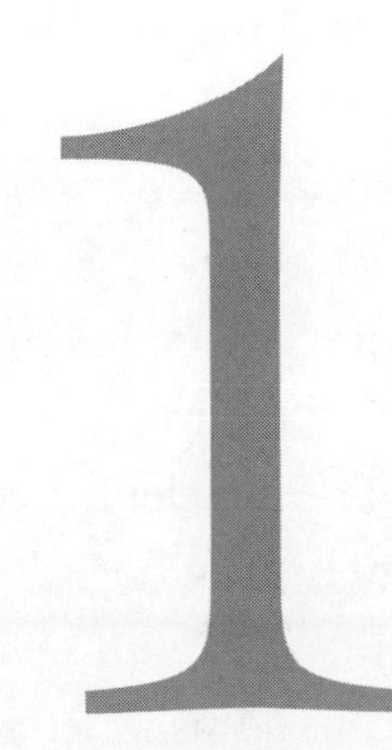

Dreams of Wealth and Glory

In November 1873 three men visited Grassy Island in the Detroit River, within sight of both the Canadian and U.S. shores, for the demonstration of a new technology. A man named Nelson W. Clark carried a large wooden box enclosing a zinc can about thirteen inches square and twenty-two inches deep. Inside the zinc can were ten trays containing fifty-four small boxes each.

At the island, George Clark furnished "the most perfect arrangements" for obtaining whitefish spawn. He placed two tanks, each about five feet in diameter, by the shore and filled them halfway with water. The two Clarks pulled whitefish from a net removed from the river and dumped them into the tanks. One of the men lifted the fish out of the tanks with a dip net while the other snatched the fish from the net and held them over an impregnation pan. One of the Clarks manipulated the abdomen of the fish. Applying a light pressure behind the pectoral fins to ripe females, he squeezed out eggs, which poured into the pan in a steady, liquid stream. A "pressure in the vicinity of the anus" inspired male fish to issue their milt into the water in one to three jets.

The men let the eggs in the pan and milt in the water stand for about half an hour. Then they poured off the milt and water, rinsing the eggs with several changes of water. As U.S. commissioner of fish and fisheries representative James W. Milner watched, the other men dipped a tablespoon into the eggs and counted about a thousand. After further lengthy preparations, the men put the eggs in the small boxes, the boxes in the trays, added a small quantity of water to the contents, and turned the case over to a baggage master for transport to a hatchery in Clarkston, Michigan, about thirty-five miles away. Milner guessed that about 1,330,000 eggs were thus put into the hatchery's troughs.

"The success attained by these persevering experiments is now complete, and the white-fish may be restored by artificial propagation, to the same extent as the salmon, or the brook-trout, or the shad," Milner reported. "The obstruction of streams is no obstacle in the way of their multiplication, because they have no necessity of ascending them, and unlike the trout and the salmon, they cannot be suspected of eating each other."[1]

It was then only about twenty-five years after commercial fishing had begun in earnest on the Great Lakes, but whitefish populations were plummeting to such an extent that a federal fisheries inspector had come to make a report. Ontario and the Great Lakes states were passing laws and devoting unprecedented attention to the condition of the suffering resource—and "artificial propagation" was becoming an accepted, even indispensable means of addressing a gap caused by overharvesting. For the first but not the last time in history, the seeming limitlessness of the Great Lakes was colliding with the actual limitlessness of human appetites.

For over two centuries, the Europeans who explored the lakes region, colonized it, and settled it had been dreaming about the possibilities of the great chain of freshwater seas that dwarfed the lakes of their homelands. Contemplating the open water horizon the way American and Canadian settlers of the 1800s contemplated the vastness of sky and land called the Great Plains region, these early visitors would project onto the lakes their hopes for wealth and glory. In this they tailored a pattern that has shaped the history of the Great Lakes to the present day.

Before the Europeans arrived, native cultures had inhabited the region after the retreat of the glaciers about twelve thousand years ago, leaving traces of their civilization but not fundamentally altering the environment. By about seven thousand years ago, a people of the Old Copper Culture were in place and continued to live across a wide part of the region for over three thousand years, developing the birchbark canoe, rudimentary agriculture, and small communal settlements. Their name derives from the assumption that they were the first miners of the Lake Superior region's abundant deposits of nearly pure copper. For thousands of years, early Americans mined copper from dozens of locations in the Lake Superior Basin, leaving behind tools and traces of campsites.[2] Copper weapons and jewelry fashioned during this period have been found not only in the lakes region, but also at great distances east and south, implying they were part of a continental trade.

About three thousand years ago, people of the Woodland Culture began to dominate the Great Lakes. Developing agriculture in the region extensively for the first time, they crafted pottery and constructed mounds, a few of which survive today. Despite the crops they cultivated, they subsisted to a large extent on fish and game. Their skill in fishing was the finest in aboriginal North America, said one researcher. While the Copper Culture peoples relied on spearing and gaffing from weirs, those of the Woodland period developed great expertise at netting fish, including the deployment of gill nets in deep water. "The northern Great Lakes fishery was unique in North America and a vitally important subsistence enterprise in the region," said historian Charles Cleland.[3]

Native population never grew much beyond fifty thousand throughout the Great Lakes. By the sixteenth century notable tribes around the Great Lakes included people now called the Odawa (Ottawa), Potawatomi, and Ojibwa (Chippewa or Anishinabek). Though meeting the Europeans with mixed feelings of wonder, fear, and mistrust, the natives of the Great Lakes often cooperated with the new arrivals in satisfying their curiosity about the region's geography and resources.

Etienne Brule, a scout for Samuel de Champlain, is generally thought to have been the first modern European to behold one of the lakes in approximately 1610. Brule spent over twenty years among the native peoples that he had befriended while pursuing France's commercial ambitions for the lakes before they killed him as a traitor. Yet, he left no record of his thoughts or impressions on encountering Lake Huron's Georgian Bay. Nor did his master, Champlain, "the first important white man in history to view" the waters of one of the lakes, turn lyrical when he looked out over the same bay in 1615:

> Champlain went into no ecstasies; he recorded no visions of the future; he erected no cross and emblazoned no arms. He only said that the blueberries and strawberries were plentiful, that his savages gathered some squashes, and that they came in handy because these improvident tribesmen, though eating but one meal a day, had as usual gorged all their food and were already facing want in this long journey. It is disappointing. The Royal Geographer, looking for the first time upon one of the mighty lakes of the earth, upon the central waterway of what was to be

the richest and busiest region of the world, wrote in his journal that he had found—squashes![4]

But others would soon compensate for Champlain's lack of grandiosity. While not always articulating their expansive visions, the French and English who swarmed over the Great Lakes region later in the century began to people it with their restless wants and ambitions.

At first the grail they sought was a passage from the farthest end of the lakes to the exotic land of Cathay. Much like twenty-first-century Western capitalists who are rejoicing at the thought of selling to the world's greatest market, almost two billion Chinese, these men sought the Northwest Passage to a land of fabulous potential commerce and profit.

As far back as the 1520s the French had sought a navigable waterway to Asia. Giovanni da Verrazano had instead blundered into the Atlantic Coast of North America. But the dream didn't die. In 1634 Jean Nicolet, another of Champlain's young braves, floated west through the Straits of Mackinac to Green Bay, disembarking from his canoe in a mandarin's robe, expecting to meet the dignitaries of Cathay instead of the Winnebago people that he actually encountered.[5]

In about 1669, still hoping to pinpoint the mythical passage, Pierre-Esprit Radisson and Médard Chouart Sieur des Groseilliers sneaked out of the colony at Trois-Rivières, Quebec, and traveled to Lake Superior by way of the Ottawa River, northern Lake Huron, and the St. Mary's River. After spending a brutally cold winter among the natives, they found no water route to Asia but instead a robust population of beaver. They returned to Montreal in the late summer of 1661 with approximately three hundred canoes loaded with beaver pelts, the largest such shipment until that time. Briefly jailed by the French authorities for violating a law against fur trading without a license, the two men went on in anger to open the Hudson Bay region to the fur trade in the name of England. But they had started a rush among the Great Lakes they left behind.

In 1750 the Frenchman Saint-Pierre departed Quebec "to achieve the discovery of the Western Sea." In 1766 Englishman Jonathan Carver traveled the lakes from Oswego to Detroit and through the Straits of Mackinac to Green Bay, and thence to today's Grand Portage, Minnesota, hoping to "discover" a major river leading west to the Pacific from the center of North America, providing a route for commercial fortune and glory for himself and His Majesty the King.[6] But the bulk of the effort among both French and English alike in the lakes region had shifted to the attainment of another object: the riches of fur.

Although the fur trade would span the continent, reaching from northern California to the Arctic, "the center of this immense, far-flung industry—its soul and throbbing heart—was always the Great Lakes Basin. Geography guaranteed that."[7] Providing a convenient route to the center of the continent at a time when land roads were primitive and railroads nonexistent, the lakes were not so much the source of wealth as the necessary avenue to reach it. In this sense they served the interests of capital the way they would serve, in a later age, as a highway for the shipment of grain and iron ore or as a receptacle for manufacturing's most noxious by-products—as a tool rather than a home.

Lasting from the latter decades of the 1600s through the first decades of the 1800s, the Great Lakes fur-trading era is remembered with romanticism. There is plenty of it in the tales of the voyageurs, the small but powerful men who paddled the canoes that retrieved the pelts from the far West and returned them to Quebec, from where they were shipped to Europe:

> Read the diaries of the Montreal fur-traders and the books of travelers on the St. Lawrence, the Saskatchewan, and

> the Great Lakes in the eighteenth and early nineteenth centuries. From their pages peal the laughter of a gay-hearted, irrepressible race; over night waters floats the plaintive song of canoe-men, swelled periodically in the chorus by the voices of his lusty mates; portage path and campfire, foaming rapids and placid fur-fringed lake; shallow winding stream and broad expanse of inland sea.[8]

But while the lifeways of the voyageur have long enchanted historians, the growing hunger of the industry he served consumed most of the natural wealth it sought to transform into money. The beaver population was nearly wiped out over a vast region that included and transcended the lakes. Its decline was hastened by the single-minded ingenuity of businessmen such as John Jacob Astor, "the paradigm of the classic American tycoon."[9]

Born in Germany in 1763, Astor migrated to New York City in 1784. He opened a fur shop in the city several years after his arrival, soon turning his eyes to the bounty of the Northwest. He sought furs in upstate New York and later traveled to Montreal to purchase furs. Finally, sensing the potential of the trade, in 1794 he joined the voyageurs on their eighteen-hundred-mile paddle nearly to the headwaters of Lake Superior, at today's Grand Portage, Minnesota. Learning there of the abundant furs available in the wild lands of western North America beyond, he determined to make his fortune. In 1808, when he formed the American Fur Company, extending his reach to the coast of Oregon explored by Lewis and Clark only five years earlier, Astor sought to dominate the industry. He failed in his Pacific Northwest adventure, ultimately concentrating his energies in the Great Lakes trade. After the War of 1812, Mackinac Island became a regional fur capital, as tens of thousands of furs traveled through the post there. Astor died in 1848 worth an estimated $20 million, making him the richest man in the United States.

But Astor left another kind of imprint. "An arrant individualist, selfish, narrow-minded, quite blandly antisocial, he went after whatever he sought and took it by fair means or foul," said one observer.[10] His dominating company also depleted the wildlife on which it depended and wrecked the native cultures that had been drawn into the trade, supplying first the French, then the English, and then the Americans with the resource they desired.

Far from an exercise in free market economics, the trade flourished in large part because of the support of monarchs, statesmen, and their governments. National military might was exercised to claim the commercial capacity of the inland seas. King Louis XIV backed the French trade by building and enlarging forts and establishing settlements, including Detroit.[11] Rival colonial power England went to war to control the Great Lakes transportation route, leading to a military confrontation that culminated in a British victory at Quebec City in 1759. England's American colonies went to war with the mother country in 1776, and the new United States fought pitched battles with England throughout the lakes region in the War of 1812. The result of the latter conflict was the division of four of the five Great Lakes roughly down the middle, separating the United States and Canada just as the fur trade ceased to be the impetus for the region's economy. But government intervention in and support for exploitation of Great Lakes resources was just beginning.

In the United States, there was the matter of which states would get access to the Great Lakes, not because of their beauty, but because of the value of their shores as potential avenues of commerce. To accommodate the dreams of boosters hoping to turn natural harbors into great ports, the existing and would-be states clawed at the Great Lakes like rock climbers grasping for handholds. To claim access to Lake Erie, Pennsylvania paid the national government $151,640.25 in 1792, acquiring the so-called Erie Triangle, including the harbor of Presque Isle. The

Northwest Ordinance of 1787 had defined the bottom tip of Lake Michigan as the southern boundary of the northern states to be carved out of the land of the Old Northwest. But before admission to the Union in 1816, Indiana insisted on claiming forty-five miles of Lake Michigan shoreline from Michigan Territory, helping foster one hundred fifty years of determined effort to construct a world-class commercial port. The border of Illinois was adjusted forty-one miles northward before its statehood in 1818, giving it possession of Fort Dearborn, today's Chicago. The final dispute over Great Lakes access between the states erupted in 1835, when Michigan and Ohio nearly went to combat over the "Toledo strip." A surveyor's error had incorrectly placed a line running directly east from the southern tip of Lake Michigan north of Toledo when it should have run south of the harbor. The error shorted Michigan of four hundred sixty-eight square miles of land to which it thought it had rights. But to win admission to the Union in 1836, Michigan ceded its claim to the strip, receiving extensive lands in the western Upper Peninsula as compensation.[12]

Settlers quickly began to crowd into the region. European settlement accelerated first in today's Ontario. American colonists still loyal to the Crown fled the United States in the 1780s and 1790s to settle along Lakes Ontario and Erie. The provincial governor settled over six thousand refugees and soldiers along the two lakes in 1783 and 1784 with free land grants ranging from one hundred acres for a civilian head of family to one thousand acres for commissioned officers.[13] Six Nations natives, allies of the new Canadians, got a reservation along the Grand River. When the British Parliament divided old Quebec into Upper and Lower Canada in 1791, Lieutenant Governor John Graves Simcoe of Upper Canada speeded the settling process. Free land continued to be the enticement to lure settlers; after the end of the Napoleonic Wars, English immigration to Upper Canada mushroomed. Between 1830 and 1833 its population in doubled.

On the U.S. side of the border, development lagged briefly, but the opening of the Erie Canal in 1825, coupled with even more liberal land policies than those furnished to the settlers of Upper Canada, soon took care of that. Populations of the Great Lakes states and territories grew at startling rates. Becoming a state in 1803 with 45,365 inhabitants, Ohio exploded to a population of 1,519,467 in 1840. The number of Wisconsin residents grew from 11,683 in 1836 to 305,390 in 1850. Finding the southern lands of the Great Lakes well suited for agriculture and the northern lands rich in timber, the settlers cleared the land as quickly as possible. With the land fast developing thanks to the subsidies and encouragement it had provided, government stepped out of the way. The ransacking of the region's resources would within a few decades terminate the new laissez-faire approach. The first victims of government's neglect of the Great Lakes public trust would be the fish.

The Living Relic

VISITING GREEN BAY IN 1871, U.S. COMMISSIONER OF Fish and Fisheries James W. Milner wrote, "The sturgeon are taken in great abundance in this region, and are almost universally destroyed. They come into the nets in great numbers in the early fall, and are pulled into the boats with the gaff-hook, and thrown upon the offal-heap."[14] Milner lamented the loss of thousands of pounds of food every year and recommended that the fishermen of Green Bay learn something from the Schacht Brothers of Sandusky, Ohio, who had learned to manufacture a "superior substitute for halibut," caviar, isinglass, and oil from the once-despised sturgeon.[15]

Like conservationists of the present era, Milner anchored his arguments for lake sturgeon protection not in the beauty of the fish—for only discerning eyes can appreciate that beauty—but in its usefulness. He argued that sturgeon, like so many fish of the Great Lakes, could be a crop. Today, the primary crop sturgeon raise is wonder. Growing regularly to more than five feet, weighing as much as three hundred pounds, and sometimes living longer than human residents of the basin, they are survivors of the worst that life can throw at them.

The lake sturgeon's ancient lineage is evident in its design. Its sharklike tail, bony armored plates, and long snout suggest its coexistence with the dinosaur. Belonging to a family of fishes that dates back over one hundred thirty million years, it has apparently changed very little in appearance in a long time. So perhaps it was revulsion as much as annoyance that prompted early commercial fishermen in the Great Lakes to kill, dispose of, and even burn sturgeon by the tens of thousands. What the anglers said was that the large, ungainly sturgeon damaged nets and interfered with their efforts to haul in the prized whitefish.

Before the commercial value of the sturgeon was recognized, the slaughter of the species undermined it. But the discovery of its commercial worth almost doomed it. In just ten years, ending in 1905, the combined U.S. and Canadian harvest of sturgeon in Lake Erie fell 80 percent. The population of the sturgeon in 2004 is thought to be 1 percent of its historic abundance.

The same characteristics that equipped the lake sturgeon to survive the extremes of natural cycles before the influence of humankind brought it to the brink of extinction in the Great Lakes. Longevity is an asset in most ways; males frequently live fifty to sixty years, while one female is thought to have lived one hundred fifty years. But with it comes a price. Female sturgeon take longer to mature sexually than their human counterparts—generally reproducing first between the ages of twenty and twenty-six. They spawn only once every four to nine years, males once every two to seven years. One fisheries manager says sturgeon are "docile as lambs" when spawning, thus making them vulnerable to human predators.[16]

There are other concerns. Living long in the modern Great Lakes requires sturgeon to outrun or outwit dams, pollution, habitat loss and degradation, poaching, and other threats. Fisheries biologists on both sides of the international border are working collaboratively to help the sturgeon in this work.

The scarcity of the fish limits the allowable catch and shortens fishing seasons. Michigan anglers, for example, can keep one large fish each season if they fish the waters of Lake St. Clair and the St. Clair River, a take not believed harmful to a local population the state Department of Natural Resources pegs at more than twenty thousand. But only five fish can be taken in an annual spearing season in Cheboygan County's Black Lake that lasted thirty-five minutes in 2001.

The sturgeon has now developed its own cultlike following. On Wisconsin's Lake Winnebago, anglers spend up to ten hours a day in ice shanties waiting for a chance to spear the single fish they are allowed to take. One of them, according to a 1999 report, had spent thirty-three winters this way without ever seeing, let alone taking, a sturgeon. "Sturgeon spearing is tantamount to religion in these parts," said Wisconsin Department of Natural Resources fisheries biologist Kendall Kamke.[17] As Michigan's Black Lake sturgeon swim upstream to spawn in the Black River during April, dozens of volunteer guardians, organized by a group called Sturgeon for Tomorrow, patrol the riverbanks to watch for poachers.

Signs of a slow recovery suggest the lake sturgeon may be defeating the most difficult adversary it has faced in tens of millions of years: the destruction and negligence of man. In September 2000 an eighty-pound, seventy-three-and-one-half-inch sturgeon washed ashore from Lake Erie in North East, Pennsylvania. The population in Wisconsin's Lake Winnebago has quadrupled in the last forty years, a success attributed to good biological management and strong law enforcement regulation. Small, young sturgeon are beginning to appear in other traditional habitats.

"The more I learn about sturgeon, the more I'm fascinated by them," says Michigan Department of Natural Resources Fisheries Division supervisor Sharon Hanshue. "World-wide the group is under terrible threat of extinction, yet they've managed to survive longer than just about anything else on the planet. What does that say about them—and about us, eh?"[18]

Still, sturgeon numbers in various reaches of the lakes fluctuate, and human knowledge of its feeding habits and other elements of its life cycle is imperfect. Its comeback is still tenuous, and its fate will be a measure of the health of the lakes and the people who live among them.

In August 2001 three anglers in the St. Mary's River near Sault Ste. Marie huddled in the front of their fishing boat when a four-foot-long sturgeon jumped into it. After calming, they snapped photos of the fish and released the sturgeon to the river. It's doubtful the sturgeon was jumping for joy, but the peaceful escape of the sturgeon—described as the "ugliest fish I've ever seen" by one of the anglers—is a reason for hope.[19]

I remember listening to the fog horn, a lake reminder no matter where you were, in the house, outside, a constant many days of the year. We would go out on the breakwater to check out the lighthouse and fog horn, sometimes daring to see if big waves would wash us off.

I also remember the cold of the lake all summer long. We just lived a few blocks from Lake Michigan and you could feel the lake even on hot days. Going just a few miles inland made a big difference.

We'd swim almost daily. The only way to go in was all at once, endure the shock, then adjust and play for a long time. There were an abundance of sand bars along the shore there and we'd swim past the deep section until you could stand up again. I also remember all the sawdust piled up on the shore, washed away from the many sawmills on the rivers or along the lakes. Manistique Paper also emitted something that smelled really bad and made the water close by ugly.

I don't think I took Lake Michigan for granted. It was always a force in our lives. I didn't always appreciate it, though, and often cursed it in the summer for the chill that eked into most days. The fishing boats, the docks, the tourists, the sound of the waves all were parts of life that reminded me of the lake. I also loved it for swimming and the endless shoreline that led to a quiet place only visited by deer, shorebirds, seagulls, and a big natural family free of human imprint.

—Paul Babladelis

Failing the Fish

Early European observers of Great Lakes fish were almost unanimous in striking a note of dumbfounded wonder at the sheer abundance of aquatic life. In the seventeenth and eighteenth centuries, French commandants and Jesuit priests marveled at the size and number of the fish pursued and harvested by native peoples throughout the upper lakes.

The St. Mary's River, linking Lake Superior with the lower Great Lakes over a rocky bed, particularly astonished observers. "This river forms at this place a rapid so teeming with fish, called white fish, or in Algonkin *attikamegue,* that the Indians could easily catch enough to feed 10,000 men," reported Rene de Brehant de Galinee after an expedition in 1669 and 1670.[1] Almost two hundred years later, American Charles Lanman reported of the fish at the Falls of Saint Mary:

> You may accuse me of telling a large story when I speak of boat-loads of *trout,* but I do assure you that such sights are of frequent occurrence at the Sault. My favorite mode of trouting at this place has been to enter a canoe and cast anchor at the foot of the rapids, where the water was ten or fifteen feet deep, but owing to its marvelous clearness appeared to be about three, and where the bed of the river or strait is completely covered with snow white rocks. I usually fished with a fly or artificial minnow, and was never disappointed in catching a fine assortment whenever I went out.[2]

A few decades later, such natural plenty was largely a memory. "In 1830," remembered George Clark late in his life of an Ohio stream feeding Lake Erie, "Maumee River probably afforded more fresh-water fish, and more varieties, than any other river known. There were some thirty odd varieties, of which the wall-eyed pickerel were the principal fish, some weighing from twelve to eighteen pounds. Maskinonge, pike, white and black bass, catfish, and many other species were caught, salted and sold fresh each year for food, amounting to some thousands of barrels yearly."[3]

The decline of a once awe-inspiring fishery moved west with the pioneer generations. By the dawn of the nineteenth century officials were finding it necessary to author (although not always to enforce) fish conservation laws. In 1801 New York legislators passed statutes limiting obstructions to the seasonal migration of the native Atlantic salmon from Lake Ontario to their spawning grounds in tributary streams.[4] The legislative council and assembly of Upper Canada enacted in 1807 and 1821 laws prohibiting the setting of nets, weirs, and other devices to take salmon or fry in or at the mouths of Lake Ontario tributary creeks or rivers and prohibiting torchlight fishing and spearing of salmon. In 1857 the legislature of Upper Canada gave protection to waterfowl and passed more stringent fish protection laws, with some enforcement power, in 1857 and 1858.[5]

But these early actions often collided with the desire of entrepreneurs to build dams to harness river power and of commercial anglers to maximize harvest and profit in the short run, with fish the losers. One of the most dramatic early losses was the extirpation of the native Atlantic salmon of Lake Ontario, which disappeared by 1900. Part of a legendary species whose range once encompassed the North Atlantic Ocean and its freshwater tributaries as far south as Connecticut in North America, and from Russia's White Sea to Portugal in Europe, the salmon was highly prized as food, but also for its mystique, a silver streak leaping high to scale small waterfalls on its journey home to spawn. Dams, other habitat alteration, and pollution contributed to its early demise. As early Canadian fish culturist Samuel Wilmot noted of the creek in which he first proposed stocking the salmon:

> But now the forest has disappeared by the labour of the husbandman, laying bare the face of the country to the rays of the sun and general influences of the atmosphere, which by the process of absorption and evaporation have almost wholly dried up the numerous springs and rills, which were the original feeders of the creek. This has also diminished the flow of water fully one-half, and increased its temperature to such an extent during the spring and summer months as to create enormous quantities of infinitesimal spores for growth of fungi and other deleterious matter. . . . These and other causes, which neither time nor space will admit of entering into here fully, had well nigh exterminated the salmon from the waters of Ontario.[6]

Laws were not the same as protection either then or now. Implementation was checked by lack of funding and the use of fisheries officer positions as political plums. Members of Parliament named candidates for the Canadian jobs. In a typical case, a Conservative member recommended his brother and another man for appointment, complaining that salaries of $200 to $300 a year weren't adequate to attract good men to the job. A Liberal administration removed the brother from his job four years later for neglect of duty.[7] Willingness of the fisheries officers to apply regulations was uneven at best. Anglers typically used double the net allowed by their licenses, according to the 1888 report of one fisheries officer, but this was a tacitly accepted practice. Inadequate funding also prevented the Canadian fisheries officers from obtaining needed equipment; until 1888 they patrolled in rowboats or sailboats.

Early enforcement of fish conservation regulations was also unpopular. The Ohio fish commission observed in 1873, "It does not accord with the prevalent ideas of humanity to imprison a person for obtaining food from 'nature's preserve,' especially when that 'preserve' is not private property."[8] A story is told of William Gibbard, who in 1859 became a part-time fisheries overseer for the Lake Huron and Superior district of today's Ontario. A believer in regulation as a means of protecting the native fish populations, he generated a wealth of enemies. On an 1863 expedition to Manitoulin Island in northern Lake Huron, where he sought to intervene in a dispute over a fishing lease, he disappeared overboard at night from the ship on which he was returning to Collingwood. His bruised body washed up on shore days later. A coroner's inquiry later determined his death the result of foul play, although no culprit was ever identified.[9]

The confederation of Canada in 1867 indirectly undermined fisheries regulations for almost thirty years, during which the federal government had responsibility for fisheries management but did little on their behalf. In 1899 Ontario regained primacy in the field by virtue of a Privy Council ruling and a subsequent enactment by Parliament, but it was years longer before fish conservation made a serious difference.

As fishing pressure exploded on both sides of the international boundary, as dams and impoundments multiplied, and as enforcement of the laws faltered, both commercial anglers and public officials began to beat a drum of alarm. A Canadian fisheries overseer, John Kerr, testified before a House of Commons select committee in 1869, "All the Salmon have been destroyed in consequences of the contraventions of the Fishery laws."[10] The Wisconsin Fish Commission told in 1875 of a decline of at least a quarter in fish harvests. The 1871 federal legislation creating the post of U.S. commissioner of fish and fisheries was prompted in part by worry over the fate of food fish. And biologist Milner, dispatched to the Great Lakes to ascertain the situation there, documented the decline:

> The impression prevails that there is an alarming diminution of the food-fishes of the lakes. This is the ordinary feeling among dealers; a majority of the fishermen, and the people generally. . . . The white-fishes are smaller now than formerly; in early times it is said that on average fifty gill-net fishes would make a half-barrel; now it requires about eighty or ninety. . . . There are no recorded statistics that show a reliable calculation of dates, but the testimony of fishermen, dependent on their recollection of their purchases of nets and changes in the mode of fishing, places the beginning of a marked decrease within about ten years.[11]

Whitefish were a primary object of worry because they were delectable—and therefore a staple of the Great Lakes commercial fishing industry. In 1888 Michigan naturalist Bela Hubbard said the whitefish were known as the "deer of the lakes" in early times. "How well I remember the time when the fishing season—at which time alone could this dainty fare be obtained—was looked forward to by the old residents with pleasure and impatience, and one of the hardships of a removal to other parts of the country was experienced in the longing after this favorite dish," Hubbard wrote. "The greed of trade outruns all sober precautions. And it is to be feared that the time is rapidly approaching when the inhabitants of our lakes and rivers, like the wild animals which were once so abundant and are now so few, will be in like manner exterminated."[12]

The stunning advancement of nets and fishing gear, as well as the increasing number of commercial anglers, fueled ever-growing fears about the fate of the fishery. In the early 1800s most fishing was conducted close to shore and fish caught were sold to local markets. But the second half of the nineteenth century revolutionized fishing techniques, enabling harvesters to target more species, capture fish in deeper waters, and fish during a greater portion of the year.

Succeeding seine and pound nets in the late 1800s, trap nets were so efficient that Michigan and Ontario banned them. An advance from pound nets, trap nets funneled fish into a small "pot," or enclosed space, anchored to the lake bottom. The nets were effective at capturing large numbers of whitefish, lake trout, and walleye.

The Erie Canal opened up eastern markets, and the salting of fish enabled their preservation until they reached those markets. Railroads also began carrying fish to distant points in the 1830s on the U.S. side and the 1850s in Canada.[13] Artificially produced ice became available to Lake Erie commercial anglers in the late 1800s, and alternative freezing, using ammonia and chilled brine systems, soon overtook salting as the principal method of fish preservation, further extending markets.

Early fishing was done from sailboats, but by 1890 steam-powered tugs and gasoline-powered launches began to replace them. Steam tugs were able to fish up to five times more net than the sailboats.[14] Evolving through the fishing equivalent of an arms race, the fleet began to deploy diesel engines in the 1890s and outboard motors around 1910. Steel-hulled boats also emerged in the late 1800s.

Fish populations responded predictably—by plummeting. Great Lakes whitefish harvests fell from about 24.3 million pounds in 1879 to just over 9 million pounds twenty years later. Lake sturgeon, regarded at first as a trash fish and destroyed, soon became commercially valuable. Recorded sturgeon production in the Great Lakes fell from 7.8 million pounds in 1879 to 1.7 million pounds in 1899. But fishing didn't slow or stop. It shifted. The decline in whitefish production turned the attention of anglers to lake trout and herring. More elusive and initially numerous than the whitefish or sturgeon, these two species supported a robust fishery well into the twentieth century before collapsing.[15]

The early decades of decline prompted only mild action to restrain overharvesting, but the increasing dismay of both commercial and recreational anglers and their call for stronger legislation were impossible for governments to ignore completely. The response typically took two forms: inquiries into the cause of fish population decline that led to marginal restrictions on fishing effort, and significant public spending on fish hatcheries as an artificial means of replenishing the fish.

An inquiry by the Dominion Fishery Commission into the state of Ontario's fisheries was an example of the fact-finding method. As markets for whitefish expanded dramatically in Toronto, Buffalo, and New York City, fishing pressure in the sheltered Bay of Quinte of Lake Ontario increased in tandem. Whitefish landings in the bay had fallen from 199,400 pounds in 1885 to 48,300 pounds in 1893. In October 1893 the federal panel held a hearing in Belleville and heard testimony from commercial anglers. Despite the fluctuating catch, witnesses from the local fishing industry were skeptical of additional regulations, supported government-sponsored fish hatching programs, and argued the bay would still provide an ample supply of fish to meet foreseeable needs.[16] The government did not take action to limit fish catch.

Contending with competing factions of commercial anglers who opposed tightened regulation of their own fishing while sometimes supporting restrictions on competitors, governments on both the Canadian and U.S. sides of the lakes had even more incentive to operate fish hatching and stocking programs.

An Ontario man was among the first in North America to experiment with the techniques of pisciculture. In 1866 Samuel Wilmot built a test hatchery on his family farm near Newcastle. He hatched four fry from spawn. The Canadian federal government began funding his hatchery the next year; in 1868 Wilmot became a fishery overseer for the Department of Marine and Fisheries. In 1876 he won the job of superintendent of fish culture, the same year he obtained a patent for his fish egg incubator and egg-picker. Wilmot's successes helped popularize government-sponsored fish hatcheries and stocking throughout the United States and Canada. By the early 1880s nearly all of the Great Lakes states and Ontario had agencies charged with boosting fish stocks.

> The Commissions were created by the state legislatures and the Congress a generation prior to the conservation movement in response to the beliefs that (1): there was an "appalling" decline of the nation's fisheries, and (2): that the decline could be corrected by artificial propagation of fish, thus overcoming a fundamental weakness in nature's schemes—the inherent wastefulness of natural

> propagation. . . . Fish culture was to bring back both the commercial harvest and replace "inferior" species with those possessing more sporting qualities.[17]

Fish propagation had begun centuries before in China, but the first modern fish hatchery had begun operation in France in 1852. Even before Wilmot's Ontario experiment, Seth Green had constructed the first American fish hatchery, in approximately 1864. Not until after the enactment of the 1871 law creating the post of U.S. commissioner of fish and fisheries, however, did American fish culture flourish. In 1872 the American Fish Culturists Association successfully lobbied for a $15,000 U.S. federal appropriation to be distributed by Spencer Baird, the U.S. commissioner. The work of addressing nature's inefficiencies moved ahead quickly. Between 1867 and 1920, governments built eighteen hatcheries on Lake Erie alone.[18]

As one critic observed, "it was apparent that the Commissions felt all rivers, lakes and creeks were either understocked or undesirably stocked."[19] For example, accusing the "wicked" pike and pickerel families of mutilating their "amiable, Quaker-like neighbors upon the 'total depravity principle,' " the Michigan commission in 1875 said it would seek to supplant them and other unworthy native fish with "the better sorts of food fish."[20] These superior fish included rainbow trout from the mountainous western United States, brown trout from Germany, and salmon from both the East and West Coasts. Trout and salmon from Scotland were distributed to the states by the federal government. Sometimes charges were staggering. In its 1875 report, the Michigan commission complained bitterly of a $518.55 charge on between seven hundred thousand and eight hundred thousand California salmon eggs, a significant chunk of its $7,000 annual budget. Still, almost a hundred years before "biological integrity" became a term with meaning to fisheries managers as well as their constituents, both sport and commercial anglers welcomed the exotic fish introductions.

There were accidents and unintentional consequences, too. The European carp, imported by both immigrants and the U.S. fish commission in the late 1800s, soon escaped from ponds and found a comfortable home in the Great Lakes, while occupying a niche formerly held by the sturgeon and failing to appeal to Americans and Canadians as a source of food.[21] Today the carp is abundant and valued largely because its bottom-feeding tendencies enable it to accumulate large amounts of toxic chemicals, making it a useful barometer of pollution hotspots.

Ultimately, imports of fish species did little to benefit the industry. "The great majority failed completely, a few had catastrophic effects on the native fish population, others proved harmless, and some have been generally acclaimed as great successes," noted two Great Lakes fisheries experts.[22]

With few exceptions, the state commissions were popular with legislators and constituent groups alike for most of their tenure. They reassured fishermen through visible effort that government was doing something to replenish the stock of fish. But by the early 1900s the combination of continued declines in valued commercial species, other threats to the health of the lakes, and a slowly dawning awareness of the fundamental laws of ecology shrunk the public budgets devoted to fish culture. Studies "failed to find evidence of significant returns from the stocking of fish fry."[23] When several of the commissions also called for unpopular, increased restrictions on fishing effort to protect fish populations, they faced legislative retaliation and ultimately backed down.

More than overharvesting was menacing the fish. Rapid development of the forests, rivers, and shores of the lakes undermined habitat and changed the face of the basin forever. Beginning in upstate New York and eastern Ontario in the 1830s and 1840s, and spreading westward to Minnesota and far western Ontario in the 1890s, a massive and reckless timber cut generated instant riches for entrepreneurs but caused ecological upheaval.

The change in the landscape was striking enough. In the mid 1830s a traveler named Anna Jameson described southwestern Ontario this way:

> The seemingly interminable line of trees before you; the mysterious depths amid the multitudinous foliage where foot of man hath never penetrated—and which partial gleams of the noontide sun, now seen, now lost, lit up with a changeful, magical beauty—the wondrous splendor and novelty of the flowers—the silence, unbroken but by the low cry of a bird, or hum of insect, or the splash and croak of some huge bull-frog—the solitude in which we proceeded mile after mile, no human being, no human dwelling within sight—all are either exciting to the fancy, or oppressive to the spirits, according to the mood one may be in. . . . How savagely, how solemnly wild it was![24]

But by the late 1870s most of the primeval southern Ontario forest was gone. Similarly, the vast forests of Michigan, Wisconsin, and Minnesota disappeared in the last decades of the 1800s.

The day's logging practices stripped the landscape of trees considered commercially valuable, the remains providing ample fuel for fires that blackened and sometimes sterilized the landscape and endangered settlers. The loss of forest canopies exposed cool-water streams to the sun, raising temperatures and undermining some fish, such as the grayling, adapted to the original conditions. The uprooting of trees also diminished the capacity of the land to store and hold water, increasing the frequency and destructiveness of floods. The rolling of cut logs off riverbanks and the running of the logs downstream to market released and stirred up huge quantities of sediment, destroying spawning habitat and leaving lasting scars on many streams.

The sawmills that converted the logs into timber also created the first significant industrial pollution. For a brief period as the timber boom peaked, the vast quantities of sawdust discharged into bays and harbors populated by the sawmills provoked official concern. In 1884 the New York Fish Commission determined that sawdust not only interfered with fish spawning, but also asserted that it jeopardized human health. The commission argued that decaying sawdust contributed to malaria, associating the pollution with the curse of "chills and fever."[25] Sawdust coated the bottom of Green Bay two miles out and dampened whitefish reproduction there and in Saginaw Bay. But early antipollution laws, while sweeping in their intentions, were ineffectual and rarely enforced against the wealth-generating, politically potent industries that violated them on both sides of the international boundary. "From at least the time of Confederation, fishery officials attempted to curb the dumping of mill wastes, but the political power of the lumber industry was able to prevent any effective reforms until at least the turn of the century," wrote A. B. McCullough of the situation in Canada.

Still, the decline of the fishery forced the fish commissions and conservationists to consider new approaches, including cooperation across state and international lines. The states and Ontario held "conference after conference," including meetings in 1883, 1884, 1891, and 1892.[26] Recommendations produced at the conferences on fish conservation reforms were largely not enacted, crushed under pressure brought by the U.S. commercial fishing industry.

Canadians, whose national heritage did not include the reflexive antipathy to regulation in which U.S. anglers were steeped, chafed at the disparity between the rules under which they operated and those of the Americans. In the early and mid

1890s the fishing industry's allies in Parliament attacked the Dominion government for tolerating the inequity between the regime in the States and the one under which they operated, which included clearly defined closed seasons, a required increase in net mesh sizes, a ban on seining and trap netting, and increasingly vigorous enforcement. But the regulations remained in place, and Canadian officials boasted of their greater success in conserving fish stocks.

The disparity in national approaches inspired renewed calls for regional and international cooperation to save Great Lakes fish. Partly as a result of controversies between the United States and Canada over saltwater fisheries issues, but also with recognition of the Great Lakes problem, representatives of the nations met in Washington during the winter of 1892. Out of this meeting came an agreement to appoint a commission of two experts, one from each country, to study, analyze, and make recommendations on threats to fish populations in boundary and shared waters. The two commissioners, Richard Rathbun for the United States and William Wakeham for Canada, spent three years in fact-finding from the Atlantic to the Pacific. In 1896 they issued their report. Margaret Beattie Bogue observes:

> In an elaborate set of recommendations for Lakes Ontario, Erie, Huron and Superior, the Detroit and St. Clair Rivers, Lake St. Clair, and Georgian Bay, Wakeham and Rathbun spelled out exactly what they believed would be essential to save the fish. . . . The report portrayed a once-bounteous natural resource seriously eroded and, Wakeham and Rathbun believed, urgently in need of constructive regulation. . . . The commissioners attributed the sorry state of affairs to overfishing and to vastly improved fishing technology used by ever-larger numbers of fishermen in pursuit of the wealth of Great Lakes waters.[27]

The two men recommended regulation as a primary response to the collapse of fish stocks. They supported universal licensing of anglers, regulations on mesh size and net numbers, protection of spawning grounds, and closed seasons for some species, among other measures. But the report failed to move the U.S. Congress and the states. Joint regulation of Great Lakes fishing implied a federal regulatory presence and threatened to undermine state sovereignty. Further, it outraged many in the U.S. commercial fishing industry, who feared the regulations would reduce their profits. The report was received by outgoing President Cleveland and a lame-duck Congress in early 1897 and filed.

The official failure to act didn't make the problem go away. Fueled in part by the rise of conservation as a political and policy issue under President Theodore Roosevelt, the U.S. and Canadian governments (the latter acting through Great Britain) dusted off the old draft treaty, altered it slightly, and embraced it in 1908. Calling for an International Fisheries Commission to promulgate regulations to conserve fish in both salt water and the Great Lakes within six months, it was never implemented. The House of Commons, after some hesitation, approved the regulations in 1910, but commercial anglers in the United States again mounted a fierce campaign against the treaty. Ohio fishermen were a key force in opposing the proposed ban on trap nets, the favorite of anglers in Sandusky and Toledo. A final effort by the Woodrow Wilson administration to win adoption of the pact in 1914 was defeated in the House of Representatives.

It seemed all hope for joint regulation was dashed. Then, the seemingly impossible happened in 1925. Harvests of lake herring, the prime commercial species in Lake Erie since just after the turn of the century, dwindled from 32.2 million pounds in 1924 to 5.7 million pounds the following year. The catastrophe prompted governments to act. Between 1927 and 1933, several of the states and Ontario met repeatedly to hash out a plan to conserve fish. Ultimately, each effort collapsed because at least one jurisdiction was unwilling either to adopt or enforce the recommended regulations because of political pressures. Instead, the governments continued to struggle independently with catches that inched downward over time.

Resistance to formal cooperation finally dissipated, but it took a threat from without to drive the region's jurisdictions together in defense of the lakes. The new menace was the sea lamprey.

Although there is some disagreement about the historical record, it appears the lamprey migrated into Lakes Ontario and Erie from the Hudson River after the completion of the Erie Canal. The parasitic lamprey, however, did not flourish in the four upper lakes until after the reconstruction of the Welland Canal in 1919. The new canal design apparently attracted the lamprey, which in its normal life cycle hatches and spawns in freshwater but migrates to salt water during its growth to maturity. In 1921 the lamprey was discovered in Lake Erie, where it did little immediate damage. But a spawning population in Michigan's Huron River, identified in 1932, was a prelude to a fishery disaster.

The lamprey feeds on fish, plunging its teeth into them and feeding for months, slowly draining them of life. In the 1930s anglers began reporting heavy scarring of lake trout in Lake Huron. The invader nearly killed off the lake trout in just fourteen years, with catches falling from 1.74 million pounds in 1935 to a mere 1,000 pounds in 1949.[28] The devastation on Lake Michigan was comparable. The lamprey also migrated into Lake Superior in about 1945 and began to attack fish there. In addition to lake trout, whitefish and ciscoes were at risk.

Faced with a common enemy, governments at all levels and in both nations began working feverishly to study the lamprey and to find ways to control it. Scientists from agencies of both Canada and the United States installed weirs to block migration to streams in the three upper lakes. Research on electromagnetic barriers forged ahead, resulting in the construction of one hundred sixty-two of the devices by 1960. Experts at the U.S. Fish and Wildlife Service Biological Station at Hammond Bay, Michigan, tested approximately six thousand chemicals in a search for one that would chiefly kill lamprey. By the early 1960s the two countries began to apply 3-trifluoromethyl-4-nitrophenol, or TFM, and a molluscicide, Bayer 73, which increased the toxicity of TFM in streams without broadening it to attack other organisms.[29]

The difficulty in spanning state and international boundaries was not quite solved, however. A 1946 convention between the two federal governments, which would have provided for a commission to fix regulations in the Great Lakes on such matters as gear, open and closed waters, and data gathering, was never ratified by Congress, again out of fears that it intruded on state sovereignty.

After sixty years of unsuccessful efforts to create joint regulation of fisheries in the Great Lakes, backers of cross-boundary cooperation threw in the towel. In 1952 they began working to amend the 1946 convention and produced a new pact in September 1954. It abandoned the idea of entrusting an international body with rule-making authority and instead recognized the value of "joint and coordinated efforts" between the two nations to address fisheries conservation. But the focus was on the lamprey. The new Great Lakes Fishery Commission was charged with the job of formulating and implementing "a comprehensive program for the purpose of eradicating or minimizing the sea lamprey populations in the Convention area." In effect, the new panel would coordinate research on lamprey control techniques and work with agencies in the two nations to implement them.

The perceived threat to sovereignty being removed, the convention was swiftly ratified by both nations. Congress gave its assent in June 1955; Canada, four months later. The treaty took effect on 11 October 1955.[30] As the fishery commissioner's former executive secretary observed, "By that time lake trout production from Lakes Huron and Michigan was 99 % lower than the average annual commercial catch in the 1930s."[31]

It took the near-elimination of one of the most critical and commercially valuable fish species on the upper lakes to lower even partially the historic barriers to intergovernmental, international cooperation. The failure of the governments to act decisively on fishery regulations was the first but not the last instance of the region's political balkanization. The long-term health of the Great Lakes suffered as jurisdictions, pressured by industrial fishing interests, guarded their prerogatives and failed to agree on a common regime. The era of fishing decline and government's incompetence in dealing with it would be paralleled in the age of gross pollution.

The Pitcher's Thistle: Prickly Beauty

THE SHORES OF THE GREAT LAKES ARE THE ONLY habitat in the world for several exquisitely beautiful plant species. Unfortunately for the plants that rely on the shores of the lakes for survival, the same habitat is coveted by a growing number of human beings. Homes, driveways, marinas, off-road vehicles, and trails continue to menace these other shoreline-dependent species. Several—the Pitcher's thistle, dwarf lake iris, and Houghton's goldenrod—are listed as threatened under the U.S. Endangered Species Act. Others are imperiled on a statewide scale and recognized as imperiled by state laws.

Pitcher's thistle may best pose the question: what price protection? And what price development? Seen from this perspective, its sharp spines may be irritating us into contemplating bigger questions than whether one more summer home on the beach or one more stand of a rare but homely plant is more valuable.

Known now at only about one hundred fifty U.S. locations and only about a dozen locations in Canada, Pitcher's thistle is unremarkable to the untrained eye for most of its life span. But in one season it reveals a strange beauty. At a point between the plant's third and tenth year, and once only, the Pitcher's thistle flowers. After flowering and fruiting, the plant dies.

Named after Dr. Zina Pitcher, who noted the plant in 1827 at the Grand Sable Dunes on the Lake Superior shore of the Upper Peninsula of Michigan, Pitcher's thistle appears to have originated in the Great Plains. Its precursor probably migrated into the Great Lakes region following the abrupt warming period known as the Hypsithermal, when many prairie species moved into the area. It dispersed slowly eastward in the sandy habitats created by Wisconsin's glacial melt waters. Sand is still its home, and Great Lakes shoreline sand provides the necessary moderate sand movement—thanks to wind and waves—and open bare areas that allow the thistle to survive and to scatter its seeds on the winds.

Lake Michigan is its favorite neighbor, according to the U.S. Fish and Wildlife Service; 77 percent of its occurrences are along the Michigan, Wisconsin, and Indiana shores of that lake. The Indiana Dunes National Lakeshore contains the southernmost known population. Extirpated from Illinois, the plant has been reintroduced to the Lake Michigan shore there by botanists. In Ontario it ranges from the north shore of Lake Superior to the southern shore of Lake Huron, growing most abundantly on Manitoulin Island.

Sand is a harsh as well as scenic habitat. But Pitcher's thistle is naturally adapted for this environment. The process of sand movement enables dunes to be maintained, and the thistle to thrive. Nothing has affected pitcher's thistle like human disturbance and occupation of its natural habitat. In addition, the non-native knapweed and baby's breath, introduced by humankind, compete with the thistle for open space.

While the plant is known to have disappeared from only seven Illinois and Indiana locations and from a handful along Ontario's Lake Huron shore, it "probably occurred more commonly along the Great Lakes shoreline prior to European settlement,"[32] says the Fish and Wildlife Service. Since nearly 55 percent of the U.S. plant sites and the majority of Canadian sites are in publicly owned, protected parks, it's reasonable to believe scores of Pitcher's thistle populations on private land disappeared, many of them before any scientists were aware of their relative rarity and significance.

Several states have enacted laws to protect the coastal habitats on private land enjoyed by Pitcher's thistle, although the plant was not the primary reason for these statutes. Yet by tradition and Constitution, U.S. statutes do not forbid development of private property; they only limit it. Sand dune protection and habitat conservation statutes may reroute development a few feet or yards from a thistle population, but that is no guarantee that the plant can survive.

Half-measures may not be enough. At one site on the Lake Michigan shore near Manistee, Michigan, two small populations of Pitcher's thistle were fenced off while scores of condominiums were developed around them. During the summer, hundreds of people live in and around the fenced reserves. And the fences themselves may retard the movement of sand the plants need to flourish.

Chris Shafer, who managed Michigan's Great Lakes shoreline protection programs in the 1990s before leaving government, says public purchase of threatened habitats is the only way to assure they endure. "There is a constant onslaught of political pressure to permit development on the shoreline," Shafer says. "The more Great Lakes shoreline we can get in public ownership or conservancy ownership, the better."[33]

The professional prescription for the plant's recovery is simple. Leave large tracts of the coastal sand dunes alone. Let the wind and water wash and blow their sands around to regenerate the thistle's habitats. Use the hand of humankind to restore the habitat of Pitcher's thistle where it once thrived and to ward off the human disturbances that would threaten it there.

While critics have questioned the value of tailoring a few of our plans to the needs of the Pitcher's thistle and its threatened and endangered plant and animal relatives who depend on the shoreline, learning to live in harmony with them would be an act of generosity to them and to ourselves. Protecting and restoring dunes and beaches is hardly unselfish; these places renew us as well. And if even the prickliest human has a right to exist, does not the prickly thistle?

When I was in high school, we lived in Evanston, Illinois, about two blocks from a beach on Lake Michigan. During the summer we went to the beach almost every day. My dad bought a small boat and we went water skiing quite often. I loved skiing on Lake Michigan and felt it was a challenge when the waves got big. One day, though, the waves got too big. My dad had a hard time getting the boat back to shore and we had to keep going farther north until we were finally able to dock it at the Great Lakes Naval Station. It was a scary, but memorable adventure.

—Michele Anderson

Being in Windsor, you're very conscious of the Great Lakes. Watching the ships pass up and down the Detroit River in summer, seeing the ice float downriver in the winter, you feel like you're really at the heart of the Great Lakes.

The mentality of living in Windsor is, first of all, you feel separated from the rest of Ontario. You can feel overpowered by Detroit. Driving around with a visitor, they'll say, "I didn't know you had such big buildings." And you have to say, "No, those buildings are in Detroit."

It does make you binational. The flow of the river is so visible, you think of what's upstream as well as what's downstream.

—John Jackson

Protecting a New Home

The majesty of the Great Lakes region was well-known to its native inhabitants and to some of the discerning European explorers in the seventeenth and eighteenth centuries. But Canadian and U.S. settlers during much of the 1800s had no time for eyeing beauty. Their imperative was to wring a living from the land. Scenery was a luxury, and the appreciation of forests, fish, or wildlife beyond their potential economic return was foreign to the new inhabitants.

To these settlers, many features of the Great Lakes landscape that would today seem rich in beauty and mystery—and important biologically—were forbidding wastelands to be tamed and harnessed for productive ends. The Black Swamp, a great wetland about fifteen hundred square miles in size that hugged the east shore of the Maumee River from near New Haven, Indiana, to Lake Erie, was a detested obstacle to transportation and settlement. "The Black Swamp was truly a wilderness greater in extent and degree than any previously experienced by most of the emigrants from the more settled East," wrote Martin R. Kaatz.[1] Probably named after the black loam that characterized the wet soils of the region, the Black Swamp not only delayed settlement of southern Michigan and northwestern Ohio for decades, but also diverted some settlers to and through Canada. Formed by the slow retreat of the glaciers, the swamp constituted a major part of the level, poorly drained plain left behind. It was a wilderness of size and scope unimaginable in today's southern Great Lakes Basin.

Following the American Civil War, the advance of drainage techniques rapidly converted the swamp to prime agriculture land. In the 1950s an observer wrote approvingly:

> Within a few decades the Black Swamp was transformed from a useless, obstructive morass into one of the most productive regions of Ohio and the Corn Belt. . . . The Black Swamp has been so transformed that an observer would be hard-pressed to estimate its former extent. . . . The countryside has a neat and prosperous look to it. Large barns, well kept farm houses, abundant farm machinery, and a sky-line interrupted by television antennas are signs, to even the most casual observer, that he is in the midst of good farm land.[2]

Settlers—and later, historians—justified much of the destruction of the native landscape as a necessary step toward a new economy based on managed land. Yet some began to regret what was happening to the most striking places along the shores of the Great Lakes. Coinciding with the dawning of the conservation movement in both countries, scattered efforts to protect the Great Lakes landscape and waterscape expressed a counterimpulse to unfettered development. One of the most spectacular geological features of the continent, Niagara Falls, served also as the headwaters of the new movement for protection.

The ages that it took to build Niagara alone qualify it as a wonder. The lip of the falls is the Niagara Escarpment, the uplifted, weathered edge of an ancient sea bottom that extends from Watertown, New York, to Manitoulin Island, Ontario. The escarpment's rocks are approximately four hundred million years old. Following the last retreat of the glaciers about twelve thousand years ago, the Niagara River became the main outlet for Lake Erie. Only thirty-five feet high at first, the falls were limited in part by the apparent damming of Lake Iroquois (today's Lake Ontario) at its outflow to the St. Lawrence River and by the smaller size of Lake Erie. But the falls gradually began to tower over the waters below as the constant flow cut through glacial debris to shape the Niagara Gorge. As the glaciers continued their retreat to the north, silt barriers broke, releasing much of the water of ancient Lake Ontario, contributing to the great fall at which the region's early human inhabitants gaped in wonder.[3]

Feminist Margaret Fuller aptly summarized the contrasting responses of members of the settling generations of the region to the roaring one-hundred-sixty-foot cataracts in 1843. Describing the "magical effects" of the veil of mist created by the then-British falls, she reported the quiet happiness that came upon her as she sat on Table Rock: "There all power of observing details, all separate consciousness, was quite lost."

A man who approached her while sitting on the rock reacted differently. "He walked up close to the fall, and, after looking at it a moment, with an air as if thinking how he could best appropriate it to his own use, he spat into it. . . . This trait seemed wholly worthy of an age whose love of *utility* is such that the Prince

Puckler Muskau suggested the probability of men coming to put the bodies of their dead parents in the fields to fertilize them."[4]

For a time, utility seemed close to robbing the falls of their grandeur. One of the greatest natural attractions in North America, Niagara's shoulders were occupied in the 1830s by those seeking to turn it to use as a tourist attraction or power source, outraging visiting English ministers Andrew Reed and James Matheson, who argued that some "universal voice ought to interfere, and prevent them."[5] By the 1870s the flanks of the falls were cluttered by ugly development and populated by hordes of photographers, peddlers, and hack drivers. Greedy innkeepers exploited visitors, and organized crime soon recognized the opportunity to make a profit from the tourist traffic. For example, U.S. émigré Saul Davis, who owned the Table Rock House overlooking the falls, employed hackmen who steered tourists into his enterprise with the assurance that the visit was free. But after their visit, tourists were presented with a $2 charge and threatened with mayhem if they didn't pay.[6] Appalled by the commercial exploitation of the falls, U.S. landscape painter Frederic Edwin Church, who put the falls on canvas in 1857, called for protection of its scenery.

While embarrassed by the disorder, governments initially responded to the crime problem rather than the degradation of the falls' natural wonder. Ontario premier Oliver Mowat disdained early proposals for a public park on the Canadian side of the falls, instead stressing a crime crackdown. Villainy threatened the reputation and business of tourism. Exploitation merely threatened the aesthetic values of the falls.

While officials struggled to cope with these pressures, the U.S. Congress in 1872 turned another natural landmark, the Yellowstone area of Wyoming and Montana, into the country's first national park. The precedent fired the imaginations of citizens on both sides of the border determined to shield the aesthetics of the falls and surroundings. Painter Church persuaded legendary landscape architect Frederick Law Olmsted, designer of Manhattan's Central Park, of the need for parks on both sides of the falls. A group of New Yorkers that included Olmsted approached officials of both that state and Ontario.

In September 1878 the governor general of Ontario, Lord Dufferin, proposed that the governments of New York and Ontario or Canada create a small international park at the falls. In January 1879 New York governor Lucius Robinson endorsed the proposal, putting pressure on Premier Mowat to do the same. After a meeting with New York officials that autumn, Mowat tepidly backed the park concept but shifted responsibility to the national government. In March 1880 the Ontario legislature approved Mowat's legislation to authorize Ottawa to acquire lands for the park.[7]

The Canadian government was forced to do something but reluctant to act on its own. Members of the cabinet of Prime Minister John Macdonald from eastern provinces balked at investing dominion funds in a provincial project unlikely to be enjoyed by their constituents. Macdonald did approach Mowat with the idea of a federal-provincial partnership, but nothing happened to advance the park for five years.

The emergence of proponents who wanted to make profit off a park generated a backlash that pushed the protection effort forward in the 1880s. Promoter William Oliver Buchanan conceived of a private syndicate that could develop the park. Envisioning a miniature railway from the falls to the whirlpool below, picnic grounds, hotels, and refreshment kiosks, Buchanan's plan was costly and potentially greatly profitable. Encouraged by Premier Mowat, he struggled to put together a set of investors. When New York suddenly began to take an interest in creating a state park on its side of the falls in 1883, Buchanan found backers, but a second contender, the Niagara Falls Railway Company, also emerged. Further complicating the campaign were new voices, belonging to citizens of Niagara Falls and nearby Stamford, who condemned the idea of a privately run park and clamored for a public one. Pointing across the international border at New York's imminent creation of a state park, they besieged Mowat with calls for a government reserve.[8]

Under 1885 Ontario legislation, a commission was appointed to select and appraise lands for the park. Surprising the premier, the commission recommended in September 1885 that the government establish a free park, under provincial control. The commission further called for protection of the area "not as a showy garden or fancy grounds, but as nearly as possible as they would be in their natural condition."[9]

When Mowat delayed, the commissioners issued a second report supporting the park. The commission's secretary, George Pattullo, noted that by creating a park on its side of the falls first, New York was reaping the profits of increased tourism and noted that most of the visitors were "what Abraham Lincoln described as the plain people," rather than the wealthy and comfortable who had previously enjoyed the natural spectacle.[10] Although he had been initially stunned by the commission's recommendation, in early 1887, Mowat agreed to the government park. A Niagara Parks Commission was established to manage the original 154 acres of parklands and to issue $525,000 in bonds to buy and develop them. New York already had a public park at the falls. Signed into law in April 1885, the Reservation State Park embraced 412 acres with a $1.4 million acquisition cost. As historian Gerald Killan notes, Mowat had taken fifteen years to address the Niagara Falls protection issue and "looked to every alternative short of public ownership" before establishing the park—in response to mounting citizen pressure.[11]

While the waterfall itself and prime viewing sites were now public, those people devoted to the ethic of utility decried by feminist Fuller were determined to harness the cataract. The potential for reaping power from the vast waters tumbling over the escarpment transfixed governments and developers alike. At virtually the same moment New York state was proclaiming its new falls park, a New York engineer named Thomas Evershed was proposing works that would generate two hundred thousand horsepower from the Niagara River, employing a canal above the falls and a runoff tunnel emptying into the stream below the falls.[12] After several false starts by predecessors, the Niagara Falls Power Company organized in 1889 and ultimately blasted away three hundred thousand tons of rock to construct the tunnel, which extended from a powerhouse one and one-half miles above the falls. Twenty-eight construction workers lost their lives in the tunnel project. In 1896 Buffalo began receiving electricity from the project, supporting the industrial development of the region.

On the Canadian side of the falls, the Niagara Parks Commission quickly faced a cash shortage for land acquisition and park development. It, too, turned to power development, leasing land for a powerhouse just above Table Rock. Three companies gained licenses to generate up to four hundred thousand horsepower. The Canadian Niagara Power Company began generating electricity from the waters of the river in 1905 with two large generators.

In the wake of the fifteen-year campaign to shield the falls from aesthetic degradation and corruption, both Canadian and U.S. officials almost immediately agreed to divert huge amounts of the waters that had formerly passed over them. They later ratified this taming of the falls. Under a 1950 treaty, all water "in excess of that required for domestic and sanitary purposes, navigation and the Falls may be diverted for power generation."[13] The treaty specifies flows not less than one hundred thousand cubic feet per second during daylight hours of the tourist season, but half that at other times. Supplying about a quarter of the power used in New York state and Ontario, the electric works of the river lower its level below the falls by twelve feet during the off-season.

The proud developers of the electric capacity of the falls viewed their massive project as more than just a service to business and residential electric customers: "By harnessing Niagara, the leaders of the power company felt they had acquired a power that, like Aladdin's, was almost magical. With it, they could transform the world. . . . The hydroelectric development of the old Niagara transmuted the character of the falling water into a controlled and focused force. Using the very power of nature, humanity was able to rise above it."[14]

The apparent mastery of the falls excited other grandiose dreams. Investor William T. Love purchased an almost ninety-square-mile tract of land reaching from the escarpment to the site of the proposed Model City that was intended to reach as far as Lake Ontario on the New York side of the Niagara River. The centerpiece of his scheme was a navigable power canal reaching from the upper river to the city site. Envisioning a population of more than one million, Love said his Model City would become a great manufacturing center and "the most perfect city in existence."

Astonishingly, Love persuaded the New York legislature to grant him authority to condemn property and divert as much water as he wanted to fuel his development. The massive project never materialized, however. One mile of the canal, a lone factory, and a few houses were all that was completed when a mid 1890s depression cost Love his investors and bankrupted his company. Love, whose origins and fate are obscure, had seemingly vaporized like his scheme. In the 1990s Model City consisted principally of a garbage landfill and a tavern, along with the incomplete canal.[15] The canal would later play a significant role in the environmental history of North America—although not for any reason Love might have imagined.

A mogul and fellow big thinker, King Camp Gillette, had an even more startling dream for the Niagara region. Before the manufacture of his disposable razor blade made him wealthy, he published in 1894 a proposal to create a giant city straddling the international border at Niagara. He dubbed it Metropolis. Spanning the entire Ontario Niagara peninsula and parts of nine western New York counties, Metropolis would form a rectangle forty-five miles by one hundred thirty-five miles and harbor sixty million residents living in forty thousand circular apartment buildings, twenty-five stories high, designed by Gillette.[16] The plan would take the gospel of industrial efficiency to its logical extreme by providing the single industrial site needed to meet all of North America's needs—powered by the waters of Niagara Falls. But the falls themselves would go. Their "wasted" falling water would be completely diverted to support the development of Metropolis, which would include a platform one hundred feet above the area's landscape, extending even out over the river. The scheme was too fanciful even for people of an age convinced of its power to bend nature to its will. Theodore Roosevelt turned down Gillette's offer of a $250,000 annual salary to head the corporation that would develop Metropolis.[17]

The history of Niagara's protection and development illustrates the often-conflicting impulses of conservation and utilitarianism, as well as the projection of grand and sometimes destructive dreams onto the dramatic landscape of the Great Lakes system. A similar mix of motives fostered another of the early Great Lakes parks of Ontario. Far less imposing than the falls, but as valuable in natural wealth as Niagara, Rondeau Provincial Park would mark a subtle change in the appreciation of Canadians and Americans for the character of their new home.

Like so many other features of the lakes, the land that would become Rondeau Park had its birth in the end of the last glacial era. Meltwater from retreating glaciers lifted the level of Lake Erie and eroded cliffs on its northern shore. The deposition of the resulting sand and gravel flows ultimately built a peninsula extending over five miles into the lake, about one-third of the way from the western to the eastern end of Erie. By the time French explorers arrived in the vicinity, giant pines towered over the east shore of the peninsula. They dubbed the landmark Point Aux Pins. The beauty of the point and its natural harbor struck missionaries who camped under the pines in 1670. Because of the natural harbor's shape, they called it Ronde Eau, or round water.[18]

The strategic importance of the site ultimately saved it from the ravages of development that cleared most of the southwestern Ontario landscape. With the potential to serve as a naval base for the upper lakes, the peninsula and harbor assumed a new role in the thinking of the occupying British. In 1790 the British government acquired a large tract of land in the area from the native inhabitants for trade goods. Five years later Lord Simcoe, the first lieutenant governor of Upper Canada, declared the peninsula to be Ordinance Land under Crown control, restricting development and settlement. In addition to protecting its military significance, Simcoe hoped to husband the pine timber for naval or other use.

After the threat of war passed from the lake, the sandy soils of the peninsula retarded use of the land for settlement and farming. But private timber harvesters scalped some of the best pines. Hunters exploited deer and other game species. And by the 1860s, as leisure time began to expand, picnickers and swimmers began to capitalize on the harbor waters.

The first step to restrain consumption of the peninsula's resources was the appointment in 1876 of a caretaker, Isaac

Swarthout, to police the illegal timber harvest. While Swarthout succeeded in managing the peninsula for a time, the construction in 1883 of a railroad link to Shrewsbury Landing on the mainland touched off a sudden tourism boom:

> Luxury hotels, cottages and modestly priced boarding houses appeared at the resort village of Erieau and around the shoreline. Rondeau's reputation spread south, and after 1880 steamers brought American vacationers from Erie and Cleveland. . . . Because of its central location, in one of the richest and most populous agricultural regions in the province, its close proximity to Chatham, and the availability of cheap transportation, middle- and lower-income people were attracted to Rondeau. Although the area had its share of "society" hotels and cottages for people of means, its predominantly lower middle- and working-class clientele set it apart from more exclusive resorts.[19]

While local business interests welcomed this growth, others began to take a more protective stance toward the changes wrought on the peninsula. Two businessmen were granted permission to construct a guesthouse on the neck of the peninsula. Two First Nations families sold a few handicrafts on the point. A new provincial caretaker permitted farmers to graze hundreds of cattle on the peninsula's fields and marshes. Several businessmen cut trees or drew resin from pines for commercial purposes. So when Ontario created its first non-Niagara provincial park, Algonquin, in 1893, a local clamor arose for Rondeau to become the second. The elected councils of Chatham, Kent County, and Harwich and Howard townships petitioned for the designation.

Although the petitioners attached some sentiment to their bid for park status, their primary arguments were commercial. A "Government Park at Rondeau," formally established by provincial statute in 1894, would assure recreation for thousands and protect the timber that helped make the bay the largest safe harbor on the north shore of Lake Erie. Ironically, given what is now known about the park's biological significance, little mention was made of protecting the peninsula as a nature preserve or wildlife sanctuary.[20]

Seeking to respond to local public opinion before a pending June 1894 election, the Mowat government of Ontario quickly agreed to the park proposal, which received royal assent in May. Still manned by only one person, now a park ranger, the park was also protected by a new set of regulations. The rules forbade settlement and prohibited timber extraction except for already downed wood, but left the door open for such tourist attractions as a dancing pavilion and the lease of, ultimately, 450 cottage lots. Without quite understanding what they were doing, provincial officials, responding to community pressure, had preserved one of the last remnant native landscapes in southern Ontario.

Today the park remains a recreation attraction but is better known among naturalists for other qualities. One of the southernmost points in Canada, Rondeau harbors plants and animals characteristic of the central portion of the eastern U.S. seaboard, the rationale for the forest's description as Carolinian. Sassafras and tulip trees, the Virginia possum, and the yellow-breasted chat live at Rondeau. The endangered prothonotary warbler has its largest Canadian breeding ground in the park. Named after religious and legal clerks who sometimes wore a golden hood and a blue cape, the striking bird ultimately found one of its last Canadian refuges in Rondeau Provincial Park.[21]

Only a few dozen miles west of Rondeau, another shoreline site of great natural significance was protected in 1918. Point Pelee, a nine-mile-long peninsula pointing south toward the United States, benefited from its obvious values as a habitat for waterfowl and migrating birds. The Migratory Bird Treaty, signed by the United States and Canada in 1916, had capped decades of efforts to conserve dwindling populations of birds that each year crossed the international boundary en route to summering and wintering grounds. Much of the peninsula had also been retained by the Crown and federal government since the early 1800s, lessening the burden of land acquisition that would retard many other park projects. A constituency of naturalists who appreciated the magnificence of the more than three hundred bird species passing through the park appealed to the Canadian Conservation Commission to support protection of the flyway. In 1915 ornithologist Percy Taverner told the commission that mining of sand from the lake bottom offshore was endangering Point Pelee, reducing the point by half a mile or more since 1905.[22]

Famed bird protector Jack Miner also fell in love with Point Pelee. In 1914 Miner wrote in a letter to the Leamington newspaper that a visit the preceding May to the area had opened his eyes to "the greatest variety of trees and shrubs that stand in any one place in Ontario. In fact I spent this day in the prettiest 'natural park' I ever saw. Let us hear from you and let us combine our forces and keep Point Pelee out of the hands of unlimited wealth and preserve it for our children's children." Organized by Miner, prominent Leamington businessmen and Essex County wildlife conservation associations contributed to the political voice for the 1918 establishment of Point Pelee National Park.[23]

In 1911 Canada had become the first nation to create a government unit devoted to national parks. The Parks Branch soon articulated a variety of reasons for creating parks, including revenues generated for local businesses and governments by the tourism they supported. But the first Dominion Parks commissioner, James Harkin, an Ontario native educated in Michigan, offered another rationale that would resonate with the generations of the twentieth century:

> To many people in cities, life means long hours of labour amidst the dust and whirr of wheels, an excessive nervous strain, and joyless, monotonous employment; to many, life is a grind, a round of labour, a season of care, on top of which are conditions of overcrowding. The dangers that threaten, the evils which have been constantly increasing in industrial centers, are a degeneration in physical type, a deterioration in mental and moral quantity. . . . National Parks are reservations of the wilderness, they constitute a national recognition of the necessity of recreation.[24]

The national parks movement in the United States began to gain critical momentum a few years after the establishment of Canada's Parks Branch. The establishment of the National Park Service in 1916 turned the eyes of American conservationists toward potential parks far removed from the rugged western landscapes that had characterized the early preserves. And it helped ignite a more than fifty-year battle to protect the Indiana Dunes. Playing out the conflict between those who wanted to put the water and adjacent land of the lakes to industrial use and those who sought to protect it virtually unchanged in perpetuity, the fight over the dunes involved science, economics, political power, and a growing passion for place. The dunes struggle sharply divided citizens, officials, and states lining up on opposing sides of the question of whether scenic Great Lakes shorelines were better put to industrial and commercial use or protected largely in their natural state.

Regarded as a wasteland and an obstacle by the pioneers of the first half of the nineteenth century, the Indiana Dunes became the last great remaining enclave of a landscape that had once reached for seventy miles around the southern shore of Lake Michigan. The dunes dated back between five thousand and ten thousand years, to the end of the last period of glaciation. Sands flowing into the lake from melting glaciers and in river-born sediments were washed to shore and over time heaped by winds into the great dunes. Consisting of high proportions of finely rounded quartz, the dune sands were the essential building block of a natural system that featured plants of great diversity and tenacity, adapted to the harsh extremes of wind and temperature along the lakeshore. The lake's influence also created "a unique crossroads" of natural communities.[25] Moderating extremes of temperature, Lake Michigan, coupled with the sandy soils, provided a habitat suitable for conifers characteristic of the north, hardwoods from the east, tallgrass prairies of the west, and cactus from the south. But to the westward-moving American settler in the 1830s, they presented a different aspect:

> The next singular scene was an expanse of sand, before reaching the lake-shore,—sand, so extensive, hot, and dazzling, as to realize very fairly one's conception of the middle of the Great Desert; except for the trailing roses which skirted it. . . . I had ploughed my way through the ankle-deep sand till I was much heated, and turned in hope of meeting a breath of wind. At the moment the cavalcade came slowly into view from behind the hills; the labouring horses, the listless walkers, and smoothly rolling vehicles, all painted absolutely black against the dazzling sand. It was as good as being in Arabia. For cavalcade, one might read caravan. Then the horses were watered at a single house on the beach; and we proceeded on the best part of our day's journey, a ride of seven miles on the hard sand of the beach, actually in the lapping waves.[26]

Shaped by water and wind into broad towers as high as two hundred fifty feet above Lake Michigan, the sands furnished vistas of open sky and water. The landscape they defined was described variously as eerie, barren, subtly beautiful, and ripe for clearing and development. Major trails and then roads skirted them; for decades, only a few fishermen and their families made homes in them.

As Chicago oozed ever outward in the last three decades of the nineteenth century, engulfing what were once small villages reaching along the lakeshore to the Indiana border, economic dreamers in the Hoosier state began to see their chance. The publisher of a newspaper in Chesterton, A. J. Bowser, in the 1880s became the first loud booster of an Indiana shoreline industrial capital tapping the power of Lake Michigan for electricity, the convenience of a harbor for shipping, and the proximity of a skilled workforce across the state line and of rail lines capable of transporting raw materials from the south. His Chicago-based Porter Home Investment Company unsuccessfully sought to lure industrial investors to locate along the lake in Porter County. Later, as a member of the Indiana legislature, he was more successful, championing a "made-land" law that permitted industry to fill in the lake and expand plant sites for free.[27]

This law and time, it seemed, were on the side of development in Indiana's lakeshore dunes. In addition to grasping toward the state line, Chicago's growth created indirect opportunities for the tax base, jobs, and prestige that Indiana officials and community leaders craved. A steel manufacturing base for decades, by the end of the nineteenth century Chicago no longer contained undeveloped land of sufficient size and isolation to make room for the larger, more economical operations the industry desired.

Standard Oil's construction of an oil refinery in Whiting, Indiana, in 1889 opened a new era in the development of the near-shore communities. Formed through consolidation in 1901, U.S. Steel began exploring for sites in Indiana's Lake County. With the help of local attorney A. F. Knotts, the company identified and purchased a relatively inexpensive nine-thousand-acre site with seven miles of Lake Michigan frontage. The land in question was a "primeval jungle," said Knotts's brother, "a barren waste of sand dunes and impassable morasses inhabited by small wild animals."[28] Construction on the former duneland began in 1906. The site became Gary, Indiana, named after the chair of the board of U.S. Steel, Elbridge Gary.

Like the altered and harnessed Niagara Falls, Gary was soon hailed as a modern wonder. The site for the massive plant was raised fifteen feet, the dunes were demolished, the lake bottom was sucked of sand to deepen the draft for arriving supply ships, and a water intake capable of moving five million gallons of water per day was built a mile into the lake. The inconvenient, winding, swampy Grand Calumet River was straightened for a length of two miles. The company deployed a thousand workers to build a huge harbor, including a canal fifty-five hundred feet long and a mile-long breakwater. "U.S. Steel destroyed the Lake County Dunes forever," said two environmental historians. But more than twenty-five miles of undisturbed dunes to the east remained to be contested.

And for the first time, a constituency to contest their destruction was forming—across the state line in Chicago. Already highly developed, the city itself had struggled over the balance between protection and commerce for years, with the greatest passion erupting over the fate of the city's lakefront. Early officials charged with selling lands to pay for improvements had in 1836 declared the city-to-be's Lake Michigan shoreline a "Public Ground—A Common to Remain Forever Open, Clear, and Free of Any Buildings, or Other Obstruction whatever."[29] But after the city's 1871 fire, debris had been dumped into the lake, extending the land hundreds of yards to the east. In the 1890s shanties, stables, railroad sheds, and a firehouse occupied the shore on what would later become Grant Park, and city officials planned a civic center there. Instead, businessman Montgomery Ward sued to clear the shoreline and block the city's plans, insisting on a public park. Although an alderman said downtown lakefront was no place for a park and that instead the land "should be used to bring revenue to the city," Ward prevailed after nearly twenty years and an expenditure of $20,000 from his own pocket. Unpopular at the time, Ward's fight would later be regarded as an example of enlightened civic leadership.[30] As Ward fought for a public lakefront, Daniel H. Burnham would defend it eloquently in his 1909 "Plan of Chicago":

> The lakefront by right belongs to the people. It affords their one great unobstructed view, stretching away to the horizon, where water and clouds seem to meet. No mountains or high hills enable us to look over broad expanses of the earth's surface; and perforce we must come even to the margin of the lake for such a survey of nature. These views calm thought and feelings, and afford escape from the petty things of life. Mere breadth of view, however, is not all. The lake is living water, ever in motion, and ever changing in color and in the form of its waves. . . . Not a foot of its shores should be appropriated by individuals to the exclusion of the people.[31]

Preserving undeveloped land far from Chicago for its value as a nature study was another matter. Scientists and Chicago civic leaders made the case for the ruggedly beautiful, revealing Indiana Dunes. "The struggle for existence always interests because our life is such a struggle," said a botanist on the University of Chicago faculty, Henry Chandler Cowles, who had studied and loved the dunes since his arrival in 1895, and who developed his world-renowned theory of plant succession there.[32] As he crossed from dunes nearest the lake to those farther inland, Cowles found he was passing through time. Plants growing on the oldest, inland dunes had changed it, setting the stage for the rise of new species. His 1899 publication on plant succession in the Indiana Dunes, said Sir Arthur Tansley, "brought before the minds of ecologists the reality and the universality of the process in so vivid a manner as to stimulate everywhere—at least in the English-speaking world—that interest and enthusiasm for the subject that has led and is leading to such great results."[33]

Jens Jensen, an internationally prominent landscape architect who, among other things, had played a hand in the design of some of Chicago's parks and began tramping in the Indiana Dunes in 1889, helped introduce scores of associates and friends to the dunes both directly and through his founding role in the Prairie Club. "If this wonderful dune country should be taken away from us and on it built cities like Gary, Indiana Harbor and others," Jensen said, "it would show us in fact to be a people who only have dollars for eyes."[34]

Sometime in 1906 or 1907 a Chicago broker named Earl Reed was walking through the dunes when he was suddenly inspired to spurn the businessman's life and devote himself to recording the peculiar grandeur of the landscape that surrounded him. Reed became the author of *The Dune Country* and other works, and in them he told of a place "not for the realist, not for the cold and discriminating recorder of facts, nor the materialist who would weigh with exact scales or look with scientific eyes. It is a country for the dreamer and the poet, who would cherish its secrets, open enchanted locks, and explore hidden vistas, which the Spirit of the Dunes has kept for those who understand."[35]

By the second decade of the 1900s the dunes were the gathering place and symbol of a movement. They were beloved by a growing number of Chicagoans and neighbors. The dunes' greatest appeal was as a community to a community—a natural community of stirring and stark beauty, capable of inspiring the rawest and most sophisticated of human emotions:

> The lure of the dunes is kin to the lure of the desert and the desire for great waste spaces. They have, however, a uniqueness of their own which admits of no comparison. They breathe mystery and romance, and appeal to the imagination. They have a temper and a charm which you come to know and feel. . . . A hundred theories may explain their appeal, but, after all, the spell they cast becomes your own to unriddle, and you answer the riddle in your own way.[36]

In addition to the destruction wrought at Gary, dune lovers had received another cautionary lesson. At the eastern end of the Indiana shore in Michigan City, a great sand pinnacle known as the Hoosier Slide had already been sacrificed to commerce. Visible as far away as Chicago itself—more than forty miles distant—the slide had for a few decades attracted tourists eager to behold a panorama of Lake Michigan. But in 1906 the Hoosier Slide Sand Company incorporated. Michigan City sand was soon heading south to factories in Muncie, Anderson, Kokomo, and other cities, serving as an ingredient in glass. Hoosier Slide also supplied material for glass insulators, iron foundry cores, and a sand trap at a private golf course. A Michigan City newspaper reported in 1913 that "much of it has gone across the lake to Chicago and found its way into the wall constructions of some of the city's skyscrapers and other buildings." A "well-known old resident of the city" lamented the loss of the dune, "one of nature's most interesting attractions in our city, furnishing food for reflection and meditation."

Deploring the possible consumption of the remaining dunes for profit, the expanding population of dune lovers formed an association to call for creation of Sand Dunes National Park, reaching from east of Gary to Michigan City. For a time, prospects for the national park seemed promising. The park idea won a critical ally in 1916—Indiana U.S. senator Thomas Taggart, appointed to fill a vacancy by a Democratic governor. Organized instate support for the park was a novelty and was soon buttressed by the formation of a National Dunes Park Association that included both Chicago and Indiana members. Taggart introduced a bill calling for purchase of the dunes as a park, then a resolution calling for a study first. Stephen Mather, the first director of the National Park Service and a former member of the Prairie Club's Conservation Committee, obliged by scheduling an October hearing in Chicago.

At the hearing, University of Chicago ecologist Cowles called the dunes "the common meeting ground of trees and wild flowers from all directions. . . . Many of these species are found nowhere for many miles outside of the dune region, so that failure to conserve the dunes would result in the extinction of this wonderful flora for all time."[37] Representatives of the General Federation of Women's Clubs, the Chicago Association of Commerce, Michigan City mayor Martin Krueger, and other Indiana park backers also testified. The *Chicago Tribune* editorialized in favor of the park on the morning of the hearing.

After the hearing, Mather endorsed the idea of Sand Dunes National Park. In his report to Congress, he called for a reserve spanning twenty-five miles of the dune shoreline to a distance one mile inland, totaling up to twelve thousand acres and costing $2.6 million. But just days later, Indiana senator Taggart was defeated in his bid for election to fill the remaining four years of the term of his deceased predecessor. Taggart's defeat was one of several crippling blows to the park movement.[38] America's entry into World War II and a general congressional reluctance to sink taxpayer money into park acquisition also blunted momentum.

Ominously, Indiana voices opposing a national park had grown louder. Publisher Bowser decried the arrogance of Chicagoans seeking to set aside land in Indiana for their enjoyment. "What's in it for Indiana?" he asked. The out-of-staters would "gradually absorb our farmland and our souls would, like lo the poor Indian, have to be kept in bondage to them."[39] Local newspapers and business interests joined the chorus. Significantly, one suggested a compromise: a state park in a portion of the undeveloped dunes, with the remainder set aside for industry. Despite the opposition, Taggart's defeat, and the illness of Mather, the park boosters organized a dunes pageant on Memorial Day 1917 that attracted an estimated forty thousand people. An orchestra supplied the accompaniment for actors dramatizing the succession of those who had inhabited and loved the dunes, beginning with indigenous peoples. Shortened by rain, the pageant was conducted in its entirety the following weekend. While a major publicity success, the event marked the climax, for nearly fifty years, of the campaign to create a national park in the dunes.

Frustrated by federal government inaction, dunes lovers turned to Indiana for help. With the assistance of Richard Lieber, the first director of the Indiana Department of Conservation, citizens maneuvered for legislation that would protect at least a portion of the area once considered for the national park. Some action seemed critical. Inland Steel bought thirteen hundred acres of dunes in 1919, and a developer named F. Randolph Chandler proposed a Dune City on twenty thousand acres among the dunes. Meanwhile, a Dunes Highway was being constructed, providing convenient access into dune country for the first time and threatening the encroachment of residences as well as businesses.

Gary resident Bess Sheehan proved to be one of the critical campaigners for a dunes state park. Chairing the Dunes Park Committee of the State Federated Women's Clubs, she lobbied untiringly for a national and then a state reserve. The fight culminated in the waning days of the 1923 state legislative session. Resistance was considerable, especially among downstate farm legislators who, Sheehan said, "could see nothing good in a hill of sand." Sheehan gave a lecture on the dunes with pictures to legislators and their wives. Clubwomen from across the state inhabited the state capitol in Indianapolis. Sheehan enlisted former U.S. senator Taggart to win over reluctant Democrats. On 1 March 1923, the final day of the session, the General Assembly approved the dunes state park bill with one vote more than the minimum required. The state would now have a park with three miles of lake frontage, down from the compromise of nine that the National Dune Park Association had sought. Sheehan wrote to a friend, "The people here all gave up the struggle; seemed I was the only one who stuck. Had I known how discouraged the others were I guess I would have given up too."[40] Having won the state park fight, Sheehan retired from active advocacy for the dunes.

Developers still had visions of industrial glory in the dunes. The construction of the eight-mile Burns Ditch in 1926, slicing through over a mile of Porter County dunes, raised new hopes among businessmen for a public commercial harbor that would give Indiana an outlet to the waters of the Great Lakes and St. Lawrence and Mississippi waterways. Weirton Steel Company purchased seven hundred fifty acres on either side of Burns Ditch, and Northern Indiana Public Service Company bought three hundred acres in the eastern part of Porter County's dunes. Yet timing was still not right for further development. The onset of the Great Depression in 1929 and resistance from the U.S. Army Corps of Engineers to various harbor proposals for nearly three decades protected the dune region. During the same time, the American conservation movement grew to become a significant political force. In the post–World War II period, as affluence and leisure time grew, the demand for public recreation lands created a new economic as well as environmental argument for parks.

By the late 1950s development of the remaining unspoiled dunes seemed imminent. Pent-up pressure for a commercial harbor and industrial expansion, coupled with increasing residential development of the dunes, made it apparent to the growing community of conservationists that a day of reckoning was at hand. One of them, Dorothy Buell, who along with her husband owned a home in Ogden Dunes, committed her full energies to the dunes struggle in 1952 at the age of sixty-five. Helping to organize the Save the Dunes Council, she "radiated a dignified presence that allowed her domination of any company. She dressed formally for public occasions, complete with hat and gloves. . . . Colleagues recall that Buell had the tenacity of a bulldog. Once she got hold of something she never let it go. When she wanted to do something, she did it; nobody stood in her way."[41]

The council operated from the homes of Buell and other supporters. Before long, hundreds of members paid dues of $1 a year. The group's first success came quickly. Buell stumbled upon news that a bog in the back dunes—believed to be one of the sites where botanist Cowles had decades before made the observations that helped developed his theories of plant succession—was available for purchase because of nonpayment of taxes by the previous owner. Scraping together funds from Sheehan and a wealthy supporter as well as Buell's husband, Hal, the new council in 1953 bought the landmark bog. Its later sale to the federal government paid off debts accumulated during the lengthy fight for a national park in the dunes.

Buell's organizing talents had impressive impact. Under her leadership, the Save the Dunes Council organized an advisory board consisting of prominent scientists, artists, conservation leaders, and philanthropists. It collected five hundred thousand signatures on a petition to save the dunes. Perhaps most important, desperate after being rejected by Indiana politicians, Buell in 1957 enlisted Illinois U.S. senator Paul Douglas as a sponsor of legislation to create a dunes park.

A former professor of economics at the University of Chicago and a onetime pacifist who enlisted in the U.S. Marines at the age of fifty to protect democracy during World War II, Douglas and his wife, Emily, had built and spent considerable time in a beach cottage in Dune Acres, Indiana. A proponent of an activist federal government, Douglas intuitively understood the value of the dunes and the need for protective legislation:

> If ever there was a case where the state approach to a regional need was grossly inadequate, this was it. Aside from the little Indiana state park of 2,300 acres that had been purchased 40 years before by generous contributions from Chicagoans, including Julius Rosenwald, the people of the Midwest were about to be shut off from access to Lake Michigan, and the beautiful Dunes would be despoiled into a jungle of steel and asphalt. . . . The worst features of our civilization threatened to invade what had been an earthly paradise. The gross national product from the area, as measured in dollars, would probably increase. But so would smoke, polluted water, crime, and sexual license. Ugliness would replace beauty. There would be more jobs, but a larger proportion of nervous breakdowns and more inmates of mental institutions. Could this be regarded as progress?[42]

Douglas introduced a bill in 1958 calling for a national monument encompassing three-and-a-half miles of shoreline. The measure deliberately included land targeted for development by the state and recently purchased by Bethlehem Steel. Almost in unison, Indiana officials, the news media, and industrial interests condemned Douglas for meddling in Indiana's business. On the other hand, the intervention of Douglas brought national attention and support to the dunes cause. "It is often fruitless and it is always difficult for a member of Congress to oppose any plan for 'development' or industrialization of an area when large individual or corporate economic interests are as directly and immediately involved as in the present case," wrote John B. Oakes in the *New York Times* in June 1958. "But if by some miracle Senator Douglas' proposal should succeed, it would be a triumph for long-range values that are frequently overlooked."[43]

Like previous dunes park proponents, Douglas needed, and possessed, impressive stores of tenacity. The national monument legislation died in 1960. The new and more sympathetic John F. Kennedy administration, which took office in 1961, was willing to take a closer look, but Bethlehem Steel was determined to move ahead in developing its dune holdings in the center of the proposed reserve. In April 1961 it contracted to sell 2.5 million cubic yards of the dune sand on its property to Northwestern University in Evanston, Illinois, for construction of a "lakefill" to add seventy-four acres in Lake Michigan to the school's campus. Douglas decried the agreement. But neither party to the sand pact backed down.

While Douglas and harbor proponents sparred over federal funding for the proposed Burns Ditch Harbor, critical to the plans of Bethlehem Steel and other industrial property holders, his legislation languished. In the summer of 1963 Bethlehem began to develop the land it had retained. Nearly one thousand construction workers leveled the dunes and filled the low wetlands, moving more than twenty thousand cubic yards of sand per day.

As duneland desirable for park development was fragmented and shrank, Douglas and Buell continued their battle. By 1966 his bill to create an Indiana Dunes National Lakeshore had grown from thirty-six hundred contiguous acres to include eight thousand acres of noncontiguous land that excluded the central dunes now developed by Bethlehem Steel and desired by the development interests. The fate of the dunes came down to the final days of a legislative session as it had in the Indiana General Assembly forty-three years before. In an effort to help Douglas win re-election to a fourth Senate term in a hotly contested race, the Johnson administration and House and Senate Democratic leaders marshaled their forces for a final attempt to pass the lakeshore bill. On 14 October 1966, over the objections of home district Indiana congressman Charles Halleck, the U.S. House of Representatives approved compromise legislation establishing the lakeshore. But in almost the same breath, the Congress sanctioned $25 million in federal support for the Burns Waterway Harbor in the middle of the dunes, forever ending the dream of a contiguous public park.

Fifty years after Stephen Mather recommended a Sand Dunes National Park to the cheers of Chicago opinion leaders and a small number of Indiana dune lovers, a fractured lakeshore was now to be created. The victory was bittersweet. As Douglas, who did not win re-election in 1966 famously put it, he had entered the U.S. Senate in 1949

> to save the world. I was into my second term and knew I'd be doing very well to save the Western Hemisphere. Now at the end of my second term they'd got me down to North America. Into my third term I realized I couldn't do a damn thing about Canada and Mexico, so I was going to save the United States, which wasn't a bad thing to do. Christ, it wasn't long before I gave up everything west of the Mississippi and south of the Mason/Dixon line. They pushed me and squeezed me and took away everything I wanted to save, but Goddamn, I'm not going to give up the Indiana Dunes.[44]

For citizen dune protector Dorothy Buell, the passage of the lakeshore legislation was the culmination of a fourteen-year fight. Soon after, she and her husband retired to California, where she died in 1976, also the year Douglas died.

"If it weren't for the Save the Dunes Council, Indiana's Lake Michigan shoreline would be nothing more than a mosaic of belching smokestacks from Gary to Michigan City," said author Steven Higgs on the fiftieth anniversary of the council's formation in 2002.[45] Despite the loss of much of the landscape envisioned as a recreation and nature preserve at the beginning of the twentieth century, the lakeshore ultimately proved larger and more admired than its supporters might have expected in 1966. Successive expansions approved by Congress nearly doubled the size of the lakeshore outlined in the Douglas legislation, encompassing fifteen thousand acres of dunes, woods, wetlands, and remnant prairies as well as public beaches. About thirteen of Indiana's forty-five miles of Great Lakes shoreline were protected. The reality of industrialization did not in fact rob the dunes of their strange beauty. "In the closing decades of the twentieth century, the fragmented, vulnerable, yet ever-renewing Dunes landscape was an apt metaphor of the struggle for community in the midst of a divided society and broken land."[46]

Two ironies attest to the significance of the dunes as metaphor. While women, long denied their full share of participation in democratic processes, led the successful fights for both a state and national park along Lake Michigan, another group of citizens who were almost disenfranchised—African Americans—were little involved in the struggle because they were still seeking a basic right to use the public Lake Michigan beaches of nearby Gary. For example, violence by whites erupted in 1953 when two carloads of young African-American women tried to desegregate the beaches of Marquette Park. In his book *Environmental Inequalities,* Andrew Hurley observes, "Most African Americans . . . lacked the necessary sense of entitlement to the shoreline to become overly concerned about the prospect of industrial encroachment. Denied the use of public beaches, most African Americans were not willing to devote their energies to protecting them."[47]

A second irony is that after a brief forty years of intensive industrial use, much of the land lost by conservationists to the steel industry was up for grabs again early in the twenty-first century. The declining domestic steel industry vacated some facilities and found the sale of other land attractive. "While the impending contraction of the steel industry is truly regrettable, we must not compound this misfortune by failing to seize the tremendous opportunity it presents," said U.S. representative Pete Visclosky in September 2002.[48] Visclosky said he hoped to capture 75 percent of Indiana's shoreline for public use.

Indiana Dunes was just one of four national lakeshores among the Great Lakes established during the 1960s and early 1970s. Pictured Rocks, whose striking, stark rock formations on the eastern shoreline of Lake Superior and second-growth forests soon attracted outdoor recreationists as well as tourists, also became a national lakeshore in 1966. Apostle Islands, with twenty-one islands and twelve miles of mainland lakeshore in Wisconsin, gained federal status in 1970. So did Sleeping Bear Dunes, a landscape of large dunes perched atop a moraine on the northwest shore of the Lower Peninsula of Michigan. Only the legislative battle over Sleeping Bear Dunes, where longtime private property owners feared being displaced by the new park, reproduced the violent clash of views that had characterized the Indiana Dunes.

Ontario and the Canadian federal government also added to the number of protected areas from the 1950s through the 1970s. Responding to the same post–World War II affluence that created demand for recreation sites in the U.S.—as well as a growing public clamor for protection of unspoiled nature—the province added The Pinery on Lake Huron, Wasaga Beach on Georgian

Bay, and Holiday Beach, Rock Point, and Turkey Point parks on Lake Erie, among others. The national government, under agreements with Ontario, created Pukaskwa National Park on the far north shore of Lake Superior in 1971 and Bruce Peninsula National Park on the Niagara Escarpment in 1986.

But no amount of parks could ultimately guarantee the long-term health and protection of the Great Lakes system. Increasingly, conservationists and scientists fretted that only improved private land stewardship could suffice if the integrity of the region was to be assured. Ultimately, every park would represent a compromise among expansive visions, private property rights, the persistent development imperative, and political realities. In that sense, the Indiana Dunes struggle offered several lessons. A monument to compromise as well as nature, the Indiana Dunes Lakeshore reflects the continuing conflict between utilitarianism and the protection impulse—and the deepening love of a growing number of the Great Lakes Basin's current residents for their home.

Diana and the Dunes

THE POETRY OF THE GREAT LAKES SAND DUNES addressed a stony audience for most of the nineteenth century. Measuring the natural world by its suitability for settlement and its potential for producing wealth, the first citizens of the new states of Michigan and Indiana found the dunes wanting on both counts. State geologist Douglass Houghton described to the Michigan legislature and governor in 1838 "a succession of sand dunes or hills of loose sand, not unfrequently attaining a considerable altitude. . . . These movable sands, which are now unnoticed, may hereafter become matters of serious inconvenience, more particularly in those portions where the timber may be heedlessly removed. These dunes are not unfrequently composed of sand tolerably well adapted to the manufacture of glass, though its value is frequently much impaired by the presence of particles of dark colored minerals."[49]

But by the time historian Frederick Jackson Turner in 1893 declared the closing of the American frontier—and described the effect of the movement west in shaping the national character—Chicagoans were turning just to the east to find a sand frontier. The question they asked: could Americans abandon the impulse of conquest in favor of a love of landscape?

Artists interpreted the dune country to a broader population. Carl Sandburg published a poem titled "Dunes" in 1916 and would later live with his family on the lakeshore just north of Michigan City, Indiana. As support for park protection of the Indiana Dunes mounted in the years after 1910, art about the wild landscape so close to the great metropolis blossomed. The Chicago Public Library sponsored an exhibit on the dunes in 1917, featuring art and photographs by members of the local Prairie Club. The Chicago Art Institute included the dunes as one of thirteen classic American landscapes in its 1919 exhibit, *Pictures of Our Country*.

If works of art were insufficient to impress the public with the wild beauty of the dunes, the fierce independence of a Chicago woman did so. Alice Mable Gray, the daughter of a Chicago physician, took a degree from the University of Chicago in 1903 and continued with on-and-off graduate study through 1912. But she escaped general notice until 1916, when Chicago newspapers reported on a lone female living and walking among the Indiana Dunes. The newspapers embellished upon the reports of fishermen who sighted her, terming her "Nymph of the Dunes" and ultimately "Diana of the Dunes." Her practice of shedding clothes to skinny-dip in the cool waters of Lake Michigan helped inspire the interest of reporters; and rumors that she almost magically disappeared at the approach of visitors only deepened their determination to pursue, overtake, and capture her in a newspaper account.

Although rumors persisted that Alice Gray had chosen to live in the dunes out of a disappointment in love, she said nothing to support this thesis. She told the *Chicago Examiner* in July 1916, "I wanted to live my own life—a free life. The life of a salary earner in the cities is slavery, a constant fight for the means of living. Here it is so different."[50] Diana of the Dunes said she had slept under the stars for four nights before discovering and occupying an abandoned fisherman's hut. She told the newspaper she lived simply, needing to buy only bread and salt for a year and living during that time on the last paycheck she had received in Chicago.

Alice won notice for more than her habit of bathing in the nude. Wearing her hair bobbed, she owned no mirror and knew when it was too long by the shadow it cast. She dressed in a "short coarse skirt," big boots, ragged waist, and a cap in winter; in summer, an old light dress and ragged waist. She did without shoes and stockings, cooked outside her hut, and had only an old coffee pot and cup as utensils.

Defying all convention in a time when the four walls of home, church, and a few civic institutions typically bound the environment of women, Diana of the Dunes excited newspapers. Within a week of the *Chicago Examiner* story, at least twenty-five versions of it appeared in the region's newspapers. Noting her celebrity status, the Prairie Club of Chicago invited her to speak at a 1917 event supporting the creation of a national park in the Indiana Dunes. She said: "So the Indiana Dune Country, like Chicago herself, is the child of Lake Michigan and the Northwest Wind. . . . Besides its nearness to Chicago and its beauty, its spiritual power, there is between the Dune country and the city a more than sentimental bond—a family tie. To see the Dunes destroyed would be for Chicago the sacrilegious sin which is not forgiven."[51]

The simple life did not, in the end, prove idyllic. The raw winds of winter scour the dunes, and the rawness of human nature and life scours the glitter from modern myths. After meeting a tall, muscular man named Paul Wilson, a fisherman and carpenter, Alice Gray boldly professed to yet another reporter (who called her "Mrs. Crusoe") in 1920 that she shared the shack with him. "Caveman Wins Dunes' Diana," reported the *Chicago Herald-Examiner.*[52]

Wilson, a rough-hewn and apparently unlettered man, was not beloved in the local country. He was suspected, although cleared, of the murder of a man whose body was found not far from the shack. Later, confronting a local deputy who had accused the couple of stealing provisions from cottages they were tending, Gray was pistol-whipped and suffered a fractured skull; Wilson was shot in the foot.

It is likely no coincidence that the popularity of Diana and her mate declined as roads opened the wild dunes to development. When the Dunes Highway between Gary and Michigan City opened in 1923, property values shot skyward. Squatters were no longer romantic but impediments to profit. In the fall of the same year, Wilson and Alice Gray set out on a twenty-four-foot boat for the Mississippi and the Gulf of Mexico, but by 1925 they had returned. On the night of 8 February, Paul Wilson asked Samuel Reck, who owned the land on which he and Alice were squatting, to summon a doctor. The next morning, Alice died of uremic poisoning. "Death Takes 'Diana of the Dunes' From the Scenes She Loved and Cloaks Forever the Motive for Her Desire for Primal Life," cried the *Gary Post Tribune,* adding that she had disdained medical treatment.[53] Wilson had run to Reck's house for help only after she slipped into unconsciousness.

Her funeral in Gary climaxed a simple life rendered sensational. A later historian said people hawked duneland souvenirs at the service. In this version of the funeral story, Paul Wilson wept over the casket, brandished a pistol, and was restrained by police officers. The threatened violence may have had greater significance than immediately realized. Alice's fatal uremic poisoning, it turns out, may have been triggered by Paul Wilson's beatings of her, which inflicted severe bruises.

Alice Gray said in 1916 that a poem of Lord Byron's called 'Solitude' gave her "the first longings to get away from the conventional world, and I never gave up on the idea, although a long time passed before I could fulfill it."[54] The line in the poem that most impressed her: "In solitude when we are least alone." What more she may have had to say, we cannot know. Manuscripts on which she worked in her shack in the sands were looted, it is said, while she recovered from her 1923 skull fracture in a hospital.

In the same year, 1923, a small patch of the Indiana Dunes was purchased for a state park. But in 1929 a division of National Steel bought seven hundred fifty acres of land, and the Northern Indiana Public Service Company bought three hundred more acres for a power station. After decades of struggle between local developers and the region's conservationists, much of the land proposed for a national park was consumed in construction of a port to serve, among other things, the steel industry. When Senator Paul Douglas finally won congressional approval of the Indiana Dunes National Lakeshore in 1966, the new park in no way matched the original proposal in quality, beauty, or scientific value. Today Diana's dunes are a checkerboard of houses, industrial buildings, and remnant hills of sand and intervening wetlands. Despite their struggles, an eerie beauty persists.

The stories of Diana, of the national park, and of the Great Lakes dunes system are both a dirge and an anthem to that inevitable struggle.

I remember learning duck hunting among the bulrushes and cattails of Saginaw Bay. As a Bay City native, I grew up along the Bay's shoreline with all the related activities that are associated with it. Duck hunting was, and still is, a major recreational activity there. As the dark, cloudy, windy days of October and November arrived, large migrating flocks of ducks and geese would be abundant and low-flying. These were the times we would drop everything we were doing, even skipping an occasional class in high school and college to get out to the marshes along the Bay.

—Jim Goodheart

The lakes always seemed so big to me. In fact, I was never really sure why they were called lakes since when you are on the water, whether luffing or listing, it often felt like you might as well be on the ocean, since you could go for a long time without seeing land. While living in Washington D.C., I used to play on the Chesapeake Bay quite a bit. I remember my friends' disbelief when I would boast that the Bay had nothing over the Great Lakes except maybe a little more rain and a lot more of the doldrums.

—Karen Trevino

Degradation

Water—the source of life and the defining characteristic of the Great Lakes region—for generations after European settlement was an afterthought. It was also a dumping ground, an open sewer, and a threat to the public health.

The rapid population growth and industrialization that transformed the Great Lakes region in the second half of the nineteenth century subjected the waters of the system to the worst insults they had ever known. Crude sewage management methods tolerable for small towns and rural areas were simply incapable of handling the wastes of millions. The early response of governments set a pattern that has persisted into the present. Applying cheap and temporary patches to existing problems in order to avoid costly, unpopular decisions about permanent solutions, they tipped communities and the lakes into crisis after crisis, correcting them only when public outrage forced their hand.

Chicago became one of the first cities on the continent to plot and construct a massive sewage system to transport wastes into nearby waters, building one hundred fifty-two miles of sewers in the ten years following commencement of the system in 1859. The system captured "the imagination of the public health and engineering communities" and was imitated by dozens of other cities.[1] But it merely diverted the problem by transferring sewage to the open waters of Lake Michigan, where residents of the city liked to bathe in the warm months, and from which they would soon draw their water supply. By the 1870s public officials throughout the Great Lakes region were beginning to worry about the danger to health that might be developing.

Robert C. Kedzie, an early leader in Michigan's public health movement, complained in a State Board of Health president's address in 1878 that Detroit had chosen to dump all of its sewage into the Detroit River. "When anything was said about the contamination of the river-water, and that this water would become unfit for use by those living on the banks of the river below the city, the reply was ready that it was not possible to pollute such a mass of water by any amount of sewage," Kedzie said. "But the country above Detroit is becoming thickly settled. . . . Just now there is no little excitement in the City of the Straits concerning contaminated water, and the fear is expressed that when the population along the river above Detroit becomes greatly increased, the water of the Detroit River will be unfit for domestic and potable use."[2]

His forecast, like others made at about the same time, did almost nothing to force consideration of alternatives. Instead, city after city constructed extensive sewer systems, with the explicit hope of dispatching sewage into rivers and away from dwellings and businesses as rapidly as possible. The problem was that downriver cities frequently used the same rivers as sources of drinking water, with deadly consequences. Sanitary engineer George Johnson observed that "a person who knowingly takes into his mouth the excrement of another human being is certainly defective. A community having a public water supply known to be contaminated by the sewage of other cities, and using it without even attempting its purification, is certainly a victim of defective civilization."[3] The Great Lakes civilization was no better than any of its time.

Sarnia, Ontario, installed its public drinking water supply intake pipe only forty-five meters away from its untreated sewage outfall pipes. Particularly in the connecting channels of the St. Mary's and St. Clair Rivers, the Detroit River, and the Niagara River, the flow of sewage began to sicken and kill people in large numbers. Typhoid death rates in the first two decades of the twentieth century ranged as high as one hundred seventy-eight per one hundred thousand in Port Arthur, Ontario, one hundred one in Sarnia, and forty-nine in Windsor. A level at or above twenty-four per one hundred thousand was considered a sign of a "compromised" supply.

For a time, despite the commonsense warnings of Kedzie and many others that dumping sewage into lakes and streams was dangerous, the practice was condoned. Sewage treatment was a new technology and was expensive. Cities were just beginning to recognize the problems generated by burgeoning populations and to consider assuming a new role as purveyors of clean drinking water and other sanitary services. There was at least one other reason for delay: protection of a community's image.

> When disease did break out, local leaders took great pains to keep the news quiet. This was an age when every city and town competed to attract manufacturing and service

> industries. Such pride made even public health officers hesitant to pursue their responsibilities fully if they might undermine their community's prestige or thwart an opportunity for growth, as would happen if their town became known as a disease-prone locale. A significant manifestation of this attitude was the tendency for local public health officers to under-report incidence of disease, especially typhoid fever. When they did inform the central Board, local health officers were quick to point out that many of the typhoid cases reported in their communities had originated outside the city limits, but that treatment in their hospitals necessitated inclusion in their returns.[4]

By 1912 pressure for reform from within the public health community in Ontario grew to the point that the provincial legislature enacted a public health law requiring municipalities to get approval from the Ontario Board of Health for their choice of water and sewage works and mandating maintenance and improvements to the systems. The new law helped correct some of the most egregious community conditions.

The signing of the Boundary Waters Treaty of 1909 by the United States and Canada provided a new mechanism for resolving boundary disputes between the two nations. It also provided a new mechanism, a binational panel called the International Joint Commission (IJC), for the investigation and analysis of the pollution problems plaguing the waters along the boundary. In August 1912 the two national governments sent a reference, an official request, to the IJC to study whether pollution had rendered the boundary waters unfit for domestic or other uses in violation of the treaty. Six years later, after one of the most comprehensive environmental investigations conducted before or since, involving sampling at over fourteen hundred points in the boundary waters, the IJC published an extensive report concluding the "situation along the frontier . . . is generally chaotic, everywhere perilous and in some cases disgraceful."[5]

The worst pollution occurred in the Detroit and Niagara Rivers. Detroit's sewage discharge fouled downstream waters used by Walkerville and Windsor in Ontario and by Wyandotte on the American side, elevating death rates from typhoid fever. Pollution of the lower Niagara River made it "totally unfit for domestic uses unless purified," the commission said.[6] Gross contamination was found to some degree in all of the channels connecting the Great Lakes.

What would it take to stop the untreated dumping and to reduce the number of deaths? The IJC estimated costs per capita for adequate modern sewage treatment at 54¢ per year in Detroit, 65¢ in Buffalo, and an average of 77¢ in smaller Ontario and Michigan coastal cities. "These charges also appear to the Commission to be reasonable, both in view of the financial standing of the towns and cities and in view of similar charges in the case of other towns and cities in the two countries," the commission declared.[7]

The commission had another suggestion. Calling the transboundary pollution "a matter of great international moment," it urged the two national governments to give it the power to develop regulations and orders to assure protection of the cleanliness of the affected waters. The IJC pointed to the "variety and possible conflict of national, State, provincial and municipal authorities" as a justification for such centralized standard setting.[8] But the two nations balked at giving the IJC such powers. Like the proposed transboundary fishing regulations that threatened state and provincial sovereignty in the late nineteenth and early twentieth centuries, a draft treaty to control transboundary pollution was shelved.[9]

Meanwhile, Chicago had found an alternative solution to its sewage woes, necessitated by runaway population growth. A city of just 4,470 in 1840, Chicago expanded to a population of 1,698,575 in 1900. Attracting immigrants from most of the nations of Europe, the city engulfed villages and towns to the north, south, and west. Proud of its central role in the commerce and culture of the United States, the city successfully competed to host the 1893 World's Columbian Exposition, honoring the four hundredth anniversary of the landing of the Columbus expedition in the Americas. Only twenty-two years after the murderous fire that consumed much of the city, the six-month exposition attracted more than twenty-seven million visitors, firmly establishing Chicago's position as one of the world's great cities—in a local slogan, the "I Will" city.

But there was another face to Chicago. During the years of the city's explosive growth, it had unsuccessfully coped with a problem that mocked lofty human pretensions—what to do with the mounting quantities of excrement generated by its citizens. Although dubbed "The First City of Filth" for its sheer quantity of waste, Chicago's problem was not unique; cities all over the continent agonized over how to protect their populations from the water-borne disease and repulsive nuisances caused by the discharge of sewage into rivers and lakes. But Chicago's solution was unique.

Chicago's position at the head of Lake Michigan had helped support its staggering growth. Providing access to Great Lakes vessels that shouldered timber and minerals from Ontario, Wisconsin, and Michigan needed to support America's westward movement, Chicago benefited from still another accident of geography. Only a few miles from the shores of Lake Michigan lay the boundary of the Great Lakes Basin. The west fork of the south branch of the Chicago River originated in a marsh known as Mud Lake, which at times also fed the Des Plaines River, a headwater tributary of the Mississippi.

For decades the proximity of these two great watersheds had fostered Chicago's advancement, making it the nexus for agricultural, forest, and mineral shipments heading west and east and supporting the development of nearby refining and manufacturing industries. Chicago was one of the nation's leading marketplaces.

Since 1848, fulfilling the dreams of its founders and early leaders, Chicago had joined with the state of Illinois in exploiting the local hydrology. In that year, after twelve years of construction, the ninety-seven-mile Illinois and Michigan Canal opened, providing a conduit for barges seeking to make a transit from Chicago to the prairie cities of Illinois, St. Louis, and beyond. Although soon eclipsed by railroads as a method of shipping such commodities as grain and lumber, the canal contributed to Chicago's prosperity.

But as the twentieth century began, facing the threat of mass sickness and typhoid-induced death caused by sewage pouring into Lake Michigan and contaminating the city's drinking water intakes, city leaders conceived a new benefit of the watershed connection. Why not reverse the flow of the Chicago River, sending the city's filth away from the lake and the drinking water supply, diluting it with the waters of the Des Plaines, and carrying it out of sight and smell?

In 1880 a Chicago citizens committee supported the idea of a sewage canal running away from Lake Michigan, proposing also that the "new river" carry ocean-going vessels. In 1886 the city created the Drainage and Water Supply Commission, which evaluated alternatives such as disposing the sewage on land, facilitating its use as fertilizer, but the panel ultimately settled on the same idea espoused by the earlier committee. In 1892 work on the Chicago Ship and Sanitary Canal began. In January 1900, racing to beat a court injunction sought by the downstream city of

St. Louis, which feared an onslaught of Chicago sewage, city officials hurriedly opened the gates.

On 14 January 1900 the *New York Times* reported, "The impossible has happened! The Chicago River is becoming clear! The stream which for a generation has been the butt of the newspaper paragrapher and the low comedian, which has been known rather as a solid than as a liquid body, which polluted the city water supply for a quarter of a century, and which twice caught on fire and had to be put out by the Fire Department, is actually approaching translucency and can be seen to move!"[10] In the eyes of many other observers, the river's reversal was a sanitary milestone, a $31 million monument to human ingenuity. The threat to the public health of Chicago was vanquished.

The diversion, which ultimately averaged thirty-two hundred cubic feet per second, only slowly awakened the resentment of Chicago's neighbors. It would be years before the seven other Great Lakes states would launch a civil attack on the Lake Michigan diversion, culminating in a 1926 U.S. Supreme Court challenge over the perceived economic damage caused by the project's lowering of Great Lakes levels.

Sending sewage away from Chicago solved the immediate problem of contamination in the city's Lake Michigan drinking water supply. Other governments were even less interested in reducing—as opposed to controlling—the sewage they generated. The reason was chlorination, soon to be regarded as a major public health success. Beginning in the first decades of the twentieth century, communities in Canada and Michigan began disinfecting drinking water supplies with chlorine. Debuting at the Bubbly Creek Filer plant at Chicago's Union Stock Yards in 1908, chlorination—especially when used in conjunction with filtration—rapidly expanded throughout the two nations. Typhoid death rates per 100,000 residents fell in Detroit from 27 in 1900 to 5.1 in 1920, in Toronto from 40.8 in 1910 to 1.0 in 1915, and in Milwaukee from 17 in 1900 to 2.2 in 1920.[11] Chlorination saved thousands of lives in the Great Lakes Basin.

Cleveland's handling of its sewage problem was typical of the basin's cities. By the mid 1870s the sewage and filth of the city rendered its water supply, drawn unfiltered from Lake Erie, a health hazard. The city in 1874 pushed the intake pipes more than sixty-five hundred feet out into the lake, seeking to isolate the water source from pollution dumped into the Cuyahoga River and the lake itself. But population and industrial growth continued to aggravate pollution. In 1896 construction began on a water inlet tunnel extending twenty-six thousand feet into the lake. Completed in 1904, the tunnel cost the lives of more than twenty-eight workers through fires and drowning. In 1911 the city began chlorinating its water supply and began filtering it in 1917. By October 1925 chlorination and filtration were complete, and "diseases caused by impure water virtually disappeared."[12] Results were similar in Ontario. Toronto's Department of Health complained after chlorination that the typical citizen "now accepts his safe water . . . without much thought as to how it came to be safe or what efforts are required to keep it so."[13]

The public health protection provided by chlorination had a second, unintended political effect. By virtually wiping out the scourge of typhoid and other waterborne diseases in drinking water supplies, chlorination reduced the pressure from outraged citizens for cleaning up pollution and made it easier for public officials to ignore worsening conditions. Writes environmental historian Jennifer Read: "just as unacceptably high typhoid mortality levels had initially spurred the provincial and federal governments to action, the decline in general and epidemic outbreaks of the disease equally reduced the demand for a legislative or diplomatic solution."[14] If sewage could be managed through the treatment of drinking water supplies rather than through pollution reduction or elimination—a policy course that would raise tax bills and generate conflicts with large municipalities—government agencies would opt for the treatment. In a time when only a relatively small community of hunters, anglers, and bird lovers would protest fish and duck kills caused by the dumping of sewage, when protecting stream health was not yet considered an important function of government, the stage was set for dramatic deterioration in the quality of rivers and lakes everywhere, but with special effects and meaning in the Great Lakes.

Conditions worsened throughout most of the industrialized lower lakes during and immediately after World War I. Industrial pollution added to the burden caused by city sewage. Saginaw Bay fishermen from 1915 to 1918 complained of foul-tasting catches that were traced back to direct discharges of chemical wastes by Dow Chemical Company, forty-five miles upstream on the Tittabawassee River. Michigan sought an injunction to stop the nuisance, and Dow built a settling basin to contain the dichlorobenzol and other wastes.[15] But overflows continued, and by the 1930s scientists again detected evidence of Dow pollution in the bay.

Clusters of industry were the more common source of harmful industrial wastes. A dozen paper mills on the Fox River, which feeds Wisconsin's Green Bay, and another dozen on Michigan's Kalamazoo River dumped their oxygen-demanding wastes into the tributaries, killing most aquatic life for miles downstream. The burgeoning steel industry of northwestern Indiana claimed the sluggish Grand Calumet and Little Calumet Rivers as waste receptacles, again killing off most life and sending chemicals out into Lake Michigan. Up and down the shores of Lake Michigan, manufacturing industries churned out vast quantities of waste, providing little treatment for years.

Other areas of the lakes were also grossly polluted. The Buffalo River, taking the wastes of major manufacturing industries—including a dye factory, a steel mill, coke ovens, a chemical plant, and an oil refinery—was among the worst. In addition to the untreated and poorly treated wastes that these businesses poured into it, the river suffered from municipal sewage and the destruction of wetlands along its banks from dredging, which limited its natural cleansing capacity. In the 1960s, before emptying into Lake Erie in downtown Buffalo, the river was a "repulsive holding basin for industrial and municipal wastes," said a U.S. pollution control agency. In language unusually poetic for a description of foul contamination, the report said the river was a "boundless mosaic of color and patterns resulting from the mixing" of the various wastes. In January 1968 the river caught fire, closing a lift bridge for several days.[16]

Ontario's Hamilton Harbor was another wasteland. The harbor's sizable marshes had originally provided rich habitat for wildlife and fish. The relatively small harbor accounted for 15 percent of the Lake Ontario fish catch in 1900. "Soup made from turtles caught in the harbour was a specialty at a local hotel," said a later report on the harbor's cleanup.[17] The industrial development and population increase characteristic of most of the basin's major urban areas plunged the harbor into chaos during and after World War II. Pollution closed beaches for the first time in the 1940s. The filling of a quarter of the harbor's water area after 1926 reduced valuable habitat and undermined the natural treatment qualities of the harbor. By the late 1960s the harbor was stained by chemical pollution, its waters reflecting the dark smoke of the industries clustered on its edges.

Lake Erie fared worst of all. Through a combination of its nature and its extensive development, mostly on the United States side, the shallowest of the lakes was destined to become a global poster child for environmental disgrace on a developed continent. The virtual collapse of the Lake Erie ecosystem in the 1950s and 1960s represented the worst that democratic governments and capitalist economies could do to an ecosystem. But the movement to reclaim the lake illustrated the emergence in both the United States and Canada of a new, compelling public voice.

Lake Effects

When 35.4 inches of snow buried Buffalo, New York, on 27 and 28 December 2001, news reports reminded the North American audience of a consequence of living among the Great Lakes. In winter, Arctic winds scoop up the relatively warmer waters of the lakes and dump them in sometimes smothering snowstorms. Seven snowbelts along the shores of the five Great Lakes take the brunt of the snow, with single-storm records ranging from 39 inches near London, Ontario, in 1977 to 72 inches just south of Buffalo during a six-day period in 1958. But stunning, localized snowstorms are just one of the phenomena associated with living near and along the lakes.

Just two months before the record-breaking twenty-four-hour lake effect Buffalo snowstorm of 2001, sustained winds of more than forty miles per hour that barreled across the region resulted in a seiche—the name for a sloshing water movement. Traveling across the narrow, shallow waters of Lake Erie, the howling winds dropped the water level at Toledo by nearly five feet, with a corresponding increase in levels at the east end of the lake. The storm drove water from one end of the lake to the other as though the lake was a giant glass tilted by its holder. And as it does in a tilting glass, the water must slosh back, sometimes creating peril for those on the shore.

In the early morning of Saturday, 26 June 1954, a squall crossed Chicago and its northern suburbs, driving Lake Michigan water before it as it charged toward Michigan City, Indiana. Arriving there with a six- to eight-foot swell at 8:25 A.M., the storm sent a rebounding wave back toward Chicago.

All was quiet at the city's Montrose Park, used by an estimated fifty anglers and lake lovers on that weekend morning. But at 9:25 A.M. the seiche pounced, and eight feet of water suddenly swamped the park's breakwater. Chester Michalik said, "I got up and was going over to my minnow bucket. The next thing I knew I was in the water." Conservation officer Herbert Riederer was near shore, writing out a summons for a man lacking a fishing license, when he "turned and saw 15 or 20 persons farther out being washed into the lake. I ran to a bathhouse and called police, then went back."[18]

The shouting front-page headline of the next day's *Chicago Tribune,* "7 Feared Dead in Big Wave," slightly underestimated the final toll. Eight died, including a swimmer off the city's North Avenue Beach. Two teenaged boys who had accompanied their fathers on the Saturday morning outing but went to shore before the seiche arrived identified the bodies of their parents.

Seiches, which also result from sudden changes in atmospheric pressure, can temporarily expose the lake bottom. A 1999 seiche at Buffalo enabled observers to view debris and rocks up to half a mile into the lake.

Exposed lake bottom in the lakes has also periodically resulted from naturally plummeting water levels. Although recurring every few decades, these low water periods interfere with recreational and commercial navigation and perplex, distress, or please lakefront property owners.

A low-water period that began in 1998 and culminated in 2001 dropped the level of Lake Michigan by four feet and expanded the beach of Bill Boyd at Wilmette, Illinois, from twenty-five feet to two hundred feet. "We enjoy walking along it, viewing it, and there's more room to play volleyball," he said.[19]

But up the shore in Wisconsin's Door Peninsula, the same phenomenon worried marina operators and tourism promoters. At a marina on Washington Island, the owner lamented that he would not recover the $170,000 he spent in 2000 to dredge his entrance channel. Most large sailboats that draw more than five feet of water couldn't navigate the shallow harbor. Another marina operator on the Oconto River said the sinking water had cost her $150,000 through July 2001. Piers in the peninsula were sometimes as much as fifty feet from the water.

The commercial shipping industry had similar complaints. For each inch the lakes recede, a ship hauls two hundred seventy tons less cargo, the Lake Carriers Association reported.

Long memories help buffer fears about the lakes—and forestall sometimes destructive actions that lakeshore residents are tempted to take. Rose O'Dowd of Erie, Pennsylvania, counseled patience in 2001, when Lake Erie fell to 570.2 feet above sea level, just 2.5 inches above its recorded all-time low. She remembered similarly low levels in the

1930s. In 1934 boat owners of the Erie Yacht Club couldn't get their boats into Presque Isle Bay. By 1945 the water had rebounded, taking out 200 feet of highway near the local lighthouse.

Even though water levels fluctuate naturally, their seemingly sudden rise and fall arouse suspicions among some lakefront property owners. Record high water levels that peaked in 1986 led a group of them to assert that the International Joint Commission, which has authority to manage water levels in the lakes system, was failing to act aggressively to combat the threat to homes on the shores of Lakes Michigan, Huron, Erie, and Ontario. Organized as the International Great Lakes Coalition, they demanded the commission shut the gates allowing water from two Ontario diversions to enter Lake Superior, with consequent effects on all the lakes below. "Superior and Ontario are regulated and the inner lakes are used as buffer zones for fluctuating levels. We're tired of it," said vice chairman Michael Walker.[20]

The commission ultimately obliged, but the effect was negligible. A U.S. government scientist pointed out that it would take twelve to fifteen years for a complete closure of the gates to lower the level of Lake Huron by one foot. Meanwhile, Michigan committed $10 million to the high-water problem, including low-interest loans for relocating private residences in danger of toppling into the lake from eroded beaches and bluffs. The state also provided free sandbags to shoreline communities fighting periodic flooding caused by winds and ice jams.

By 2001 the complaint was different: the allegedly unsightly plant growth on the exposed lake bottom of Michigan's Saginaw Bay was repulsive to shoreline owners, who complained of stagnant water odors and insect infestation.

Many cut the weeds or plowed the former lakebed. In a time when the lake bottom was no longer wet, they had understandable difficulty viewing it as a wetland. Organizing as Save Our Shorelines, they turned out at a November hearing of a Michigan Senate task force to demand the right to eliminate the "weeds." The U.S. Army Corps of Engineers had threatened to prosecute those who intruded on the exposed lands, which by law belong to the public.

Ernie Krygier of Save Our Shorelines, a property owners group said "our mission is to keep beaches. People have vegetation over their heads and they're walking through muck."[21] Terry Miller of the Lone Tree Council, an environmental group, retorted, "If by shoreline we're talking about preserving, preventing erosion and preserving habitat, if we're talking about filtering the water, then what they're doing is just the opposite. Their intent is to destroy it."[22]

A bulletin prepared by Michigan State University Extension seemed to agree with Miller, pointing out the values of the exposed lands, including the production of soft-stem bulrush and other plants that provide food for waterfowl and replenish habitat when the waters climb again. "Plowing and mowing may destroy large parts of these important wetlands, negatively affecting both the diverse wildlife inhabitants and coastal landowners," the bulletin observed.[23]

The cycles of water and associated politics are likely to stop only under two circumstances. Great Lakes states and Ontario can follow the example of the state of Oregon, which effectively stops development on its coast by owning more than 90 percent of the shoreline. Climate change may offer the final solution, however. Forecasted three to five foot declines in water levels during the twenty-first century will, if they materialize, halt worries about homes toppling into the lake and lessen the fury of seiches. But such changes will undoubtedly spawn a new batch of unanticipated lake effects.

I still remember the first time I saw Lake Ontario. I was 9 or 10. We came down Highway 115, and came around a curve, coming out of those big hills. The concept of "sublime" describes how I felt. I was overwhelmed by the size of that lake.

—Jennifer Read

We moved to the Cleveland, Ohio area from New York in 1950, when I was 16. The thought of leaving western Long Island Sound sailing was sad for me. I became a good sailor and seaman on salt water—the thought of a lake did not appeal. When my family completed the move to Cleveland, I was pleasantly surprised at the boating activity, good sailing weather and friendly people.

I recall that weather and heavy chop could build fast and without heavy wind activity. This, of course, was attributed to the relative shallowness of Erie. I soon became involved in a regular racing schedule, crewing for owners of larger boats than mine. Of course in the 1950s all boats were wood, steel or aluminum. Fiberglass was still on the horizon.

I remember racing out of Rocky River on the west side of Cleveland—crewing on boats out of Cleveland where I became a non-voting junior member with dues of $2 a month. I participated in annual race events "around the marks" as well as long distance events to the western Lake Erie islands—Kelly's Island, Put-in-Bay, Bass Island—also a distance race across to Canada—Pte. Aux Pins and Erieau.

—Bill Ardizone

Indignation

It had been assumed even Lake Erie, relatively small in comparison to the other lakes, was large enough to break down most of the wastes dumped into it without significant impact. But signs of stress began to accumulate after World War I. Blooms of green algae became a nuisance in the 1930s. Counts of mayfly larvae, an indicator of water quality, plummeted dramatically in the western end of the lake early in the 1950s. A 1953 report by the Ohio Department of Natural Resources found conditions grim: "At the mouths of most of the tributary streams there exist for long periods pollution barriers to fish in the form of toxic material, phenol, or deficient oxygen. . . . All evidence indicates that the marginal waters of Lake Erie along the Ohio shore and its tributary streams are in a condition which demand [*sic*] concerted cleanup action."[1] But instead, conditions worsened. By early in the next decade, scientists concluded that a massive area of the lake bottom, more than fourteen hundred square miles in size, was starved of dissolved oxygen.[2] The reason? In the jargon of scientists and industry and government technicians, it was excessive nutrient loadings.

Vast amounts of sewage pouring into the lake from Detroit, Toledo, Cleveland, and other cities, coupled with the wastes of industry and runoff from agricultural lands, especially in the western end of the basin, were overstimulating the lake. "Evidence is accumulating . . . which indicates that human activity is greatly accelerating the eutrophication of all of the lakes but Lake Superior. This evidence is most spectacular for Lake Erie."[3] The result was a growing and repulsive decline in the lake's health.[4]

The surge in Lake Erie pollution was mimicking eutrophication, a natural aging process taking thousands of years in most lakes. But eutrophication is a mostly benign phenomenon, and the effect of human activity on Lake Erie in the middle of the twentieth century was not benign. In the word of scientist Henry Regier, Erie was undergoing "pseudo-eutrophication"—a harmful human facsimile of a natural process. As lake nutrients increased in concentration, plants such as algae were stimulated to grow. Dying off, they consumed oxygen in the process of decaying, starving other organisms of the supply they needed. And the algae itself, clinging to swimmers as well as structures, made water unfit for recreation or drinking.

Such was the case in the early to mid 1960s. The regional director for the U.S. Bureau of Commercial Fisheries termed Erie a "dying lake," a phrase soon popularized by outraged citizens and the news media. While the lake was in fact teeming with *too much* life, the point was sound: the life cycle of the lake was accelerating due to human influence. People could see the difference. Some reported dead rats and raw sewage, and the floating mats of algae washing up on beaches were visible to all.

The first response of governments was largely defensive. In the 1920s four of the Great Lakes states had established commissions charged with limiting water pollution. State sanitary engineers working for the commissions had worked closely with municipal and industrial officials to manage what they termed "effluent." The effectiveness of the commissions was modest, particularly in light of the lack of broad-based public support for a crackdown on pollution and the tradition of negotiating rather than insisting on compliance with strict laws. Elected state officials were typically more concerned with the effect of stringent water quality standards on industries rather than the harm caused by pollution. Now that citizens were loudly protesting the gross conditions of many Great Lakes water bodies, the engineers were startled and sometimes angry to find their work denounced as inadequate and to be accused of coddling municipalities and industries.

Another characteristic official response was to propose treating the symptoms rather than the disease. For example, Cleveland officials proposed blasting sewage-infested effluent from an east side plant with chlorine in order to kill infectious organisms. "A small area of Lake Erie will be safe for swimming this summer—bacteriologically speaking—if you don't mind oil, hops, logs and other floating debris," the *Cleveland Press* archly reported.[5]

Despite evidence visible to the naked eye, officials insisted the problem wasn't as bad as the public thought. The chairman of the Ohio Water Pollution Control Board, Ralph Dwork, said in a formal statement that conditions at some water intakes were improving, although he conceded the Cleveland area was still a problem.[6] The board chided Cleveland officials in 1962 for failing to make progress toward eliminating its large sewage discharges—but issued the city a new permit to continue the dumping. Dwork's assessment and the state's continued deadline extensions for the city didn't satisfy a growing number of critics.

Into the breach stepped a Cleveland automobile dealer named David Blaushild. A fisherman and boater, Blaushild was an unusual clean water crusader. He first won local fame for launching a "U Auto Buy A Car Now" campaign in 1958 in an attempt to combat the U.S. economic slowdown, winning a commendation from President Dwight Eisenhower. In 1962, disgusted by the condition of the local Shaker Lakes, Blaushild paid for a billboard along a Cleveland freeway that said, "Let's Stop Killing Lake Erie." Later he explained his motives: "When I was a kid, the lakes had salamanders, crawfish and panfish. Now there are only maggots and carp. I decided if something wasn't done during my generation, my daughter's generation wouldn't know the difference and would accept pollution as a way of life."[7]

Although the billboard generated headlines, it didn't clean up the pollution. Blaushild grew increasingly impatient with the response of governments to the deterioration of the local waters. In 1964 he began a newspaper advertising campaign that encouraged readers to contact Blaushild Chevrolet. Those who did were asked to collect signatures on informal petitions to be forwarded to public officials. Blaushild also drafted a resolution opposing the pollution of Lake Erie that he asked Cleveland and nearby communities to adopt. Approximately fifteen did so, but Mayor Ralph Locher of Cleveland balked, citing the potentially harmful impact on industry of strict enforcement and the impact on the city's budget of tougher pollution control requirements.[8] Locher and others, including Ohio governor James Rhodes, feared Blaushild's campaign would invite the federal government to step in and direct cleanup. When public opinion in favor of the cleanup continued to grow, Locher backed down, and the Cleveland City Council approved the antipollution resolution in the autumn of 1964.

But that didn't guarantee immediate action. Under laws then in effect, the U.S. government could directly intervene only in water pollution cases with a clear interstate origin. Although Detroit was almost certainly a major source of the nutrients entering Lake Erie, the traditional American deference of federal to state governments in matters of pollution control would persist until a Michigan, Pennsylvania, or New York contribution to the lake's problems was conclusively demonstrated.

The combination of grassroots pressure from activists such as Blaushild, continuing publicity about the lake's decline, and new data about lake pollution released by the U.S. Public Health Service in March 1965 began to turn the tide. Local newspapers and TV and radio stations, which for years had been increasing their coverage of the apparent decline of Lake Erie, now made it consistent front-page news. The "Save Lake Erie Now" campaign of the *Cleveland Press* gained new momentum. Reporter Betty Klaric, who won several awards for her role in spurring Lake Erie's recovery, reported in the spring of 1965 that to boaters in Greater Cleveland, pollution was "no abstract problem. Its thick oil coats expensive hulls. Collisions with submerged logs, tires and debris do thousands of dollars of damage yearly."[9]

Blaushild was still at it, buying more ads, including one that urged the public to support an Ohio Water Pollution Control Board crackdown on Cleveland sewage overflows. His persistence made politicians uneasy. In February 1965 the auto dealer complained that he couldn't get an appointment to present one hundred eighty thousand antipollution signatures to Governor Rhodes. "There is no possible way that this can be included in the governor's schedule as his calendar is completely committed at this time," said Rhodes's secretary.[10] Accustomed for decades to negotiating arrangements among local and state governments and industry without vigorous public oversight, officials perhaps hoped the new activists would go away. But Blaushild and others didn't. At a public hearing later in 1965, Blaushild would say he was representative of citizens "weary of the banalities and lethargy of public officials. Of citizens weary, too, of the negative, snide, condescending attitude of some of our major industries who keep wantonly infecting our water at the complete expense of an ever-angering public."[11]

Not directly accountable to voters, appointed officials sometimes counterattacked the critics. For example, Dr. D. W. Arnold, director of the Ohio Department of Health, condemned "extremists who were trying to stir public indignation into action for a clean water program. We admire the motivation but deplore the exaggeration. Lake Erie is, in fact, still a magnificent body of water with some soiled edges."[12]

But politicians began getting the message, declaring their firm support for clean water—while often pointing their fingers at others to pay for the tab. Though resisting a federal "takeover" of the waters they had traditionally managed, state officials clamored for federal aid. At an interstate conference on the pollution of Lake Erie held in Cleveland in May 1965, Ohio Governor Rhodes called for the establishment of a Clean Great Lakes Authority administered by the states but funded by Washington. "The demand for federal aid can hardly be met with raised eyebrows," Rhodes said. "Forty-one percent of the people of the United States are directly affected because they live in the Great Lakes region. These people pay 47% of the taxes."[13] At the same meeting, however, New York governor Nelson Rockefeller touted a $1 billion state clean water bond issue that would appear on the November 1966 ballot. Its ultimate passage, and the subsequent approval by Michigan voters of a $335 million clean water bond in 1968, put several of the states out front in seeking to curb the pollution of Lake Erie and other waterways.

The May 1965 conference in Cleveland and others held in the mid 1960s illustrated the growing public coalition supporting the cleanup of Lake Erie and all the Great Lakes. In addition to prominent opinion leaders such as Blaushild, representatives of organized labor, the League of Women Voters, and federal officeholders attacked the gross water pollution and impatiently demanded action. The league's work was particularly thorough. Typical of its Ohio members was Edith Chase of Kent, who described the Cuyahoga River as it flowed through her city in the 1960s as green "like pea soup. . . . As a member of the League, I learned about water issues, what was and wasn't being done, and how citizens could participate in cleanup."[14]

Studying and documenting the hazards created by pollution, the league issued several reports in 1965, including "Pollution—The Other Side of Progress." Said the league: "The little rivers and creeks of the Lake Erie Basin have not been adequate to dilute and assimilate the voluminous wastes they receive." The Rouge River in Michigan was coated with oil; the Maumee, Sandusky, Black, and Huron Rivers turbid with silt running off from agricultural lands; the Cuyahoga River "practically devoid of oxygen from five miles below" the Akron treatment plant and the Cleveland plant. The sober scholarship of the league prevented pollution control officials from dismissing the criticism as unfounded and emotional.

Newspaper editorials backed the league up, prodding politicians to act. The *Cleveland Press* called pollution of Lake Erie "the greatest threat to health and security the whole area continually faces" and added, "Something must be done. It is many years overdue."[15] The *Plain Dealer* said: "Lake Erie and the Cuyahoga River contain the lifeblood of Cleveland. Each day that lifeblood—the waters which were the very reason for the settlement and growth of this city—becomes more contaminated. This lifeblood must be cleansed if this community is to survive and grow, and the *Plain Dealer* will continue campaigning for this until it is accomplished."[16]

Despite public opinion and the clean water bonds—including a $100 million sewer bond approved by Cleveland voters in

1968—progress was far from immediate. Other cities and several Great Lakes states still struggled to marshal funding for improved sewage systems and to control industrial pollution. Interstate conferences on Lake Erie and Lake Michigan pollution, the only federal remedy then available, led to new vows of commitment and forecasts of future progress, but the public remained skeptical. When federal official Murray Stein said he could see light at the end of the tunnel as the conferences closed, a reporter likened his words to those of U.S. Army generals in Vietnam who were issuing forecasts considered less than credible.

A sudden blaze on the Cuyahoga River on 22 June 1969 won national media attention and, by provoking further public outrage, stiffened the resolve of public officials to press for cleanup.[17] The river had been suffering for years—and had endured much larger conflagrations before without large-scale notoriety—but the brief fire, noted in *Time* magazine, ignited a comparable flame of anger as Americans and Canadians worried about the survival of their societies and the planet.

One response to the public indignation was government reorganization. Three Great Lakes states created environmental protection agencies in the late 1960s, while four created "superdepartments" merging traditional conservation with the new environmental health functions. Only Indiana continued to operate largely as before, assigning water pollution control to its Board of Health. The new agencies had both written and unwritten mandates to correct the visible pollution of the Great Lakes region's streams and lakes.[18]

At the same time, government agencies, particularly the U.S. Environmental Protection Agency, created by executive order in 1970, showed a new willingness to confront polluters—in court, if necessary. In February 1971 the U.S. Justice Department filed historic lawsuits against U.S. Steel and the DuPont Corporation for poisoning the Grand Calumet River near Chicago. EPA administrator William D. Ruckelshaus said the partnership of federal and state agencies and citizens groups "typifies the cooperative spirit that is being developed in the common fight against water pollution."[19]

A member of the U.S. Congress even took a law into his own hands. U.S. representative Henry Reuss of Milwaukee, Wisconsin, dug up the obscure Refuse Act of 1899, which required a permit from the Army Corps of Engineers prior to the discharge of any refuse material into a lake or stream. The law provided a fine of $1,500 for each violation, with half the sum going to those who reported it. Enacted primarily to support navigation, the statute had new meaning in the late 1960s, as "refuse" began to clot the lakes and streams in Reuss's home state. The Wisconsin Department of Natural Resources had listed two hundred seventy firms openly dumping wastes into the surface waters of the state.

Reuss prepared affidavits using the facts in the state's list of dischargers and filed them with the state's U.S. attorneys in April 1971. While the U.S. attorney for the western district of Wisconsin filed four lawsuits, won each, and turned half the fines over to Reuss, the U.S. attorney for the eastern district took no action. Reuss was particularly incensed by the failure to litigate after residents of a neighborhood in Milwaukee tried to clean up the Little Menomonee River just downstream of a plant that had been dumping creosote into the stream. "Nine people who waded in the stream were badly burned by the creosote pollution, some so severely that they required hospitalization. This too failed to move the U.S. Attorney from the Eastern District of Wisconsin," Reuss complained. But the congressman was undeterred, preparing a Reuss Handy Kit explaining how citizens could deploy the Refuse Act to stop pollution.[20]

There was also an angry and determined spirit in many of the new citizens' organizations that had sprung up to combat pollution. Students were an important part of the new clean water brigades. The University of Toronto became the birthplace of Pollution Probe in early 1969. Responding to a Canadian Broadcasting Company documentary on air pollution, Pollution Probe expanded its agenda to deal with the general problem of pollution and health. University faculty, drawn particularly from the Department of Zoology, supported the students who comprised the heart of Pollution Probe.

> The students' youthful enthusiasm and idealism propelled the organization. They orchestrated Probe's publicity events, such as the mock funeral held for the "dead" Don River. They canvassed door-to-door and took every opportunity to present their message citywide, even nationally, through the CBC and Toronto newspapers. It was to this group of energetic and dedicated young people that [professor Donald] Chant referred when he urged "Let us heed the voice of youth."[21]

The newly energized and organized public represented by Pollution Probe was decisive in building support for new, binational measures to protect the Great Lakes. One of the most important issues it addressed—and one that would prove pivotal in reversing the decline of Erie and several other Great Lakes—was the matter of detergent phosphorus pollution. Pollution Probe responded skeptically to the claims of industry representatives that a switch from phosphate additives in laundry detergents would result in dirty laundry and cost too much. In a brief submitted to a 2 February 1970 hearing of the International Joint Commission in Hamilton on the IJC's proposed phosphate limitations, Pollution Probe argued for a ban on the manufacture, sale, and use of high-phosphate detergents.

Perhaps more important, the group worked with University of Toronto civil engineering professor Phil Jones to test major detergents for phosphorus and publicize the results, beginning with a 8 February broadcast on CBC's *Weekend* show. Some detergents tested by Pollution Probe had phosphorus content of as much as 50 percent by weight, when limits of 0.5 percent were recommended to protect water quality. The list of high-phosphate detergents received extensive national publicity, generating seven thousand consumer requests for the list by the end of March. The use of scientists and hard data strengthened the emotional arguments advanced by environmental advocates. "The group piqued public interest and support by challenging the problem-solving style of the traditional wise-use conservation experts," wrote Jennifer Read. "Pollution Probe's strength lay in its use of scientific expertise to educate the public and offer well-considered alternative solutions to those suggested by the government scientists and manufacturers."[22]

At the same time newly energized citizens were pointing the finger at phosphorus as a prime culprit in the decline of Great Lake waterways, scientists and public officials were converging on a plan to control the nutrient. The United States–Canada Great Lakes Water Quality Agreement, signed by President Richard Nixon and Canadian prime minister Pierre Trudeau in Ottawa on 15 April 1972, provided the framework that turned almost a decade of promises into action.

The agreement was a response to recommendations made by the International Joint Commission in 1970. The IJC had found that the waters of Lakes Erie and Ontario and the international section of the St. Lawrence River were "seriously polluted on both sides of the boundary to the detriment of both countries and to an extent which is causing injury to health and property on the other side of the boundary." Significantly, the IJC also noted that 70 percent of the phosphorus in U.S. sewage and 50 percent of the phosphorus in Canadian sewage originated from detergents and recommended a crackdown on the problem, including both improved sewage treatment by municipalities and industries and a reduction in the phosphorus content of detergents "to the maximum practicable extent at the earliest possible time."[23] The commission said its recommended cleanup objectives for the polluted waters should be the basis of standards set by the states in the Lakes Erie and Ontario watersheds and the province of Ontario, and should be embraced in an agreement between the two nations.

The IJC's recommendations had particular strength because of general consensus in the regional scientific community on the cause and cure of the nutrient problem—with studies dating back to 1960 providing ample documentation—and because of the IJC's generally sound reputation as a nonexcitable binational institution. The agreement set the stage for a decisive recovery of the lakes, but individual battles still remained to be won.

The Soap and Detergent Association, representing manufacturers of the high-phosphorus cleaners, had a tradition of fiercely fighting government mandates about its product ingredients. The association had headed off one batch of threatened controls in the mid 1960s when the public and lawmakers had complained of massive sudsing in streams caused by the use of a nonbiodegradable chemical base in the detergents. After estimating the cost of switching to biodegradable ingredients at $100 million, the industry did so voluntarily in 1964.[24]

Nearly eliminating phosphorus from its laundry detergents was a different matter. The association successfully fought federal legislation, including an all-out ban on phosphorus in detergents introduced by U.S. representative Henry Reuss in 1969. It denied that laundry detergents were a major source of the problems of Lake Erie and other water bodies, blaming phosphates in fertilizers and human waste, among other sources, as larger contributors. If control was needed, it could be more efficiently applied by improving treatment of sewage containing phosphorus at municipal plants, the association said. In congressional testimony before Reuss, the vice president and technical director of the association, Charles G. Bueltman, argued that the "elimination of detergent phosphate alone could not possibly mitigate or diminish excessive algae growth." But the association had paid for the $5,000 scientific study he cited to back up the claim, Bueltman admitted under questioning.[25]

More independent technical findings leading to the Great Lakes Water Quality Agreement provided a new impetus for controls on phosphorus at the state level and in Ontario. The province legislated a limit of 8.7 percent phosphorus by weight in detergents beginning 1 August 1970 and a 2.2 percent limit beginning in 1973. An Indiana state law banned the sale within the Lake Erie Basin of detergents containing more than 3 percent phosphorus by weight after 1 January 1973. New York enacted a statute banning any phosphorus content after the same date. Michigan enacted a 0.5 percent laundry detergent phosphorus limitation in 1977.[26] Another contributor to a cleaner Lake Erie was the enactment, over President Richard M. Nixon's veto, of the 1972 Clean Water Act. The act paid a generous 75 percent of costs for municipalities improving their sewage treatment, spurring a construction boom across the nation. In the Great Lakes region alone, spending on sewage treatment exceeded $10 billion U.S. from the late 1960s to the 1990s.

The phosphorus controls and improved municipal sewage treatment measurably improved the water quality of the Great Lakes and especially the supposedly moribund Lake Erie. In 1983 the Water Quality Board, established by the IJC to monitor the health of the lakes and in compliance with the 1972 and 1978 Great Lakes Water Quality Agreements, reported that municipal sewage plants on both the Canadian and U.S. sides of Lake Erie had achieved on average the target concentration of 1 milligram of phosphorus per liter. Detroit's contribution of phosphorus to the Lake Erie Basin had plummeted from 4,720 metric tons in 1975 to 515 metric tons in 1982.[27] Algae blooms were noticeably reduced; oxygen levels in the lake were rebounding; swimming and fishing were once again not only possible but desirable. Cleanup of unsightly Great Lakes pollution was an international success story.

One reason was that by the early 1970s, controlling water pollution had been fully institutionalized as everyone's cause. Perhaps no better measure of this was the tale of a Cleveland man, Gilbert Pugliese, told in the *Cleveland Press.* A millwright at a facility operated by Jones and Laughlin Steel Corporation, Pugliese told a reporter that he had begun a "quiet rebellion" in the 1960s. He would no longer push a button sending wastes collected from the tempering mills into sewers and from there into the Cuyahoga River. His mutiny was not detected. Just two weeks before the river caught on fire in 1969, Pugliese was given an order to pump out a sump hole and refused. Ordered to an office by his foreman, Pugliese requested his union committeeman assist in his defense. "I said this was polluting the river and endangering people's health. If they suspended or reprimanded me, I told them I would go to the authorities." Although not disciplined on that occasion, Pugliese was suspended for five days in 1970 after balking at pumping out a flooded basement contaminated with wastes. The suspension was later rescinded. "I guess I'm just an average kind of working guy," Pugliese said. "I try to be a good citizen. . . . When you read and hear about all the pollution and industries don't seem to be taking heed but go on stalling and alibiing and getting permits from authorities, well, then you feel there is only one alternative. . . . That's the people."[28]

Although the visible pollution of the Great Lakes would dwindle throughout the 1970s, there was much left for the people to do. A new and troubling pollution was menacing the lakes' health—and public health.

Fireproofing the Cuyahoga River

SOMETIMES IT IS THE LEAST IMPORTANT FACT ABOUT A river, like the least important fact about a person, that commits it forever to memory.

When the Cuyahoga River, a major tributary of Lake Erie, briefly burst into flames in downtown Cleveland near noon on Sunday, 22 June 1969, its misfortune attracted relatively little notice at first. Although the flames may have been as high as five stories and putting out the fire required the work of three fire battalions and the fireboat *Anthony J. Celebrezze,* locals had seen far worse on the river before.

Coverage in the next day's Cleveland *Plain Dealer* included a story five paragraphs long and a photograph. Headline: "Oil Slick Fire Damages 2 River Spans." The newspaper estimated the twenty-four-minute fire had caused $50,000 damage to two "key railroad trestles," closing one to traffic. Although the photo appeared on the front page, the story was tucked inside.[29]

If the coverage was lackadaisical, this was only because the fire was far from unprecedented. Blazes in 1936 and 1952 had created much more dramatic flames and smoke. "It was a strictly run of the mill fire," William E. Barry, chief of the city fire department in 1969, later said. [30]

No cause of the fire was identified in the article or another in the *Plain Dealer* on the twentieth anniversary of the blaze, but it is known that this stretch of the river was smeared with oil and choked with debris, logs, and household waste sent downriver by storms and sewers. A train passing over one of the trestles may have ignited the oil with a spark.

The Tuesday, 24 June, edition of the *Cleveland Press* took a tougher line. Reporting on a visit by Cleveland mayor Carl Stokes to one of the damaged trestles, the newspaper quoted him: "This is a long-standing condition that must end." The paper noted that an estimated 875 million gallons of raw sewage had recently gushed out of a broken city sewer and that white wastes were flowing into the river from a chemical plant. Stokes, the paper said, would demand enforcement of antipollution laws and sue the state of Ohio, industries, and cities that were dumping wastes into the river. "There may be some wry humor in the phrase 'the river is a fire hazard' but it's a terrible reflection on the city surrounding it when it does indeed become one," said Stokes.[31]

More than a month later, in a story headlined "The Cities: The Price of Optimism," *Time* magazine called national attention to the sick Cuyahoga. "Some river! Chocolate-brown, oily, bubbling with subsurface gases, it oozes rather than flows. 'Anyone who falls into the Cuyahoga does not drown,' Cleveland's citizens joke grimly. 'He decays.'"[32]

Time noted the blaze: "A few weeks ago, the oil-slicked river burst into flames, and burned with such intensity that two railroad bridges spanning it were nearly destroyed." That was enough to install the Cuyahoga River in the national memory. It would be almost three years before the U.S. Congress would enact the Clean Water Act—and insist on putting it into law over the veto of President Richard Nixon—but the marriage of the river and the law would never permit divorce. In 2000 a federal civil servant appointed to promote the river's recovery told the *New York*

Times, "The river catching fire brought national attention and ridicule to Cleveland, but it also proved to be the instrumental rallying point in the passage of the Clean Water Act of 1972." [33]

Fire may not have been the river's worst affliction. In several stretches of the river, including the one that belched fire and smoke on 22 June 1969, pollution had starved it of oxygen, killing almost all fish and other aquatic life.

By the time the *Times'* 2000 retrospective appeared, the Cuyahoga had become a national symbol of a different nature. Now the story was that a federal, state, and community commitment had helped restore America's waters. In the flats along the river in downtown Cleveland at the beginning of the twenty-first-century, nightlife had replaced a dead stream. Restaurants and clubs dotted both sides, luring thousands downtown on warm summer nights.

But in some ways that was only a revival of a far distant past. In a native tongue, Cuyahoga means "crooked river," referring to its one-hundred-mile course first south, then north, in a corner of Ohio. Before the day of Christ, the first Americans had found the river a benevolent source of food and avenue for transportation. The Cuyahoga continued to support this people for more than a millennium and a half. When Europeans began settling near and along it in the 1700s, conditions first slowly, then rapidly deteriorated. The river was destined to be a key in the development of Ohio. George Washington said so, arguing at one point that the Cuyahoga would be critical to communication with "the invaluable back country."[34]

After Washington's day, the river became a chief artery for shipments of goods from inland areas to the developing port of Cleveland. During the Civil War, citizens petitioned to make Cleveland a naval depot, arguing that the mouth of the Cuyahoga assured that "between the Detroit and Niagara Rivers on the American shore, there is no harbor which has a safer and better ingress, in all weathers, than that of Cleveland." [35]

When railroad bridges spanned the river in 1878, the area near the river mouth became even more critical to commerce. As mills, foundries, lumberyards, and manufacturing plants settled along its banks in both the city and suburbs, and as the population of the metropolis mounted, waste poured into the river. In 1884 the mayor of the city termed the Cuyahoga an open sewer. That was eighty-five years before the decisive fire.

But the fire itself happened a year after the city of Cleveland made a commitment to restoring the river. In 1968 the city's director of public utilities, Ben Stefanski, got Mayor Stokes's blessing to organize a campaign to pass a $100 million sewer bond. Voters approved it by a margin of two-to-one even though it doubled low sewer rates to pay off the bonds. "It became like apple pie and motherhood," Stefanski said. "No one could be against it." [36]

While the fire wasn't needed to galvanize Cleveland, it did galvanize the American public. "The trouble," *Time* explained, "is that pollution rarely gets a high priority until profits are affected or people are killed."[37]

The federal law that the fire helped inspire changed that. It considered stream sickness, not just human death or economic injury, a wrong in itself. And it set ambitious goals. By 1983, Congress decreed, all of America's waters would be fishable and swimmable. By 1985 the discharge of pollutants to the nation's rivers and lakes would end. No one could envision how much better the country's water resources would be more than three decades later—and how far from achieving the goals of the Clean Water Act the nation, and the Great Lakes, would remain.

The Cuyahoga itself is not clean. Declared one of forty-two Great Lakes "areas of concern" under an International Joint Commission program, forty-five miles of the lower river and approximately ten miles of Lake Erie shoreline at its mouth are still in need of care. PCBs contaminate fish such as white sucker and yellow bullhead, and fish populations are rated as "fair" to "very poor" in some stretches of the river. But populations of the tiny invertebrates at the bottom of the river's food chain have recovered significantly. The greatest remaining challenges to the river are habitats—millions of cubic yards of poisoned river bottom muds and the paved, walled, dammed, and destroyed riverbanks that once supported various forms of life. Restoring both of these will be far more tedious and far less photogenic tasks than putting out a summer fire. But they are the work of this and future generations.

I remember [Cleveland's] White City Beach from early childhood the most. This beach was in the city and easily accessible. There was an amusement park, Euclid Beach, in the city as well located on the Lake. I spent summer holidays playing in the sand and swimming at family picnics and going to Euclid Beach Park. I remember going there one summer day to swim and being unable to because the beach was totally covered in dead fish. I remember that day very clearly. The fish were all the same silvery color with white bellies and medium sized. It was shocking and unexpected because like many beaches there was the trail to the beach that one had to walk carrying all of the beach gear. The anticipation is always hopeful and when we got there the beach was closed and covered with dead fish.

In 2001 White City Beach reopened. I was boating with my uncle and we passed the area and I remember saying to him "Is that White City Beach?," and he replied that it had recently re-opened.

—Cathy Square

I recall those treasured weekend visits as a law student to my mother's house on Lake Michigan north of Leland. The house was built close to the beach, before new (and wise) set-back restrictions, so you are always keenly aware of the lake. Each time I pulled into the winding drive, shut off the engine and opened the door to the peaceful sounds of the water and trees, I swear I could feel the tensions of my daily life released from my body into the gentle and fragrant air. Walks along the beach, by myself or occasionally with friends, lost in thought intermittently mingled with wonder at the magnificence of the lake. Finally, tearful departure, knowing I was leaving peace, quiet and solitude for stress and frenzy.

—Tracy Dobson

Manipulating the Lakes

To some, the Great Lakes have never been quite great enough.

While quick to recognize the Great Lakes as a treasure for human commerce, American and Canadian governments and some citizens still saw a need for significant improvement on nature's endowment, and they advanced policies to fulfill this vision from the early nineteenth century to the latter decades of the twentieth. They were impatient to straighten crooked rivers and natural channels, to harness the power of tributaries through dams rather than permitting them to be "wasted" by flowing unfettered, to fill in the wet "wastelands" that lined many of the shores, and especially to open by force a route permitting ocean-going vessels to penetrate to the heart of the North American continent at Duluth. Whether the impulse to master the lakes for strictly human ends through great schemes has died away is debatable; some of the most ambitious plans have been charted, and a few implemented, since the 1960s.

The first and one of the most spectacular manipulations of the plumbing of the Great Lakes was the building of the Erie Canal, begun in 1817 and opened in 1825. Championed by New York governor DeWitt Clinton, the three-hundred-sixty-three-mile canal helped alter the development of the United States while making the Great Lakes a major thoroughfare for commerce and settlers. The largest public works project of its time, the canal linked the Hudson and Niagara Rivers. It vaulted New York state into the lead in a competition along the eastern U.S. seaboard for the business of the growing Midwest. It inspired many less-successful imitators.

"Internal improvements," as they were often called in the new states of the Great Lakes region, began to multiply. The young state of Michigan in the 1830s quickly recognized the potential for economic gain in a plan to run a canal directly from the southeastern part of the state to the western shore, eliminating a four-hundred-mile diversion for vessels around the Lower Peninsula. The idea was just one of many teeming in the restless minds of officials in the region.

In fact, the proposed Clinton-Kalamazoo Canal, a two-hundred-sixteen-mile long waterway connecting Lake St. Clair and Lake Michigan, stalled well short of its destination. Begun on 20 July 1838, with the ceremonial turning of shovels of dirt, the canal penetrated only sixteen miles inland before funding ran out. Like almost all of the state's proposed improvements, it was the victim of over optimistic economic calculations and a revenue base too small to support the massive bonding necessary to finance the construction.[1] It was also only twenty feet wide, too narrow for easy passage, and four feet deep, too shallow for profitable freight. The canal had cost $350,000 by the time of its abandonment, earning only $90.32 in tolls. Yet even thirty years after its failure, another booster would challenge his listeners to support completion of the canal. The $10 million needed to construct the canal in 1876, H. A. Shaw said, would be more than justified by the saving of lives made possible by routing ships across the peninsula rather than out on the open lakes, and by huge gains in the length of the shipping season.

Other such dreams were born in great optimism and died hard. The father of one was also the father of the United States. Having surveyed the old Northwest prior to the War of American Independence, George Washington envisioned a canal linking the Ohio River with Lake Erie, opening up the great central interior of the growing nation to the East. In the early 1800s Ohio officials imagined vast potential in the shipping of goods from New York City to New Orleans through the canal, avoiding the risky ocean route that had prevailed in the early decades of the new republic. Excited by the opening of the Erie Canal the same year, the Ohio Legislature approved the construction of the Ohio and Erie Canal in 1825. The canal was completed in 1832, linking Clevleand and Portsmouth. The three-hundred-nine-mile long canal, nicknamed "The Big Ditch," included one hundred forty-six locks and fourteen aqueducts.[2] In the 1870s competition from railroads doomed the canal, which was formally abandoned in 1909.

The first generation of Indiana state officials and community boosters also envisioned greatness achievable by removing the barriers to freight transport and shipping imposed by nature. A historic portage between the Maumee and Wabash River systems in the northeast part of the state provided the most convenient opportunity to create a long-distance waterway. Samuel Hanna, a Fort Wayne merchant, judge, and legislator, organized a campaign to convince the U.S. government to support a canal linking the two river systems and thus connecting the Great Lakes to the Mississippi. In February 1832 work on the canal began. A section of the canal linking Fort Wayne to Huntington, Indiana, was completed in 1835, but the two rivers were found inadequate to support the large-capacity boats that would make the route profitable. While the canal was ultimately extended to the Ohio River at Logansport, it was only briefly useful, peaking during the 1850s before railroads eclipsed it. It was abandoned in 1874.

Illinois also hoped to open up a new path to the seas. Eager to become the newest and strongest link between the lakes and the East, and the Gulf of Mexico and the West, state and Chicago officials clamored for construction of a canal linking Lake Michigan and the Mississippi River from the state's admission to the Union in 1818. Begun on 4 July 1836, with the typical fanfare, including the turning of dirt by Canal Commissioner Colonel William B. Archer, the proposed Illinois and Michigan Canal moved forward at the height of the American fervor for internal improvements. However, the panic of 1837 and subsequent depression undercut financing for the project, which halted in 1843. But financing was arranged and the dream was realized with the opening of the ninety-seven-mile canal in 1848.[3] Ironically, the canal enjoyed only a few years of undisputed financial success: "The canal was facing obsolescence almost as soon as it was completed, as railroads began to lure passenger service away from the slow canal packet boats." The canal for some years continued to carry bulky cargoes for which speed was not the primary consideration.[4]

The lakes would not achieve their full capacity as a corridor for commerce, however, until three other major natural obstacles were breached. The most obvious and the first to be breached was the Niagara Escarpment. The giant drop of the Niagara Falls was a formidable barrier to upstream movement in the Great Lakes. But it tempted dreamers and builders. As early as 1699, a

French engineer had proposed a canal cutting across what would become Ontario's Niagara Peninsula. It took the opening of the Erie Canal to propel the idea into construction. Afraid that the New York canal threatened the market supremacy of Montreal over the Great Lakes, backers of the proposed Welland Canal pushed ahead with the project in the 1820s, based on a survey that underestimated the height of the escarpment by about half. The Welland Company nevertheless managed to surmount the three-hundred-thirty-seven-foot ridge with thirty-nine locks. In 1833 the canal was extended to Port Colborne and was expanded to accommodate ever-larger ships in 1845, 1887, 1932, and 1959. Dramatic alterations of the natural system were required to accommodate shipping. The fourth Welland Canal, opened in 1932, was accompanied by construction of an artificial harbor reaching one and one-half miles into Lake Ontario near Port Weller.[5] Another massive engineering feat was required for the final realignment of the canal in the late 1960s. Expropriating sixty-five hundred acres of land, the Welland Canal Authority removed sixty-five million cubic yards of rock, dirt, and silt to modernize the waterway, opened in 1972. By then it had served for nearly a century and a half as a force for both economic and ecological transformation in the Great Lakes Basin.

The non-navigable rapids of the St. Mary's River, a connecting channel between Lakes Superior and Huron, had long impeded movement. Dropping twenty-one feet over a bed littered with rocks, the St. Mary's required a portage for the voyageurs. In 1797 the Northwest Fur Company built the first lock permitting a bypass of the treacherous currents. The discovery and exploitation in the 1830s and 1840s of massive deposits of copper and iron in the western Upper Peninsula of Michigan strengthened calls for a modern canal and lock system to make the St. Mary's commercially navigable. In 1852 the U.S. Congress granted seven hundred fifty thousand acres of public land to

Michigan to compensate the St. Mary's Falls Ship Canal Company, which undertook the two-year project of building locks big enough to accommodate the booming trade that would soon require a link between Lake Superior and the lower lakes.[6] Michigan officials sought a one-mile canal with two locks at least three hundred fifty feet long and seventy feet wide. They inspected the result and approved it on 21 May 1855.[7] The completion of the project threw open the entire lakes system to shipping of heavy cargo, ultimately forging new ties among the iron ranges of Minnesota, the grain ports of Ontario, and the manufacturers and merchants of Chicago, Cleveland, and Detroit.

In the early twentieth century, as technology seemed to promise unlimited benefits to civilization from the harnessing of nature, the head of Northwestern University's College of Engineering offered a six-point plan for "the best use of the waters of the Great Lakes." Dr. John F. Hayford argued for a ten-thousand-cubic-foot diversion at Chicago (more than three times what the U.S. Supreme Court would later allow); dams with movable parts at Buffalo and in the St. Lawrence River to regulate Great Lakes levels; a submerged dam at Niagara Falls to halt its gradual retreat and to prevent "the wasting of the water where it does no good, either for scenic purposes or for power"; full use of the three-hundred-foot drop between Lakes Erie and Ontario for power; and a combination power and navigation project in the St. Lawrence River, opening the lakes to ocean trade. "Man's progress is dependent largely upon his development of good transportation, upon his use of mechanical power and upon his success in conquering disease," Hayford said. "The chance to use the waters of the Great Lakes in the best way for sanitation, navigation and power is the greatest opportunity to do a good service that is now open to the peoples of the United States and Canada."[8]

Although Hayford's entire plan has not yet come to pass, the St. Lawrence project engaged the energies of both nations for decades. The right of U.S. ships to traverse the Canadian-controlled waters of the St. Lawrence River, guaranteed in 1871, helped promote binational talk about making the waterway capable of introducing oceangoing vessels to the Great Lakes. The United States and Great Britain, acting on behalf of Canada, jointly formed the International Waterways Commission, which advocated the development of the St. Lawrence. But for years to come cargo would be routed from Montreal to the upper Great Lakes in a cumbersome three-stage process. The steps included lake navigation in ships with up to twenty feet of draft; navigation through the Welland Canal in ships with a fourteen-foot draft; and navigation by ships with a thirty-foot draft from Montreal to the sea. A deeper Welland Canal, opened in 1932, left only the one hundred eighty-three miles of the St. Lawrence between Lake Ontario and Montreal to be conquered. The two-hundred-twenty-five-foot fall between the lake and Montreal was a significant but not insurmountable engineering barrier. A more imposing wall was the difficulty of allocating costs among the nations and shipping interests and, in the United States, the resistance of railroads and the Atlantic states to a new competitor for cargo. In 1927 it was estimated the project would cost up to $238.6 million.[9] Soon after, the Great Depression made government allocations of this size unthinkable unless a political consensus on the merits of the waterway could be achieved.

World War II further postponed consideration of the project until 1949, when Canada and the United States formed another commission to analyze a deep waterway in the St. Lawrence. By 1954 both nations had enacted legislation authorizing the St. Lawrence Seaway project at a combined cost of $470.3 million. Construction on the project began that fall. In addition to relocating bridges, blasting rock, and digging new channels, the project involved the relocation of approximately sixty-five hundred residents from over one hundred square miles of land flooded to promote power generation from the seaway.[10] The project replaced a fourteen-foot-deep waterway with thirty locks with a twenty-seven-foot deep channel with fifteen locks. In April 1959 the icebreaker *D'Iberville* became the first vessel to traverse the new system. But like previous Great Lakes improvements, the new seaway required a formal ceremony heralding a new age of navigation. It took place in the presence of President Dwight Eisenhower and Queen Elizabeth on 26 June.

In 1983 the seaway marked the passage of the billionth metric ton of cargo since its opening. President Ronald Reagan declared 1984 "The Year of the St. Lawrence Seaway," resorting to the hopeful rhetoric that had marked its opening: "Since the French explorers of the Sixteenth Century, people have searched for a reliable way to sail into the heart of our continent. The opening of the St. Lawrence Seaway in 1959 made this dream a reality and opened North America's agricultural and industrial heartland to deep draft ocean vessels. The Seaway forged the final link in a waterway extending over 2,000 miles from Duluth, Minnesota to the Atlantic Ocean."[11]

In the same decade, a new chorus of voices began to ring out against unanticipated environmental damage caused by one hundred fifty years of engineering and "improving" the lakes—and the potential for even more damage. The damage fell into two categories: the direct destruction of valuable habitat for fish and wildlife in the construction of locks and canals, and the accidental introduction of harmful exotic species through the new routes opened to shipping by human action. To understand the public outrage against new government schemes to alter the lakes beginning in the 1980s, it is important to review the history of their sometimes calamitous effects.

The very first large-scale manipulation of the lakes was likely the source of a mild-seeming scourge known as the alewife. Fish culturist Seth Green is believed to have unintentionally introduced the alewife to Lake Ontario, mistaking it for the young shad from the Hudson River that he had planned to raise at his hatchery at Caledonia. First spotted in Lake Ontario in 1873, the alewife was native to the Atlantic Coast from South Carolina to Newfoundland. There it spent its prime years feeding and growing in the open ocean, migrating into freshwater rivers and lakes to spawn. It would prove adaptable to living its entire life cycle in the freshwater of the Great Lakes.

Only about six inches in length and four ounces in weight when fully grown, the alewife gradually crept through the lakes, taking advantage of the Welland Canal. Although initially welcomed as a potential forage fish for larger, native species, the alewife soon exploded in numbers while populations of the native lake herring, lake trout, and Atlantic salmon plummeted in the 1880s and 1890s. A modern theory holds that the alewife, which contains thiaminase, an enzyme that breaks down thiamine, may have rendered the Atlantic salmon thiamine deficient when consumed by the larger fish.[12] At about the same time, the exotic sea lamprey began to appear in Lake Ontario. The lamprey probably also used the Welland Canal to reach the upper lakes.[13]

Alewives swam up the canal and established themselves in Lake Huron by 1933, Lake Michigan by 1949, and Lake Superior by 1954. Perhaps delayed in their arrival by the feeding of large predator fish such as the lake trout, alewives suddenly burst into great numbers when the predators declined. With their abundance came a phenomenon disturbing to Great Lakes lovers—the annual spring die off. Sharp changes in water temperature, characteristic of spring weather patterns, are thought to be a chief cause of the mass deaths. Although peaking in the 1960s, the die off continued into the 1990s.

> Alewives—the silvery fish that have become a yearly malodorous blot on Lake Michigan beaches—have been washing ashore once more. . . . Millions of stinking alewives have littered the shoreline for miles in the last few weeks, shooing away picnickers, beachcombers and swimmers. At Kohler-Andrea and Harrington Beach state parks, workers have spent many days dealing with mounds of dead alewives. Some park officials haul alewives away with the garbage, while other spread them on fields because they're such good fertilizer.[14]

One manipulation begets another. With the commercial value of the lake fishery dominant but small when measured against the economy as a whole, some fish biologists toyed with the idea of converting the Great Lakes into a sport fishing resource. Doing so, they argued, required an intervention by humankind to repair the damage caused by the passage provided through the Welland Canal, as well as the hyperefficiency of the technologically advanced commercial fishing fleet. After his appointment in 1964, Michigan fish chief Howard Tanner and assistant Wayne Tody decided to challenge the supremacy of the Great Lakes commercial fishery by introducing salmon imported from the Pacific Northwest. If successful, the fish would create an eye-popping opportunity for sport fishing while controlling the exotic alewives, on whom the salmon were expected to feed.

The shocking decline of the lake trout had driven sport anglers from the upper lakes. Said conservation writer Ben East:

> In the summer of 1955 a fisherman could have dragged a trolling spoon across the best lake-trout grounds in Lake Michigan 1,000 times without the faintest hope of getting a strike. And he wouldn't have done much better on

> rainbows. So far as deep-water fish were concerned, that giant lake was a desert. Less than 10 years before, Lake Michigan had held lake trout in such numbers that the commercial catch was running about 6½ million pounds annually and sportfishermen could get Grade A action on deep-trolling gear, or on ice lines in winter, almost any time they went out.[15]

For once, results of a field experiment in altering the ecology of the lakes were largely favorable, at least in the short term. Tanner and Tody submitted an impact assessment to the other Great Lakes states and Ontario, then moved ahead with introduction of coho salmon. Soon after, without the benefit of meaningful consultation with their Great Lakes neighbors, they introduced chinook. Michigan released over six hundred fifty thousand smolts into Lake Michigan tributaries in the spring of 1966 and hoped for the best. The same fall, the first young salmon returned to their "birth" streams, whetting the appetite of anglers for more.

The autumn of 1967 fulfilled all their hopes. Averaging over ten pounds, the returning coho were the best sport that Great Lakes anglers had ever seen. Fighting furiously when hooked, the salmon were a true trophy when reeled in. Men and women excited about the chance to test themselves against the salmon sought the fish in the open lake during the summer, and in the autumn off the mouth of the streams in which salmon had been stocked, putting money in the pockets of hotel and restaurant owners and linking the fate of the fishery to the tourism industry. Wisconsin, Illinois, and Indiana soon followed Michigan's example, launching their own salmon stocking programs and adding chinook to the mix. Tanner won the 1968 Conservationist of the Year Award from the National Wildlife Federation. Henceforth, the health of the lakes would be measured in large part by the productivity of the salmon fishery in the Great Lakes. Hundreds of thousands of anglers who had previously found no use for the lakes and pursued their sport only on inland waters now had a stake in the health of the open waters.

Affection for the salmon program was not universal. Douglas Dodge, an Ontario fisheries biologist, objected to Michigan's virtual unilateralism. He said years later that he had suggested to an Ontario Ministry of Natural Resources official that "maybe we should plant freshwater sharks." He added, "The salmon were supposed to be like policemen. You put 'em in, take care of a problem [alewives], and pull them out. We were appalled."[16] Some environmentalists also criticized the salmon program because it was yet another exotic species introduction, because the fish had large stores of fat that concentrated persistent toxic chemicals, and because the salmon undermined support for restoration of the native lake trout. But for the first thirty-five years of the salmon program, enthusiasts among the sport fishing community far outnumbered opponents.

New exotic threats to the lakes continued to emerge. Instead of swimming upstream through canals and locks, however, these species hitchhiked in oceangoing vessels permitted into the four westernmost lakes by the St. Lawrence Seaway. In 1993 an estimated 30 percent of all exotic aquatic species in the lakes had been admitted through the seaway.[17] None caused a larger immediate uproar than the zebra mussel, first detected in the lakes in great numbers in 1988.

The mussel had probably stowed away a few years earlier in the ballast tank of one or more vessels originating in harbors of England or the Baltic. Though thumbnail sized, the mollusk quickly created problems for whole communities and the entire food web of the Great Lakes. Reproducing rapidly and copiously, the mussels spread to each of the lakes and up tributaries. Thirty tons of mussels clogged the intake pipe at an Ontario drinking water plant. A layer of mussels two inches thick covered screens on water intakes at five power plants of a Canadian utility. The city of Monroe, Michigan, closed its drinking water plant for three days when mussels restricted water flow, and a nearby electric utility plant had to reduce its power generation because the mussels coated its pipes. News media sent the story out globally:

> It may lack the girth of the Blob or the menacing chirp of Hitchcock's birds, but the zebra mussel is staging a classic creep-show routine on the western shores of Lake Erie. . . . The prolific mollusks are now entombing boat hulls and beaches, disrupting a large fishing industry and clogging waterlines that support cities and factories. Unless the invasion is stopped, experts speculate, 26 million people could lose their water supplies within five years. . . . The voracious youngsters have increased water clarity threefold—but they've done it by grabbing up the plankton and algae that support the rest of the aquatic food chain.[18]

While the threat to drinking water supplies was controlled at first by chlorine treatments and later dwindled as mussel populations reached equilibrium in the lakes, the threat to the aquatic food chain was genuine, if difficult to tease out from the natural and other unnatural cycles affecting the ecosystem.

The mussel was not the only species invading the lakes in the last years of the twentieth century. The ruffe, a small fish with no commercial value from northern Europe, was introduced into the Duluth-Superior harbor on Lake Superior in the mid 1980s. In 1989 the U.S. Fish and Wildlife Service estimated a ruffe population of three hundred seventy thousand in the harbor and St. Louis River.[19] The fishhook water flea, a half-inch long crustacean from eastern Europe, showed up in Lake Erie in 1998 and 1999. Accumulating on trolling lines and blocking the first eyelet on fishing rods, the flea hampered fishing. But it had the potential to become more than a nuisance, feeding on the same zooplankton on which larval fish of the lakes dined. "At this point, we have no idea how this nuisance species may affect sport fish in Lake Erie, but any exotic species is potentially trouble," said Gary Isbell, an Ohio Department of Natural Resources spokesperson.[20] In 2001 another exotic, the tubenose goby, a fish native to the Black and Caspian Seas, traveled aboard a vessel from its first Great Lakes home in Erie to Superior. Biologists hoped it would not spread as far or fast as the round goby, a cousin also new to the lakes, which had already established itself throughout the system.[21] In the summer of 2002 fishery authorities warned of yet another attacker—this one swimming north on its own from the Mississippi River after escaping from aquaculture pens in the southern United States. Bighead and silver carp from Asia, the latter reputed to grow up to one hundred pounds and forty inches, were within twenty-five miles of Lake Michigan. Capitalizing on the artificial route first blazed by the Illinois and Michigan Canal in 1848, stories of the carp's voracious appetites and capacity to drive out native species terrified governments and the public. The Great Lakes Fishery Commission urged the U.S. Congress to appropriate an immediate $360,000 to operate an electronic barrier in the Chicago River and $340,000 in annual operating costs, and work soon began on the carp blocker.[22]

But while experts and anglers fretted over the unknown future harm that would result from these species, the zebra mussel remained the supreme visible example of invasive exotics. Small heaps of mussels periodically littered Great Lakes beaches. Mussels clung to the bottom of recreational boats operating in the open waters of the lakes and damaged underwater shipwrecks frequented by divers, weighing down the timbers of old vessels until they collapsed. Several of the lakes achieved startling new clarity—the result, scientists hypothesized, of the mussel's ability to filter fine particles from the water.

The lessons of manipulating the Great Lakes system without adequate predictive capacity and caution by governments still did not take hold. In fact, schemes to make the system more useful continued to multiply even as the invaders did so.

A Canadian named Tom Kierans in the mid 1980s advanced one such plan. His Great Recycling and Northern Development (GRAND) Canal project proposed diking James Bay to turn it into a freshwater lake, moving the water fifty miles through reservoirs and canals to the Great Lakes, and passing the margin on to the arid U.S. Southwest through the Chicago diversion and new transfer canals in Minnesota, Wisconsin, Ohio, and New York. Although the $100 billion price tag of the project rendered it fantastic in the eyes of some, Quebec premier Robert Bourassa endorsed the concept as a way of developing the northern part of the province while serving thirsty American customers. And the problems of the pesky Great Lakes could be eased, too:

> In dry periods, when the waters are low, pollution is concentrated and shipping is slowed or even stopped, the James Bay waters would be used to raise the level to normal. And in wet periods, when the Great Lakes are flooding and causing erosion, the excess could be drained. . . . adding clean, oxygen-rich water could reduce pollution in the Great Lakes and give some species of fish a better chance to survive.[23]

Although cost and incredulity at least temporarily doomed the GRAND Canal scheme, another plan to tinker with the lakes moved ahead in the 1960s. In 1965 the U.S. Congress directed the Army Corps of Engineers to evaluate the feasibility of extending the navigation season on the Great Lakes past its traditional 15 December closing date. Long a dream for those who chafed at natural limits on the usefulness of the inland waterways, the so-called winter navigation proposal at the time seemed a logical extension of the St. Lawrence Seaway system itself, opened only six years earlier. But in the minds of skeptics, it was actually the first round in an unpublicized and costly plan to blast away the last limits on the lakes' capacity to compete for oceangoing commerce.

From its 1959 debut, in fact, the seaway's ability to make the Great Lakes a fourth coast for the U.S. had been seriously limited. Most of the U.S. fleet at the time required a channel at least thirty-five feet deep, eight to nine feet deeper than the St. Lawrence and connecting rivers. The seaway system's locks had a maximum length of seven hundred thirty feet, while by the late 1970s the commercial navigation industry was building one-thousand-foot ships to achieve economies of scale. But addressing those obstacles would require an investment calculated in the tens of billions of dollars. A still massive but far less daunting investment would be required, seaway supporters thought, to cancel a final restriction on the system: winter.

Through the 1970s the northern portion of the lakes typically froze for three months each winter, creating formidable difficulties for shipping.

> Ice problems are most difficult on the St. Lawrence River, connecting channels, harbors, and bays; anywhere open water connects to a narrow channel. Under normal winter conditions, storms break up lake ice and blow large cakes into the narrower channels and bays where they create ice jams. At times, these jams reach 30 ft. depths as the fresh ice fastens to the under side of the solid ice cover. Only the most powerful icebreakers are capable of breaking such ice.[24]

Like other phenomena on the lakes, even the seemingly destructive annual ice buildup served an important constructive purpose. The ice helped stabilize the levels and flows of the lakes.

Plowing through the ice to keep navigation open during most or all of the winter had the potential to erode shorelines, disrupt or destroy fish and wildlife habitats, and harm power generation. The army corps acknowledged these drawbacks in a 1969 preliminary report but recommended pressing ahead. By now a strong political constituency had emerged to support winter navigation. Developing a new technology to reduce the moisture content in taconite pellets, a condensed form of iron higher in grade than iron in its natural state, engineers promised to keep the lakes busy shipping the product from Minnesota and the Upper Peninsula of Michigan during the hard winters, reducing both storage and transportation costs.[25]

The new technology and a revision in Minnesota's state constitution taxing the new product at a lower rate stimulated major new investments by companies in the Iron Range of Minnesota and in Michigan, topping $1 billion by the late 1960s. Taconite pellets grew from 35.2 percent of Great Lakes ore shipments in 1963 to 63.6 percent in 1969. To accommodate the industry, the United States built and opened a new lock for one-thousand-foot ships at Sault Ste. Marie, Michigan. The steel industry ran its ships into December of 1969, producing a record for annual ore shipping.[26]

Thus the corps' study of winter navigation was watched with great interest. In 1970 the Detroit district of the corps determined that an extended shipping season was feasible and could serve the public interest. Politically dormant in the mid 1960s when Congress had authorized the study, the Great Lakes shipping community in 1970 strongly supported not only a full-blown feasibility study but also a "demonstration program" that would begin implementing winter navigation. Congress approved the $6 million initiative, and federal agencies opened an ice navigation center in Cleveland.

From 1971 to 1975 the Winter Navigation Board (WNB) established by eight U.S. federal agencies promoted an extended season, culminating in year-round shipping in 1975. State officials and industry representatives joined the WNB in championing the demonstration project. Only one politician, U.S. representative Philip Ruppe of the Upper Peninsula of Michigan, challenged the program, arguing that residents of islands in the St. Mary's River shipping channel, in his district, were being stranded by ice jams created to clear a path for the freighters. He also suggested the high speeds at which the vessels operated damaged the shoreline environment and structures, pushing ice against docks and vegetation. In 1973 Ruppe also requested a report from the U.S. General Accounting Office (GAO) that found the project had not conformed to the 1970 National Environmental Policy Act, and questioned both the environmental and economic assumptions deployed by the army corps.[27]

Ruppe was successful in winning a congressional directive to the corps to conduct mitigative studies. But Congressman James Oberstar of Minnesota, representing the Iron Range, continued to press for year-round navigation, arguing that it would protect sixty-five thousand jobs and 50 percent of the nation's steel production. It was not until New York state began demanding an environmental evaluation of the effect of winter navigation in the Thousand Islands region of the St. Lawrence River and citizens organizations from New York and Michigan rose up against the demonstration project that it began to hit choppy water.

A confluence of forces threatened the winter navigation dream. Residents of Michigan's Sugar Island, downriver from Sault Ste. Marie, spent much of the winter of 1976 marooned because ice booms deployed by the corps were unable to contain broken ice from drifting and jamming their ferry dock. Ice fishermen noticed a decline in their catch in the river, and they and snowmobilers feared venturing out onto the river because of the danger posed by passing vessels. At the same time, a newly energized environmental and conservation movement had begun challenging assumptions about the benefits of army corps projects and their effect on ecosystems. Michigan's largest conservation organization, the Michigan United Conservation Clubs (MUCC), formally opposed the demonstration program at its 1977 convention. MUCC staff ecologist Wayne Schmidt was the author of the resolution opposing winter navigation. He called the proposal a "colossal boondoggle that would have retooled the Great Lakes to the interests of shippers at a horrendous environmental cost."[28] Schmidt worried about the effect of churning ship propellers and the waves they generated on spawning and nursery beds for fish, mayflies, muskrats, and other important links in the ecosystem. The risk of oil spills in frigid weather and disruption of nesting bald eagles along the St. Mary's River also bothered Schmidt.

At the other end of the Great Lakes system, an activist named Barry Freed helped organize a new advocacy group, Save the River, to stop winter navigation on the St. Lawrence. Freed—later unmasked as 1960s antiwar activist Abbie Hoffman, operating under an alias after his flight from a jail sentence—had moved to the Thousand Islands region with a companion whose family owned a cottage there. In August 1978 Hoffman and Save the River packed a public hearing called by the corps at Alexandria Bay, New York, with more than four hundred opponents of winter navigation. Working with MUCC's Schmidt, Save the River stepped up pressure on the corps, demanding compliance with the National Environmental Policy Act through a full, predictive environmental impact statement. They were able to point to an explosion in the corps' estimated initial cost of winter navigation from $330 million to $1.6 billion, including thirty new icebreakers stationed throughout the shipping lanes. A New York state–commissioned study had also predicted disruption of critical fish and wildlife habitats, including wintering habitat for the bald eagle, the stirring up of pollutants in the bottom sediments of the connecting channels, and the possibility that booms would admit enough ice to raise the level of Lake Ontario up to one foot in winter, threatening shoreline property owners.

The anti–winter navigation lobby suddenly attracted regional newspaper coverage. This translated into political potency. U.S. senator Daniel Patrick Moynihan of New York announced his opposition to winter navigation on the St. Lawrence in 1979. U.S. representative David Bonior, whose Michigan district included the St. Clair River and the western shore of Lake St. Clair, and whose constituents were also feeling the effects of the demonstration project, joined forces with MUCC and Save the River to plot a strategy to defeat the permanent season extension in the U.S. Congress. Bonior played a pivotal role in killing winter navigation.

In 1979, with public and congressional opposition mounting, the demonstration winter navigation program that had begun in 1971 came to a sudden halt. Plummeting traffic on the seaway during a steep recession that began in the late 1970s further undermined the case for year-round shipping. But proponents would not quit. Sensing it was losing the fight, the corps changed tactics, saying it was proposing a "season extension" of six to eight weeks, ending January 31, rather than year-round navigation. But its formal studies continued to discuss the full-blown proposal, phased in over ten to fifteen years. In 1983 U.S. House members from the Great Lakes region tucked authorization for winter navigation into a massive public works bill. Yet only U.S. representatives Arlan Stangland of Minnesota and Carl Pursell of Michigan openly supported the extension. Meanwhile, Bonior was joined by Representatives Dave Martin, whose New York district included the St. Lawrence River, Bob Davis of Michigan, who had succeeded Ruppe, Henry Nowak of the Buffalo area,

For a time in the 1980s and 1990s, nongovernmental organizations and individual citizens packed the biennial Great Lakes water quality meetings of the International Joint Commission. But the turnout generated a backlash from governments and industries on both sides of the international border, prompting both sectors to begin bypassing or ignoring the Commission's repeated calls for Great Lakes cleanup. Photo courtesy of Ann and John Mahan.

In Ashland, Wisconsin visitors to Lake Superior's shore are warned to stay away from the water. Disputes between agencies and with the party thought responsible for the contamination, Xcel Energy, have stalled short of cleaning up the contamination. Photo courtesy of Bob Olsgard.

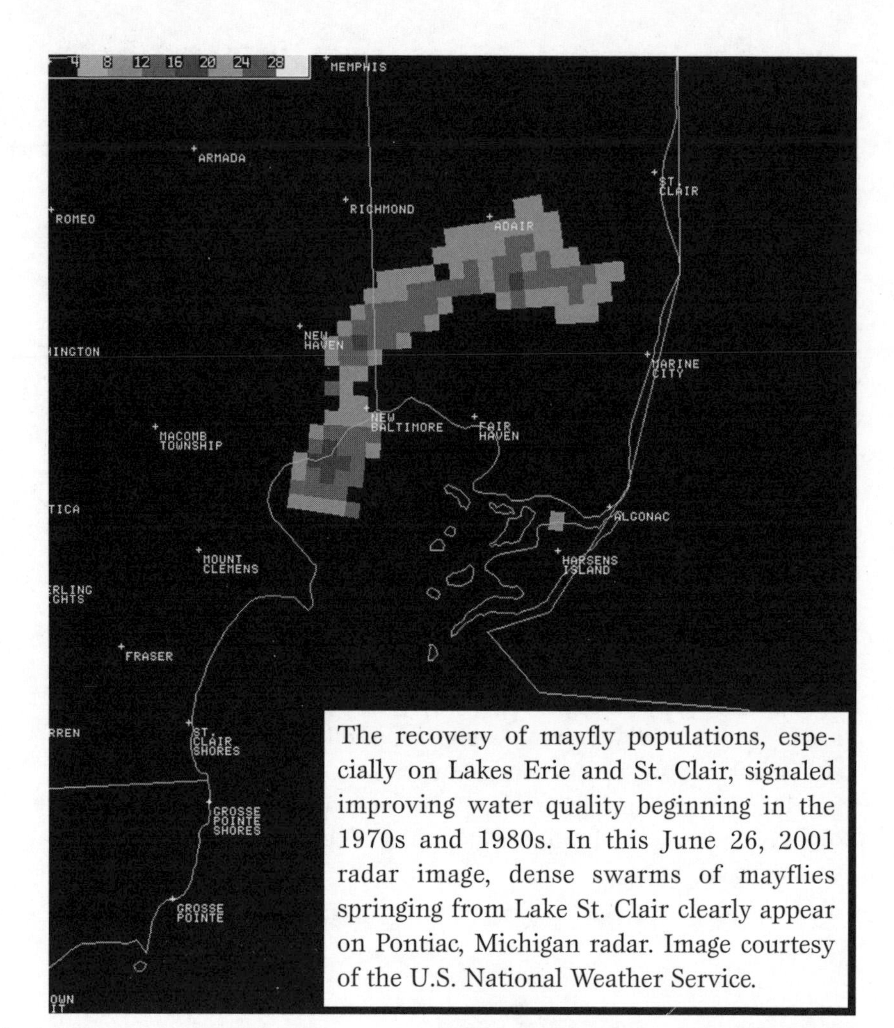

The recovery of mayfly populations, especially on Lakes Erie and St. Clair, signaled improving water quality beginning in the 1970s and 1980s. In this June 26, 2001 radar image, dense swarms of mayflies springing from Lake St. Clair clearly appear on Pontiac, Michigan radar. Image courtesy of the U.S. National Weather Service.

University of Chicago botanist Henry Chandler Cowles articulated his globally significant theory of plant succession based on observations he made in the then-wild Indiana dunes, along Lake Michigan. Cowles championed the idea of a Sand Dunes National Park at a 1916 hearing in Chicago, but dreams of Indiana developers and industry boosters thwarted establishment of a scaled-down Indiana Dunes National Lakeshore until 1966. Photo courtesy of the Joseph Regenstein Library at the University of Chicago.

The stunning advancement of nets and fishing gear, as well as the increasing number of commercial anglers, took its toll on native fish species in the latter decades of the 1800s and early decades of the 1900s. Still, effective controls on fish catch were never uniformly adopted, even in the face of steep declines in such species as whitefish, lake sturgeon, and herring. Photo courtesy of the Great Lakes Fishery Commission.

Science and passion combined to stop the decline of Great Lakes ecosystem health beginning in the mid-1970s. Illustrating both was Canadian scientist Dr. J. R. (Jack) Vallentyne, who not only played a pivotal role in deliberations of Great Lakes science advisors that led to a strengthened Great Lakes Water Quality Agreement in 1978, but also roamed classrooms in his retirement as Johnny Biosphere. Photo courtesy of J. R. Vallentyne.

Mike Thomas, a Michigan Department of Natural Resources biologist on Lake St. Clair, clutches a lake sturgeon. Growing as long as five feet and weighing as much as 300 pounds, the sturgeon of the Great Lakes belongs to a family of fish that dates back over 130 million years. Dismissed in the 1800s as a nuisance fish and discarded, then later over harvested, the sturgeon's population is at about one percent of its historic abundance but is slowly recovering. Photo courtesy of David Kenyon, Michigan Department of Natural Resources.

The Pitcher's thistle is a globally rare plant that grows chiefly along the shores of the Great Lakes. Humans increasingly favor the same habitat. As a result, the U.S. Fish and Wildlife Service list the thistle, dwarf lake iris, and Houghton's goldenrod as threatened species. Photo courtesy of Michigan Natural Features Inventory, photographed by Susan R. Crispin.

Sea lamprey populations have been reduced by 90% from 1950s levels in most areas of the Great Lakes. Male lampreys are captured during their spawning migrations in tributaries of Lakes Michigan and Huron and transported to a sterilization facility at the Lake Huron Biological Station. At the facility, lampreys are sterilized, decontaminated, and released into streams where a substantial number of sea lamprey larvae routinely survive lampricide treatments. Photo courtesy of Marc Gaden.

After almost 75 years of unsuccessful efforts to coordinate fisheries management in the Great Lakes, the onslaught of the exotic sea lamprey finally prompted the signing in 1954 of a Canada-U.S. convention that created the Great Lakes Fishery Commission. Photo courtesy of Great Lakes Fishery Commission.

Beginning in the late 1940s, the Reserve Mining Company at Two Harbors, Minnesota dumped an average of 67,000 tons per day of taconite tailings into the waters of Lake Superior. Citizen outrage and a complicated lawsuit finally brought the dumping to an end in 1980. Photo courtesy of Minnesota Historical Society.

The arrival of the zebra mussel in the Great Lakes Basin in the late 1980s was a signal of failed government policies. Reluctant to confront the powerful shipping industry, both the U.S. and Canada failed to shut the door on additional exotics for the next 15 years. The mussel clogged water intakes, lined the bottom of boats, and caused upsets in the Great Lakes ecosystem. Photo courtesy of the *Windsor Star*.

Fires broke out occasionally on Ohio's Cuyahoga River and other Great Lakes tributaries as a result of oil and chemical pollution and floating combustible debris. A 22 June 1969 fire on the Cuyahoga was the first to capture national attention, highlighting the decline of North American waterways. News coverage of the 1969 fire is credited with helping galvanize political momentum for the U.S. Clean Water Act. This fire, however, took place in 1952 and escaped national attention. Photo courtesy of Cleveland State University Library.

Great Lakes water levels fluctuate naturally. Although in the late 1990s lakefront property owners complained about unsightly "weeds" that grew up in lake bottoms exposed by near-record low waters, a dozen years earlier near-record high water levels had caused millions of dollars in property damage. This mid-1980s Chicago scene shows Lake Michigan waters, aided by a northeast wind, storming over Lake Shore Drive. Photo courtesy of Laurie Leigh.

Rondeau Provincial Park, the second in Ontario, was designated in the late 1800s because of its importance as a summer resort destination. Its extensive waterfront and southerly location in Canada make it a rare and important habitat, especially for migrating birds. Photo courtesy of Rondeau Provincial Park Archives, Ontario Ministry of Natural Resources, © 2003 Queens Printer Ontario.

and Michigan governor James Blanchard and New York governor Mario Cuomo in opposing winter navigation. Congressional field hearings during the fall of 1983 in Michigan demonstrated widespread public opposition to the proposal. In June 1984 the U.S. House approved the water projects bill without winter navigation, effectively killing it. Coupled with the organizing of environmentalists, the major force stopping the massive retooling of the lakes to accommodate winter vessels was that it had "become too controversial for pork barrel politics."[29]

But that didn't mean dreams of improving the lakes through engineering were abandoned. Instead, they simply went underwater. The Army Corps of Engineers and port interests throughout the lakes yearned for the chance to manipulate again.

Islands Aplenty

SEPARATED FROM THE MAIN, LIKE CHUNKS OF ANCIENT planets blasted into asteroids and floating mysteriously through the chasms of outer space, islands have long excited the human imagination. In the Great Lakes, islands have warped that imagination as well as enchanted it; they have reaped dividends of suffering as well as riches for tourism's boosters.

The islands themselves are treasures. Approximately thirty thousand of them are scattered across the five Great Lakes and through their connecting channels. Ranging in size from hunks of rock to Manitoulin, at eighty miles long the largest island in a freshwater lake anywhere in the world, their customary isolation often makes them castles of natural wealth guarded by moats from a world of degraded biologic integrity.

"The geography of islands, their varying degrees of isolation, varying sizes, and their very 'island-ness,' create conditions that are quite different from those occurring naturally on the mainland," wrote Dr. Judith Soule, head of Michigan's Natural Features Inventory, in 1993. "The key point is that our Great Lakes islands, and particularly those in eastern Lake Michigan, are a natural resource to which the often over-used word 'unique' is aptly applied."[30]

Soule offered several reasons why islands are valuable for biological research:

- Because islands often lack some of the flora and fauna found on the mainland, they provide an ideal research setting for comparing interactions among coexisting species. The natural absence of deer on a Great Lakes island, for example, may make it possible to study unique patterns of floral development among species that the deer would otherwise eat for breakfast.
- Because mainland habitat is increasingly checkered by human development—creating "islands" of forest or prairie, for example—studies of effects of isolation of plants and animals on islands can help promote understanding of the effects of mainland sprawl and habitat fragmentation.
- Islands have clear boundaries, through which many groups of organisms find immigration and emigration difficult or impossible. Islands thus not only tend to retain their biological integrity, but also serve as prime research laboratories that can be fully inventoried.

An example of the island effect in promoting biological diversity is the history of the Lake Erie water snake. As Great Lakes levels rose dramatically about four thousand years ago, populations of the northern water snake were marooned on the Lake Erie islands that now straddle the United States–Canada border. Natural selection helped differentiate the new subspecies from its mainland counterparts. Now occupying a habitat consisting chiefly of rocky shorelines, the non-poisonous one to five foot long snakes evolved into a dull gray color, without bold markings. In contrast to the northern water snake, which feeds chiefly on amphibians, the Lake Erie water snake developed a talent and taste for catching fish in waters up to thirty feet deep. Safe from most predators, the Lake Erie water snake population also grew dramatically until the twentieth century. The combination of commercial and residential development of both shoreline summer habitat and inland hibernation habitat, and human disgust with snakes that prompted an eradication campaign, drove populations down. In 1999, the U.S. Fish and Wildlife Service listed the Lake Erie water snake as a threatened species. The Canadian Wildlife Service considers it endangered, as does the Ohio Department of Natural Resources. About five thousand snakes are thought to remain in the United States, and an unknown number in Canada, all on nine U.S. and seven Canadian islands in Lake Erie. The vulnerability of the snakes has begun to change human attitudes toward them. Ohio wildlife biologists worked with students on South Bass Island to create posters urging residents and visitors to "Save Our Snakes. Don't Kill Our Snakes."

"As a kid, we swam in the lake and saw them all the time," said Lisa Scott, the executive director of the Put-in-Bay Chamber of Commerce and a lifelong resident of South Bass Island, in 1996. "They scared us. It was like, 'Ooo, gross.' But I never heard of one biting anyone. . . . You have to feel sorry for anything that is endangered. Although it doesn't mean we have to like them."[31]

Considerations of biological diversity were not much in the mind of James Strang when he established his kingdom on Lake Michigan's Beaver Island in 1850. Determining that the islands of the Great Lakes were a Mormon inheritance, Strang declared himself monarch of thirteen-by-seven-mile Beaver. His reign lasted six years, ending in his assassination by non-Mormons who violently objected as much to the king's polygamous customs as to his rule by decree.

A much different island reign aroused civil—but still fierce—passions in the late 1990s. Developer David V. Johnson sought to consolidate his private ownership of roughly two-thirds of South Fox Island, part of the Beaver Island archipelago in northern Lake Michigan. Intermingled with Johnson's scattered holdings was public land owned by the state of Michigan. Johnson argued that a land swap with the state that he proposed would simplify management of both the public and private acreage. The Michigan Department of Natural Resources (DNR) agreed, twice cooperating with Johnson to expedite the land exchange.

Others passionately disagreed with both Johnson and the state. The DNR proposed to give up the best part of the island and take land that Johnson has no use for,charged Brian Upton, an attorney representing the Grand Traverse Band of Ottawa and Chippewa Indians, who claim ancient ownership rights to the island. Upton sued to stop the exchange, and a coalition of sportsmen who enjoyed hunting on the island's public lands and environmentalists who objected to the proposed transfer to Johnson of a majestic sand dune complex on the island's west side organized to halt the exchange. Pointing out that Johnson had once proposed to build a resort on the island, the "Nantucket of the West," they said the state couldn't trust the developer's assurances that he simply wanted to make his existing private home on the island more secluded and his landholdings easier to manage.

Johnson said he had treated his land with respect. In early 2003 he received title to the former state lands he sought in exchange for lands permitting the DNR to consolidate its holdings.

Manitoulin, the great island that marks off Ontario's North Channel of Lake Huron, has lore as well. Named by the native Chippewa, Ottawa, and Pottawatomi peoples in honor of the Kitche Manitou, or Great Spirit, the island has a three hundred-foot-high bluff topped by Dreamer's Rock, where tribal young came for generations to take a spiritual voyage, fasting and praying and awaiting a vision.

A more recent legend, reflecting an utterly different culture, is of Daniel Dodge, son of the founder of the Dodge automobile empire. Dodge owned a lodge on Manitoulin's Maple Point. On 15 August 1938, honeymooning with his bride, Lorraine, Dodge and two other men allegedly had an accident while playing with dynamite in the garage of the lodge. Badly injured, the men somehow climbed into a speedboat with Lorraine and the wife of another of the men and set a course for a nearby town with a physician but encountered roiling waters. The story goes that Daniel Dodge accidentally fell out of the boat and drowned. The coroner's jury declared the death accidental. Lorraine Dodge inherited over $1 million after a court fight.

The island way of life is more often characterized by visions of peace. The physical remove from the stresses of everyday life on the mainland has created monumentally popular resorts out of Beaver Island, Mackinac Island in

Lake Huron, and the Ohio islands of Lake Erie. The most famous spot on the Erie islands may be South Bass Island, also known as Put-in-Bay. Some say this is a corruption of the original European name of Pudding Bay, supposedly chosen because a British ship's captain had only flour for food on arrival there in the 1780s and, mixing it with water, created an unappetizing dish that vaguely resembled pudding. Now the island attracts a stew of tourists, some seeking to make contact with Lake Erie's military history at the Perry's Victory and International Peace Memorial on South Bass Island. Others come to dine and drink without mainland restraint.

But many of the islands have resisted such colonization. Their natural development equals or exceeds that of humankind. "We can now say with certainty that the natural biological diversity of the islands of the Great Lakes is of global significance," said Karen Vigmostad, organizer of a 1996 conference on the resource. "Islands are uniquely rare at the same time they are supremely vulnerable. . . . Islands are absolutely dependent on humans to ensure their biological integrity. They need us to better understand and protect them, especially those that are still wild and 'undeveloped.'"[32]

Vigmostad's conference team manufactured a small but ambitious batch of recommendations. Governments and others should facilitate island and archipelago conservation strategies; concerned researchers and citizens should increase the sharing of information and experiences on island protection initiatives; and governments should assemble all existing scientific information on Great Lakes islands as a basis for planning the conservation strategies. Unfortunately, protection of the islands has not yet become a priority for any government. But Vigmostad optimistically concluded, "It is not too late. . . . People really care about islands and change is in the air."[33]

The biggest change, which conservationists hope for but dare not proclaim, is the cherishing of islands not only in the hearts of individuals, but in the policies and projects of the governments charged with protecting our common heritage.

I was born and raised in Minneapolis in 1924. When I was about five years old, a family friend who owned a cabin on the north shore of Lake Superior (near Lutsen) invited our family to spend a week at their cabin. It was June and cold but fun to explore the bluff and rocks and crashing waves, Split Rock Lighthouse, eat smoked cisco and learn about Paul Bunyan. One day we took a picnic lunch to Port Arthur—now Thunder Bay—in Canada.

—Edith Chase

Lake Michigan brought my family's two homes together—Milwaukee and Leland. It was a great transportation link. We gathered often at Good Harbor beach for picnics and bonfires. The clear, cold waters of Lake Michigan served as our refrigerator and kept the watermelon we always had with us, ice cold. My aunt would take us down to the lake every day during the summer. What a big sandbox we had.

—Frances Lederle Schulte

7

The Comeback

In the late twentieth century, it became commonplace to talk about the Great Lakes as a single vast ecosystem. Politicians and top-level environmental officials in national, provincial, and state governments and the news media regularly referred to the interconnections of the lakes and of all the living things in their basins. But this way of thinking and talking is only about the same age as the notion of Spaceship Earth, popularized when astronauts snapped photos of a vulnerable blue-and-white disc drifting through space in the late 1960s. In fact, in approximately 1968, the same year that the U.S. *Apollo 8* mission first photographed the earth rising above the horizon of the moon, something shifted in the way citizens, scientists, and a few of the most concerned governmental officials regarded the Great Lakes.

It was a year and an era in which old assumptions about life perished, some to be replaced by new, compelling ways of interpreting and explaining reality. Convulsed and deeply divided by U.S. involvement in the Vietnam War and by the assassinations of Senator Robert F. Kennedy and Martin Luther King, the publics of both the United States and Canada saw the evident decline of the Great Lakes as another symbol of a society in decline and groped for methods of reversing the plummeting tide. Treating individual symptoms no longer seemed to work. First scientists, then advocacy organizations, and finally governments began to imagine the Great Lakes as an immense, complicated ecosystem. Looking back more than twenty-five years later, Ontario scientist Henry Regier commented that "Western culture apparently crossed a great historical divide" in the late 1960s, with profound implications for the protection of the Great Lakes.[1]

The term "ecosystem" was coined in 1935 by British ecologist Arthur Tansley. "The universe, in Tansley's view, was a vast number of overlapping physical systems, each tending toward a state of maturity characterized by equilibrium," Stephen Bocking has written. "The ecosystem was one of many such systems, and the one of special interest to ecologists. As the 'basic unit of nature' for ecologists, the ecosystem asserted the unity of ecology."[2]

Scientists studied and refined the ecosystem concept in the post–World War II period. The U.S. Atomic Energy Commission (AEC) funded one of the largest-scale ecosystem research projects in the world at the Oak Ridge National Laboratory in Tennessee. The AEC supported the work in part to contribute "to the AEC ideal of establishing a technological, nuclear-powered basis for American society."[3] Explaining the natural world in ways analogous to the engineered nuclear systems that the AEC promoted, the scientists were able to commandeer considerable public funding. In Canada, ecosystem studies got their first significant foothold in the late 1960s at the Experimental Lakes

Area in Ontario. Researchers began to comment on the effect of human activities on large as well as small ecosystems. In the early 1970s, as Great Lakes research suggested that the stability of the fishery hinged on healthy fish communities, which in turn signaled stresses imposed by man, the region's scientists began to converge on the idea of protecting "ecosystem integrity," not just cleaning up the water.

At the same time, the public was getting an education on ecosystems with a wave of chemical controversies that fouled both physical and political waters. Rachel Carson had begun the schooling of the general audience with her 1962 book, *Silent Spring*. Provoking a storm of controversy, a counterattack by pesticide manufacturers, and a steadily increasing level of general public concern about the environment, Carson's book illustrated the danger of persistent pesticides that don't break down in the environment but instead accumulate in fish and birds, with magnified effects. Carson alluded to research done at Michigan State University beginning in the late 1950s that traced the sharp decline of campus robin populations to the use of the pesticide DDT on trees to stop Dutch elm disease.

Carson wrote of the great natural system that pesticides were affecting in unintentional ways:

> this is a problem of ecology, of interrelationships, of interdependence. We poison the caddis flies in a stream and the salmon runs dwindle and die. We poison the gnats in a lake and the poison travels from link to link of the food chain and soon the birds of the lake margins become its victims. We spray our elms and the following springs are silent of robin song, not because we sprayed the robins directly but because the poison traveled, step by step, through the now familiar elm leaf-earthworm-robin cycle. These are matters of record, observable, part of the visible

> world around us. They reflect the web of life—or death—that scientists know as ecology.[4]

Mortified by the prospect of dwindling bird and other wildlife populations, Audubon Society members and a new breed of determined environmental activists mobilized to stop the almost indiscriminate use of DDT to treat Dutch elm disease in communities throughout the United States and to combat the use of other "hard," or persistent, pesticides. Concerns about the effect of pesticides on the health of the Great Lakes made the region the centerpiece for a monumental battle based on ecological concepts. Scientists, public officials, and citizens challenging pesticides as a threat to the lakes often invoked the "food chain" as the basis for their arguments, underscoring the interconnection of plants, fish, and wildlife, and humans.

Brought to Michigan in 1967 in part by one of its founders, Kalamazoo College professor H. Lewis Batts, the Environmental Defense Fund (EDF) chose to use the courts to challenge government policies promoting heavy use of pesticides. The EDF filed two suits, one to challenge the state's approval of dieldrin to control Japanese beetles infesting fruit and vegetable crops and another to stop local use of DDT as a treatment for Dutch elm. Although the Michigan Supreme Court dismissed the dieldrin suit, the delay it prompted prevented use of the chemical in 1967. Every local government sued over DDT use agreed to discontinue its use for Dutch elm disease.

The loss of seven hundred thousand salmon fry in a Michigan hatchery in 1968, which the state Department of Conservation said was probably due to DDT residues that had leached into rivers and Lake Michigan, awakened new fears about the unintended consequences of persistent pesticides. Organized by Michigan conservation agency chief Ralph A. MacMullan, the directors of the natural resource agencies of the four states bordering the lake developed a joint pesticide statement, warning that without action to curb pesticides, "Lake Michigan's usefulness will shrink to a fraction of its potential—indeed to the point of disaster."[5] But in September 1968, over the fierce objections of a coalition of citizens groups but to the applause of farm and chemical interests, the traditional constituencies for government agricultural agencies, Michigan's agriculture commission approved the use of dieldrin and chlordane to control Japanese beetles in southwestern Michigan's Berrien County.

The EDF launched another attack on dieldrin, this time filing a lawsuit in Wisconsin to overturn the Michigan decision, alleging that the chemical's use menaced Lake Michigan. The EDF charged that Michigan's dieldrin was impairing the lake, thereby interfering with its use and enjoyment by Wisconsin citizens—an implied recognition that the lake was a system shared by states, rather than a territory carved into separate domains by political boundaries. Although the EDF's Wisconsin lawsuit was dismissed, the publicity it provoked galvanized more citizens to act, urged on by MacMullan, who had called for a state law giving him increased authority over pesticides. "Lake Michigan is big, it's deep, and it looks unpollutable—but it isn't. It is measurably contaminated. This is the clearest kind of warning bell. If my Department and the people of Michigan don't listen and don't take corrective action, our complacency will be our shame," said the fiery director.[6] Typical of citizen concerns was testimony by Joan Wolfe, a founder of the West Michigan Environmental Action Council in Grand Rapids and an officer of the Michigan Pesticides Council, which sought to limit chemical pesticides:

> Never before in history have we inadvertently distributed poisons all over the earth. Never before have we been so single-minded that we have risked destroying huge facets of this earth on which we all depend. Never before have

> we expected our children and our grandchildren to bear the burden of mixtures of poisons building up in our bodies. . . . We have already denied our children the right to a clean environment, but we can let them know that we are trying to right things as fast as possible.[7]

The tide soon turned, beginning with DDT. Still authorized for most agricultural uses despite its abandonment by many cities as a treatment for Dutch elm disease, DDT was a symbol to conservationists and environmental advocates of humanity's abuse of the web of life. In the winter of 1969 the Michigan Department of Agriculture found alarmingly high levels of dieldrin in coho salmon captured at weirs as they migrated into tributary streams the previous fall. The agency embargoed five hundred thousand pounds of the fish from sale. Shortly thereafter, the U.S. Food and Drug Administration seized fourteen tons of Lake Michigan coho salmon with high levels of DDT. The action and resulting publicity threatened the new salmon fishery that had resulted from Michigan's planting of coho and chinook in Lake Michigan. Michigan State University's Agricultural Experiment Station removed DDT from its recommendations to farmers in February 1969. With the university's support removed, and responding to pressure from sport fishing and tourism interests, the state agriculture commission cancelled most uses of DDT in the state in April 1969. The *Ann Arbor News* alluded to the systemic issues raised by persistent pesticides: "there is an awareness now that Michigan's ecological situation must be preserved in a balanced state. Overload an area or a body of water with contaminants and the effects are wide-ranging."[8]

Pesticides were just the first in a series of chemicals to taint portions of the Great Lakes ecosystem, compounding public alarm and raising awareness. The discovery in the spring of 1970 of high mercury levels in fish taken from the St. Clair River, Lake

St. Clair, the Detroit River, and western Lake Erie caused a near panic among government officials and fishing groups, stirred by prominent news media coverage. Levels of mercury in the fish were only slightly below those in fish and shellfish believed to have caused the death and deformity of over one hundred persons in Minamata, Japan, in the 1950s. Ontario and Michigan temporarily banned fishing in the affected waters. Tracking down the industrial sources of mercury accumulating in the fish—primarily chemical plants along the Ontario side of the St. Clair River and the Michigan side of the Detroit River—both the province and the state worked quickly to jawbone the firms into reducing their mercury dumping, issuing orders to the few who refused.

Only a year later, the new persistent chemical generating news and stirring government and public worry was a family of compounds known as polychlorinated biphenyls, or PCBs. Used to de-ink paper wastes and as a fire retardant, PCBs were suspected of contributing to miscarriages, stillbirths, and liver cancer. PCBs spurred a continent wide search for sources. Governments asked Monsanto, the major manufacturer of PCBs, to discontinue sales of the compound; in 1976 the U.S. Congress banned their manufacture, although some remain in use to the present day.

The ecosystem concept slowly began to win a public constituency, in part because each pollution problem solved seemed only to lead to the next. Environmental thinkers began to question whether it made sense to approach pollution threats as water quality issues, or whether bigger issues of pollution prevention were involved. Even more, given that each successive pollutant had exposed differing regulatory and public health approaches among the Great Lakes jurisdictions, critics of the status quo wondered whether arbitrary political boundaries were adequate to protect major shared ecosystems. University of Indiana government professor Lynton K. Caldwell, a scholar who had a hand in enactment by the U.S. Congress of the National Environmental Policy Act of 1970, wrote, "Implicit in the ecosystems concept is a recognition that the maintenance of the ecosystem depends upon the consistency of man-made standards, laws and boundaries with those that have evolved through natural processes."[9] In time, responding to the persistent advocacy of the expanding Great Lakes community, governments would institutionalize the ecosystem as the basis for Great Lakes protection in a series of impressive binational agreements and state-provincial pacts—although not all of them were implemented.

Despite nearly a decade of vocal, passionate debate about the pollution of all the lakes, but especially Erie and Michigan, only modest changes had taken place by the end of the 1960s and conditions seemed to be worsening. The elected officials and news media of the region, aware of public disgust, pointedly took note. U.S. representative Charles Vanik told a June 1968 Lake Erie water pollution enforcement conference that the "talkathon" was going nowhere and that his constituents wanted action to clean up unusable beaches. The *Chicago Tribune* ran a banner front-page headline in September 1967, during a Lake Michigan enforcement conference, "LAKE POLLUTION GROWING." The same year, the newspaper launched a Save Our Lake campaign and compiled its articles into a booklet, complete with vivid photos of foul water pollution.[10] Its environmental reporter, Casey Bukro, observed appalling pollution conditions from the Cuyahoga River at Cleveland to the Rouge River near Detroit to the Indiana Harbor Canal "that flowed like a chocolate bar" and reported on them. It began to seem that not just one lake but all the lakes were in jeopardy.

Like a single wave sweeping through the basin, public outrage about the possible doom facing the lakes suddenly altered the conditions under which municipal and industrial polluters had operated for decades. In the words of environmental historian Terence Kehoe, "the regulatory system of cooperative pragmatism collapsed like a house of cards" between 1969 and 1972. Buoyed by palpable public outrage, new environmental organizations were hatched and pressed insistent demands for action rather than negotiation.[11]

Although young people, particularly college students, played an important role in articulating and raising the profile of environmental issues, many of the movement's leaders were already well into adulthood. A defender of the Buffalo River and Lake Erie, jeweler Stan Spisiak was fifty years old in 1966 when he forced President Lyndon B. Johnson to pay attention to dumping in his favorite Great Lakes. Honored that year at a ceremony in Washington, D.C., as water conservationist of the year by the National Wildlife Federation, Spisiak urged Johnson's wife, Lady Bird, to visit the Buffalo area to observe the pollution problem. In August she brought her husband for a tour of Buffalo Harbor on a U.S. Coast Guard cutter. Handing a bucket of sludge to the president, Spisiak reportedly said, "They're dumping 175,000 cubic yards of this slop right out in the lake every year from the Buffalo River." Johnson subsequently ordered the Army Corps of Engineers to stop the practice. Spisiak continued for the next thirty years to fight for the recovery of the Buffalo River and Lake Erie.[12]

Women were also key members and often leaders of the environmental community. Beginning in the 1950s, Lee Botts of Chicago devoted her energies to lakefront preservation. In the late 1960s she turned her focus to the proposed construction of as many as seven nuclear power plants on the shores of Lake Michigan. Using the proposed Palisades facility at South Haven, Michigan, as a test case because it was the first large plant to be sited, Botts and allies challenged the assertions of Consumers Power Company and state and federal officials that Palisades would be safe. They charged that the lake water used to cool the plant's core would harm Lake Michigan when discharged, its high temperatures disrupting fish populations. Listing other water quality concerns, the plant's opponents demanded an environmental impact statement be prepared under the new National Environmental Policy Act. Although unsuccessful in stopping Palisades, the movement Botts helped spark contributed to halting three of the proposed plants and mitigating some of the environmental harm that was done by the remainder.

Hired by the Open Lands Project, a Chicago-area conservancy, to launch environmental education programs, Botts organized a Chicago meeting in April 1969 whose theme was "To Prevent an Unnatural Death." The conference led to formation of a Lake Michigan group within the Open Lands project, and in September 1970, to announcement of the freestanding Lake Michigan Federation (LMF), dedicated to protecting the lake.[13] But the same new laws and programs to implement them fought for and won by the new citizens environmental movement posed challenges for Botts and other activists. To contest the positions of industry and government officials on water pollution and nuclear plant siting, public interest organizations needed more technical expertise and legal skill than part-time volunteers could offer.

> Botts strongly believed that LMF's mission should be to provide information to citizens groups in the four-state region. She understood that a broad network of groups provided the legitimacy and pressure necessary to move policy in a democracy, and she had a sense of how to, in her words, "make things happen" by working the network. But LMF also had its own professional staff, which had reached six full-time employees by 1973. In order to provide information—whether on "NPDES" permits, nuclear plant safety, or the erosion effects of shoreline

> structures—LMF had to develop the staff expertise to acquire and understand the technical information provided to its constituency. LMF thus faced the tension between a constituency versus a staff-oriented method of operation.[14]

Botts grasped the need for and potential of a movement to protect the Great Lakes as a whole. When she left the federation in 1975, it was in part because she was unable to convince the organization's board to expand the group to become an advocate of all the lakes, not Lake Michigan alone.

The values of the movement had by then become embedded in both Canadian and U.S. law. A prominent figure in the region's environmental movement, University of Michigan professor Joseph L. Sax, who authored Michigan's 1970 environmental protection act, said in 1975, "Earth Day was a necessary first phase to dramatize our environmental ills. It got the attention of the legislators. . . . We are now in phase two—institutionalizing change. The environmental movement has matured."[15]

But 1975 was also a year in which the Great Lakes region weathered a severe economic downturn. For the first time since the birth of the new movement, some lawmakers and industries counterattacked, claiming the regulations imposed by national, state, and provincial pollution control laws were restraining needed growth. The environmental protection act authored by Sax was loudly, if unsuccessfully, targeted by mining companies in the state's Upper Peninsula. The laws endured, but the age of unquestioning public support for toughening environmental protection statutes had ended quickly.

The mining industry was itself the target in another historic antipollution battle over the daily dumping of sixty-seven thousand tons of taconite tailings by the Reserve Mining Company of Silver Bay, Minnesota, into Lake Superior. That Lake Superior could become a stage for a landmark pollution case was in itself an anomaly. The most remote of the lakes as well as the most magnificent, Superior remains to the present day the cleanest; the cold climate that contributes to its grandeur has proven more effective than strict laws in protecting it from human settlement and degradation. But the mineral riches not far from its shores spawned the only large industry in the Superior Basin, creating thousands of jobs and one great controversy.

Reserve Mining in 1947 had asked Minnesota officials for permits to turn low-grade taconite from the state's Iron Range into valuable fuel for steelmakers in Indiana and Ohio.[16] The technology making this possible promised to employ three thousand workers at Babbitt and Silver Bay, where the taconite would be crushed, iron would be separated out, and a huge quantity of waste tailings would be hurled into the lake. In December 1947 Reserve got its permit over what one state official termed the "Communist" objections of the sportsmen.[17] In October 1955 production at Silver Bay began. By the next year, commercial fishermen on Lake Superior were reporting huge swaths of water degraded from pure blue to murky green, of slimes on their nets, and of a drop in fish catches. In 1957 they complained that the cloudy water reached more than thirty-five miles down the shore from Silver Bay to the southwest.

In 1968 Charles Stoddard, a regional coordinator for the Department of Interior, drew the assignment of assembling a study group to examine the effect of the taconite dumping. The group sought more data, and scuba divers descended into the frigid lake to examine where the taconite went. Although much of it settled out on the bottom of the lake, as the company had said it would, clouds of it whirled out of the downward current, reducing the visibility of the lake by more than 80 percent. By the fall of 1968 the group prepared a draft report for Stoddard that estimated Reserve "discharged more sediments into Lake Superior in 12 days than all the lake's U.S. tributaries discharged into it in an entire year," and that Reserve could afford to deposit the tailings on land.[18]

The company put intense pressure on the Department of Interior, lobbying Secretary Stewart Udall not to release the report. Local congressman, U.S. representative John Blatnik, a powerhouse on the Public Works Committee, was especially insistent that the agency should suppress the findings. But in the final days of the outgoing Democratic administration, as Stoddard and Udall both prepared to leave public service, the fifty-six-year-old Stoddard released the study without informing his boss. On 16 January 1969 the *Minneapolis Star Tribune* and other papers reported on the study. Partly as a result of the publicity, in one of his last official acts, Udall called for the convening of an interstate enforcement conference on pollution of Lake Superior. Officials of the incoming Nixon administration presided over the first meeting of the conference in Duluth in May 1969.

Until now, Minnesota residents, mostly silent on the company's dumping in light of the jobs created by its operations, began to speak out. Grant Merritt, co-chairman of the platform committee of the state Democratic-Farmer-Labor Party, successfully inserted a plank in the document for the 1968 campaign that condemned "the use of Lake Superior as a dumping ground for mining or industrial wastes," overcoming the opposition of Blatnik.[19] Along the lake's Minnesota shoreline, twenty-nine-year-old Arlene Lind Harvell was the spark plug for the new Save Lake Superior Association, founded in early 1969. Harvell and allies sold fifteen thousand "Save Lake Superior" buttons, organized chapters in Ashland, Wisconsin, and Ironwood, Michigan, and quickly assembled a citizen coalition to attend and speak out at the enforcement conference. Citizens spoke out emotionally in defense of the lake, decrying pollution by Reserve and others. Paraphrasing the sentiment of her members, Harvell said, "No, we don't want that use made of the lake any more. We are sorry, but we have changed our minds." Grant Merritt put it differently in his testimony: "Even my daughter can recognize this kind of pollution and realize it must be stopped. Would I permit her to wipe her muddy feet on a clean carpet? No more readily will I stand by and allow taconite tailings to soil Lake Superior without protest."[20]

A native of Michigan's Upper Peninsula named Verna Mize, then living in the Washington, D.C., area, had learned of Reserve's pollution one evening in 1967 while in Michigan visiting a friend. The next morning she phoned a reporter to confirm the pollution. "We owe it to the children to save Lake Superior," she told a reporter later. "I want them to know the lake as I saw it as a little girl. . . . If ever there is a place to feel divinity, Lake Superior is that place. . . . You can't call Lake Superior just another lake any more than the Grand Canyon is just another ditch."[21]

Mize became a letter-writing machine, contacting newspapers throughout Michigan, public officials, sportsmen's groups, and the League of Women Voters. In 1970 she devoted her two-week vacation in the Upper Peninsula to the gathering of over five thousand signatures on an antipollution petition, which she sent to President Nixon. Dissatisfied with the noncommittal response she received from officials in the Nixon administration and some members of Congress, she began trooping to their offices, leaving behind stones she had plucked from the shores of Lake Superior. She sat like one of the stones in some offices, demanding to see such notables as William Ruckelshaus, the first administrator of the new U.S. Environmental Protection Agency (EPA). The news media found Mize irresistible and gave wide coverage to her effort to persuade Congress to stop the dumping and the EPA to sue Reserve Mining. "Can you imagine a government secretary taking on Armco and Republic Steel? It was so ridiculous," Mize said, but reporters found it great copy.[22] The *National Observer* said, "From her story emerges a picture of how a 'nobody' can tackle industrial giants, stir the feelings of thousands of persons who share her concerns, and help force a change in company practices."[23]

The publicity may have contributed to the decision Ruckelshaus announced in January 1972 to sue Reserve Mining. Grant Merritt, by 1972 the director of the new Minnesota Pollution Control Agency (PCA), credited Mize with organizing U.S. senators from Michigan, Illinois, and Indiana to write the EPA chief supporting a lawsuit. As news media interest in the spectacle of pollution reached an all-time high, coverage of the campaign by Reserve and its parent companies to stop the litigation through private lobbying of Nixon administration officials probably also emboldened Ruckelshaus. The new EPA had a popular mandate to curb the pollution-spewing excesses of the industrial age.

A case of mammoth pollution generated a court history of stunning complexity and significant duration. Reserve and the government battled over the discharge of the tailings. U.S. circuit judge Miles Lord presided over a trial that pivoted on whether asbestos-like fibers in the tailings posed a significant human health risk if ingested as drinking water by residents of Duluth and other communities. With the science uncertain, it was left to the activist Judge Lord, who took a personal dislike to the company's chronic denials that the Lake Superior dumping posed any kind of threat, to make national news. On 20 April 1974 Lord found the Reserve water discharge substantially endangered the health of Duluth residents and those of other communities, and that its air discharge substantially endangered residents of Silver Bay and other communities in the western arm of Lake Superior. He shut the Silver Bay plant down as of 12:01 A.M. the next day. Reserve successfully appealed the order and persuaded the U.S. Eighth Circuit Court of Appeals to remove Lord from the case. But Judge

Lord first declared, "The Court has said there are no heroes or villains in this case. I sometimes feel like Reserve may have found the villain: it's the judge who exposed them for what they are."[24]

In 1975 the appeals court ruled that Reserve would have to build a basin and treatment process for the tailings to keep them from Lake Superior, but would have reasonable time to do so. Reserve's $375 million on-land disposal project began in 1977 and was completed in 1980, at last ending the taconite dumping.

As the Reserve Mining dispute lurched toward its consummation, a site in the Great Lakes Basin became a worldwide synonym for a legacy of abandoned industrial wastes. Niagara Falls, New York, seized attention in 1978 when more than twenty thousand tons of chemical wastes buried and abandoned by Hooker Chemical Company were discovered in Love Canal. The would-be industrial tycoon William T. Love had built the incomplete, three-thousand-foot-long canal in the late 1800s as part of a scheme to harness the power of the river through a bypass from the upper to lower reaches. It formed a suitable trench for Hooker's brew of toxic pesticides, PCBs, solvents, and other chemical wastes. Sold by the chemical company to the Niagara Falls Board of Education in 1953, the land above and around the canal provided space for more than eight hundred single-family homes, two hundred apartments, and an elementary school by the time the wastes were found to be leaking into basements and the air. Neighborhood resident Lois Gibbs, after reading a newspaper article about the old dump, "became concerned about the health of my son, who was in kindergarten at the 99th Street School. Since moving into our house on 101st Street, my son, Michael, had been constantly ill. I came to believe that the school and playground were making him sick. Consequently, I asked the school board to transfer Michael to another public school, and they refused, stating that 'such a transfer would set a bad precedent.'"[25]

Angered by what she regarded as the insensitivity of the school board and other government officials, Gibbs went door-to-door gathering signatures on a petition to shut down the school and discovered, she said, that the "neighborhood was sick."[26] Indications of high rates of cancer, birth defects, and illness attracted news media coverage and forced New York state health officials to act. On 2 August 1978 the state department of health declared a state of emergency, shut the school down, and recommended that pregnant women and young children evacuate the area. But citizens continued to regard the response of local, state, and federal agencies as condescending and demeaning and demanded a more complete solution. A second order in 1979 expanded the relocation recommendation to another six hundred sixty families. Pressuring President Jimmy Carter to act, the appalled neighborhood residents ultimately won public funding for all who wanted to leave the neighborhood, with costs of cleanup and relocation eventually topping $60 million.[27]

Even bigger than the immediate, urgent issue of protection for the residents of the Love Canal neighborhood was the significance of the discovery. As governments throughout industrialized North America began to look for abandoned dumps and other contaminated sites, they found staggering numbers. In the Niagara River region alone, governments eventually pinpointed more than sixty-five dumps leaking from groundwater into air and surface water, "the greatest concentration of toxic dumps anywhere on the North American continent."[28] Over the next twenty years, cleanup of these and other sites would cost approximately $382 million, and cleanup of other dumps would run in the billions in both the United States and Canada.

A downstream bed-and-breakfast owner named Margherita Howe of Niagara-on-the-Lake, Ontario, launched her own crusade. Appalled by the pollution leaking into the Niagara River from the dumps on the U.S. side, the nearly sixty-year-old Howe became the leader of Operation Clean Niagara, a citizens organization. Clean Niagara pointed out that the river was the drinking water supply source for Howe's community. Operating without an office or staff, the organization worked out of its members' homes. Howe said she "phoned everyone but God" to publicize the cause. Although a Youngstown, New York, chemical company built the waste pipe discharging into the river that Clean Niagara opposed, Howe's group had successfully increased public concern about the river's problems. When the two federal and two provincial governments signed a Niagara River cleanup plan in February 1987, Howe and her group received much of the credit.[29]

Blunt to the point of rudeness, Howe insisted that governments in both nations and at all levels make and keep commitments to the public trust. Howe explained her lobbying technique: "I know that I strike people the wrong way and I can't help it. If it's important, it doesn't matter what people think of you. You can't worry about your popularity."[30]

The double blow of toxic pollution discoveries—first chemicals released by agricultural and industrial processes directly into the Great Lakes environment in the 1960s and early 1970s, then the slow leaking of chemicals from the dumps and poorly managed industrial plants into groundwater, lakes, and streams in the late 1970s and early 1980s—helped drive many to think in ecosystem terms. Increasingly vocal citizens organizations were beginning to articulate a basinwide philosophy of Great Lakes protection, but they did not yet have a central organizing principle. It came in 1978, however, when the United States and Canada negotiated a new Great Lakes Water Quality Agreement, replacing the 1972 version.

The first pact had been credited with a visible improvement in the health of the lakes. "The sparkle and freshness are slowly returning to the pollution-tinged Great Lakes, the largest reservoir of fresh water in the world," said *U.S. News and World Report* in 1976. "'It's one of the greatest success stories in American history,' says Russell Train, head of the U.S. Environmental Protection Agency. . . . The turning point for the Great Lakes was in 1972. It was then that the United States and Canada, embarrassed and concerned by the degradation of the lakes, signed an agreement to stop polluting them."[31]

Such glowing reviews made it possible for the two nations to revise and toughen the agreement. In addition to other important changes—including a new focus on persistent toxic chemicals, rather than the "conventional" pollutants such as phosphorus that had been the central concern of the earlier document—the 1978 agreement committed the two nations to the principle of restoring "the chemical, physical and biological integrity of the waters of the Great Lakes Basin Ecosystem," a term based on parallel language in the U.S. Clean Water Act. Crucially, the agreement defined the Great Lakes Basin ecosystem as "the interacting components of air, land, water and living organisms, including humans."[32]

The important new language in the document was the direct result of a report released earlier in 1978 by the International Joint Commission's Great Lakes Research Advisory Board. The board's scientists strongly recommended moving from concentration on a single or small number of pollutants entering water to the ecosystem approach.[33] The board's spokesperson, Dr. J. R. Vallentyne, championed the board's finding that an ecosystem approach "includes the concept of carrying capacity, the notion that there are limits in ecosystems to the abundance and activity of particular species at particular times and locations. It also includes the concept of man as a species with internal (biological) and external (technological) components of mass and metabolism. Jointly considered, these imply ecosystem and biosphere constraints to growth of population and technology."[34]

While the agreement, like its predecessor, had no binding effect or implementing mechanism, it carried the authority of the two nations, and the IJC would continue to serve as an evaluator of and chronicler of government performance in keeping the document's commitments. The IJC's role in watchdogging the agreement proved indispensable to the formation and growth of a Great Lakes community of citizens. From 1978 to 1992 IJC's biennial water quality meetings provided the only basinwide governmental public forum for public concern about the cleanup of the Great Lakes.

But citizens needed their own basinwide organization. The notion of an advocacy group spanning the two nations and the basins of all five lakes was an outgrowth of the work undertaken by organizations on the American side to combat the U.S. Army Corps of Engineers' winter navigation proposal in the 1970s. The Michigan United Conservation Clubs (MUCC) and Save the River had teamed in that battle, and heads of each, MUCC's Tom Washington and Save the River's Abbie Hoffman, were among those who pushed for creation of the new Great Lakes organization. But Washington and Hoffman were prickly personalities of different cultural backgrounds who sparred with each other. Other environmentalists were suspicious of the motives of each, supposing they might be trying to take over the lakes by creating a hierarchical organization. Many potential members of the new organization were appalled at the idea that either Washington or Hoffman would strong-arm or speak for them on Great Lakes issues.

The disputes were bitter, and the labor required to give birth to the organization was time-consuming. Meeting first on Mackinac Island in May 1982, activists agreed on the need for the organization but not even on its name. In November 1982, after resolving the power struggle, the new group was created with a mandate to coordinate and support, rather than supplant, existing organizations. Robert Boice successfully proposed its name: "I suggest we call ourselves Great Lakes United. The name says we each maintain our autonomy, but we're working together for a common cause. And its acronym is GLU—the group that holds the lakes together."[35]

The region's private foundations also played a significant role in strengthening the Great Lakes citizens' community. The Joyce Foundation of Chicago, the George Gund Foundation of Cleveland, and the Charles Stewart Mott Foundation of Flint provided generous funding for the nongovernmental organizations, giving citizen advocates the resources needed to pressure the governments to move forward. The foundations also supported projects of some governmental coordinating institutions, leading directly to the creation of the Great Lakes Protection Fund.

For a time, the success of the governments in cleaning up the Great Lakes made the work of GLU and other citizen advocates relatively easy. Politicians rushed to embrace the cause of Great Lakes protection and restoration with a series of high-visibility summit conferences and agreements. Michigan governor William G. Milliken hosted a 1982 conference on Mackinac Island to focus attention on the long-term threat of water diversions out of the basin. In 1985 his successor, James Blanchard, created an Office of the Great Lakes to advocate the interests of the ecosystem in state, federal, and international policy. Ohio governor Richard Celeste created a Lake Erie office in 1987. And all of the basin's governors and the premiers of both Ontario and Quebec participated in the drafting of the Great Lakes Charter of 1985, an agreement to build defenses against harmful water diversions and exports. The governors followed up with a Great Lakes Toxic Substances Control Agreement in 1986 and a $100 million Great Lakes Protection Fund, an endowment devoted to research on lakes issues, in 1989. Fanfare accompanied the signing of each document, and the officials responsible basked in the glow of their commitment to better the basin. Typical of their rhetoric was the statement of Blanchard at the charter signing: "This is a clear signal to the Sun Belt that we stand united to protect the greatest fresh water resources in the world."[36]

By the mid 1980s Great Lakes protection issues had become impossible for chief executives of the basin states and Ontario to ignore. But while the leaders convened task forces and produced agreements, the organized Great Lakes community of citizens demanded more. Now wedded to the rhetoric and promise of ecosystem integrity, they termed the interstate and state-provincial agreements helpful but inadequate. Each new proclamation by a government official of Great Lakes recovery was followed by disclosures of new and worrisome problems. In the early 1980s, after congratulating themselves for banning PCBs and DDT, governments in the basin were forced to admit that levels of some persistent toxic chemicals were stabilizing or even increasing because of a phenomenon dubbed "toxic fallout" by environmentalists. Chemicals in use in distant parts of North America, or even on other continents, were being lifted toward the Great Lakes on high-altitude winds and landing in the ecosystem. Thus even the most aggressive action by the basin governments would ultimately prove inadequate to rid the lakes of the toxic scourge.

Basic environmental enforcement also lagged behind the promises of politicians on both sides of the border. A tradition of vigorous public participation in the United States had helped propel environmental agencies forward in requiring compliance with the laws of the 1970s, but Canadian jurisdictions were more inclined to rely on the old approach of cooperation and negotiation with business. As *Maclean's* observed in 1985, "the Ontario government has never been vigorous in controlling industrial pollution. A recent report by Ontario's ministry of the environment documented the widespread discharge of untreated industrial wastes into municipal sewage systems that are incapable of filtering out toxic chemicals. Most observers say that U.S. laws, which require industries to obtain permits to discharge wastes, have been more effective. Declared University of Toronto ecologist and Great Lakes [Fishery] commissioner Henry Regier: 'If Canada owned the whole of the Great Lakes, maybe the problems would be worse.' "[37]

To force more fundamental change, the citizen activists turned to the IJC. In 1989 the groups began to organize and turn out at the commission's biennial meetings reviewing the progress of governments toward meeting Great Lakes Water Quality Agreement commitments. The result was dramatic—and ticklish. "It is difficult for a primarily technical and expert-oriented body to incorporate more public participation, especially as the public is not generally held to the same level of professionalism and accountability as is expected of experts," writes Jennifer Read. "In many ways, this has been the most delicate aspect of the IJC's adaptation to the environmental era, incorporating the public without offending participating experts."[38]

Incorporate, the IJC did. More than one thousand members of the public, most from environmental and citizens organizations, attended the 1989 biennial meeting in Hamilton, Ontario. The Lake Michigan Federation organized a bus to take passengers from Wisconsin, Illinois, and northwestern Indiana. Carpools from across the basin brought others. "By contrast with the usual polite and quiet IJC affairs, this meeting was noisy, in part because of the crowd and in part because of the nature of the presentations by the environmental organizations and dozens of individual citizens of both countries. . . . Signs and songs added theater to substantive statements on issues presented with intense emotion. At times the noise level made it seem like a sporting event as the audience responded to presentations."[39]

The 1991 IJC biennial meeting in Traverse City, Michigan, attracted sixteen hundred registrants, including the first significant industry representation. The environmental group Greenpeace hung a banner from the outside of the meeting's hotel tower denouncing EPA administrator William Reilly and Environment Canada minister Jean Charest as "Great Fakes" for allegedly failing to deliver on Great Lakes cleanup promises. The 1993 meeting in Windsor, Ontario, was attended by more than two thousand. Fireworks were common by now as mothers, students, and professional advocates sparred with industrial representatives in front of the IJC about the necessity of cracking down on Great Lakes pollution. The chair of the U.S. Section of the IJC, Gordon Durnil, was an interested observer of one incident:

> At the [IJC meeting in 1993], spokesmen from industry baited the environmentalists with words the speakers thought were true but, in some cases, were not. When those businessmen heard the hoots from the audience, reacting to the bait, they thought they were being attacked by discourteous, ill-bred, uncivil people with marijuana-damaged brains. . . . Most of the hoots were coming from just one person: a mother who testified before the commission that she had lost her one-year-old child to what she believed was the callous discharge of persistent toxic substances by the chemical industry. The industry folks, accustomed to the confines of their paneled and imitation leather offices, presumed she was just another hippie malcontent.[40]

While business advocates may have found the demonstrative environmentalists distasteful, they were astounded and outraged by the recommendations that Durnil helped bring forward from the commission as the result of the biennial meeting testimony and advice from the IJC's boards. A longtime Republican Party fundraiser and campaign manager in Indiana and an associate of Vice President Dan Quayle when he was appointed by President George Bush to the IJC, Durnil seemed to industry at first just the most recent in a long line of largely anonymous commission members, operating in the collegial, quiet traditions that had governed the panel since its 1909 formation. Instead, prompted by concern about a potential link between pollution and the impaired health of a member of his own family, Durnil championed dramatic changes in the approach of U.S. and Canadian society not only to the regulation of commerce, but also to management of the lakes.

Under Durnil's influence, the IJC made a visionary proposal in its 1990 report, challenging the United States and Canada to make Lake Superior a "demonstration zone" for the concept of zero discharge of persistent, bioaccumulative toxic chemicals. Even more boldly, the commission called for a policy of "reverse onus" regarding the introduction of toxic chemicals into commerce—essentially, shifting the burden of proof from government, which has traditionally had to demonstrate the harm of a chemical to stop its use, to the makers of chemicals. Reverse onus meant the chemical manufacturers would have to prove the absence of harm before winning approval to introduce a chemical to widespread use. The commission's *Sixth Biennial Report* in 1992 declared flatly, "it is clear to us that persistent toxic substances have caused widespread injury to the environment and to human health. As a society, we can no longer afford to tolerate their presence in our environment and in our bodies." The panel noted that approximately half of the 362 toxic chemicals confirmed in the Great Lakes system were chlorinated organic compounds. Arguing that these substances had common, injurious characteristics, the IJC then urged the governments to "develop timetables to sunset the use of chlorine and chlorine-containing compounds as industrial feedstocks and that the means of reducing or eliminating other uses be examined."[41]

The recommendations on zero discharge of toxins and the chlorine phaseout delighted environmental advocates but attracted open contempt from industrial advocates, including some who had belatedly organized as the Council of Great Lakes Industries to counteract environmentalist influence on the IJC and other institutions. Reacting to a 1994 petition filed by environmental groups to enforce zero discharge in Lake Superior, James Buchen, vice present of Wisconsin Manufacturers and Commerce, said "There's always the potential that you are precluding beneficial economic activity in the mistaken belief that it's necessary to protect the environment."[42] The Chemical Manufacturers' Association warned that bans on chlorine and related compounds could cost four hundred thousand jobs and $11 billion in annual wages.

In part, the difference between the perspective of citizens and the IJC on one hand and industry on the other reflected a difference in temperament and philosophy. Should the lakes be viewed as remarkably improved from their low point in the 1960s, or as simply enjoying a temporary recovery that would be terminated by massive ecological breakdown? Environmentalists such as Lois Gibbs condemned what they regarded as cosmetic half-measures to protect the lakes. "All the politicians and people are serving industry," Gibbs said.[43] Meanwhile, the business community of the region pointed to drops of more than 70 percent in phosphorus, PCB, and DDT levels in the lakes since the early 1970s, while arguing that further reductions in these and other pollutants were in many cases not practical.

As governments on both sides of the border were forced to choose whether they should press ahead with stringent toxic cleanups, industry and right-wing politicians were organizing to help them say "no." Ecosystem integrity sounded nice in theory, but its political and economic costs would soon prove too high for the governments to pay.

Johnny Biosphere

DEPLOYING THE SCIENTIFIC METHOD TO ADVANTAGE, government, university, and industry researchers played a significant role in the revolution that led to the Great Lakes water quality recovery of the 1970s. Collecting data, testing hypotheses, and publishing their conclusions in refereed journals, these scientists identified excess phosphorus as the culprit in the decline of Lakes Erie and Michigan; sounded the first alarms about the widespread penetration of toxic chemicals such as PCBs in the Great Lakes system; and followed up by demonstrating that many of the chemicals were traveling thousands of miles on the wind to contaminate the lakes, fish, and other living things in distant ecosystems.

While most of these scientists shunned outright advocacy and disdained what they derided as an emotional approach to the problems of the lakes, several were sufficiently aroused and disgusted to emerge as public spokespersons for a new way of thinking about the ecosystem. They risked professional acceptance, but for them this was a small cost when measured against the urgency of the Great Lakes crisis—which, they thought, illustrated the menace facing the larger ecosystem of the planet. Perhaps none of these men and women was more clearly radicalized than the one who would become known as Johnny Biosphere.

An important part of the scientific research consensus about phosphorus pollution that had made possible the 1972 U.S.–Canada Great Lakes Water Quality Agreement and its war on detergents and sewage was Dr. J. R. "Jack" Vallentyne. Working for the Canadian Department of Fisheries and Oceans at the Canada Center for Inland Waters, Vallentyne was also a member of the Great Lakes Research Advisory Board, which evaluated the pact as it came up for review in 1977 and 1978. As Vallentyne later remembered, "The Great Lakes Water Quality Agreement of 1972 was a major political innovation; however, it contained a hidden flaw. It assumed that water quality problems could be resolved by dealing with water alone. To an ecologist, that was absurd; it contradicted the 'law' of ecology that everything is interconnected."[44]

Vallentyne's committee recommended adoption of an ecosystem approach to the problems of the Great Lakes. A political breakthrough, the concept simply meant considering humans as part of a complex natural system that includes air, water, land, and other living things; addressing the decline of the lakes holistically; considering the possibility of unanticipated consequences from proposed actions; and dealing with the problems of the ecosystem by addressing their causes rather than treating symptoms.

Described as modest and even introverted by colleagues, Vallentyne had perhaps begun to put caution aside after his first experience in helping shape Great Lakes policy. Convinced by his own laboratory experiments that phosphorus was the agent responsible for the chain reaction resulting in gross blooms of algae and oxygen deprivation in Lake Erie, he had been challenged repeatedly by scientists who claimed that phosphorus was not the limiting factor to algal growth in Lake Erie. He suggested that his opponents were right—

nitrates had become the limiting factor in the western end of Lake Erie because of the excessive use of phosphates in detergents. Using the evidence of his opponents to make his case, he demolished the arguments of the U.S. Soap and Detergent Association and helped drive detergent cleanup.

In July 1978 Vallentyne presented the arguments for an ecosystem approach to the International Joint Commission in an unorthodox manner. Standing in front of the commissioners and onlookers, he produced a bottle of whisky and four glasses from under a table that served as a bar. He poured a shot of whisky into the first glass, two into the second, four into the third, and eight into the fourth glass.

"Commissioners," he said, "you and our leaders of government and industry believe that constant growth is a good thing. I am sure you are right. I am going to drink this whisky the way you say our society should grow."[45] He promised to drink one glass each ten minutes, and began making his formal presentation. It discussed growth as an exponential function—constant growth meaning a doubling of the initial quantity over constant intervals of time. Just like his body, Vallentyne said, the Great Lakes Basin had limits of adaptability to the stresses of population growth and technology.

Vallentyne took a second drink, blinked, and cleared his throat. He explained the ecosystem approach, citing acid rain, road salt, and toxic chemicals as examples of problems affecting water quality that couldn't be addressed by considering only water.

After the third drink, a reporter in the front row of the audience gasped loudly, "My God, it really is whisky!" Growing more theatrical with his ingestion of the liquid, Vallentyne demonstrated that there is no "away" in nature by crumpling a piece of paper and throwing it to the floor in front of the commissioners.[46]

"After the fourth drink my hands instinctively went to my chest as the whisky burned down my throat. After regaining my breath, I spent the better part of a minute looking unsuccessfully for the summary sheet of my text."[47] The Canadian co-chair of the Great Lakes Research Advisory Board came to his assistance. Knocking himself on the head, Vallentyne realized the summary sheet was the one he had wadded up and hurled to the floor. He read it "cool and collected" to the commissioners.

The commissioners verified the validity of Vallentyne's stunt by sniffing the bottle—which did contain whisky, though diluted by tea. The chair of the Canadian section of the IJC told a Canadian Broadcasting Company reporter that Vallentyne's presentation had been "a simply staggering performance."[48]

Other dramatic events educated governments during the summer of 1978, including the discovery of buried industrial chemicals in the Love Canal neighborhood of Niagara Falls, New York, which led to public protests, evacuation of residents, and international headlines. Disposal of wastes on land, it seemed, could affect water quality; before long dozens of leaking chemical dumps would be found to contaminate the Niagara River and Lake Ontario and water bodies around the world.

The timing was right for the ecosystem approach. Responding to a request from a Canadian official renegotiating the U.S.–Canada Great Lakes Water Quality Agreement, Vallentyne brandished two sheets of paper with recommended language to implement the approach. The two nations incorporated virtually all of the changes into the agreement, signed 22 November 1978. Since that time the agreement's ecosystem approach has been cited as a model for other regimes, nations, and planetary protection, even if it has yet to be fully implemented in the Great Lakes themselves.

By the time Vallentyne retired from government service in 1992, he had helped popularize the controversial idea of sunsetting—or phasing out—chlorine-based chemicals as a method of protecting the web of life in the Great Lakes ecosystem. The idea helped spur more than a decade of discussions about the role and responsibilities of chemical manufacturers and governments in preventing harm to human health and the environment. But by then Vallentyne was on to a new mission as Johnny Biosphere.

Speaking to as many as one hundred community and student groups throughout Ontario in a year, Vallentyne dressed in an explorer's outfit and carried on his shoulders a globe roaring like thunder and issuing animal sounds. Mesmerizing children, he sought to awaken them and their elders to the unprecedented danger that humans posed to their own survival through unthinking devotion to growth and self-blinding to its consequences. Having come to admire the environment as a teenager growing up as a "river rat" along the Grand River in Brantford, he advised teachers and students that "there is no substitute for experiences in nature" when learning about ecosystems.[49]

People tend to have "egosystem" reactions as individuals and groups when they react to immediate and local threats around them, Vallentyne told audiences. People don't react to long-term threats to the species that develop slowly and, because they are global, may have little or no local impact. "We are egocentric, reacting to more immediate threats and changes, and we physiologically adjust to common, slow environmental changes," he said.[50] He found hope in the increasing participation by women in society and increasing awareness about the environment in children.

Vallentyne's career points the way toward hope. Trained as a scientist to disdain emotion and quiet by nature, Vallentyne was compelled to speak out at critical times in the history of the Great Lakes. He was not "a major actor at the level of policy," he said. "Nevertheless, my scientific credentials and understanding of ecology made it possible for me not only to raise fundamental questions, but to have them taken seriously. In effect, I was at the right place (governmental research) at the right time (when problems were getting out of hand)."[51]

In his post-1992 retirement, Vallentyne became the first Canadian to win the Rachel Carson award from the Society of Environmental Toxicology and Chemistry and continued to speak out in defense of the Great Lakes and the biosphere. He told a reporter for a Hamilton newspaper in 1996 he worried about the risk of a radioactive release from one of the many nuclear plants lining the lakes: "A lake is not like a river. Entire river courses can clear themselves of pollution in months to years. In large deep lakes, the same process can take decades to centuries."[52] In a 1998 column for the same newspaper, he decried the "cosmic trap" into which humanity has fallen. Humankind's mastery of technology is leading to runaway population growth, he said, and mushrooming populations are promoting an explosion of technology: "Constant growth is an illusion. It's the myth of technological society. It's an illusion in the sense that nothing ever grows without limits, nothing ever grows constantly. It kills itself if it does."[53]

His luminous vision for the future is based on what worked in the Great Lakes in the 1970s. The International Joint Commission's tradition that persons serving on its advisory boards represent not the organizations that employ them, but their own capacities as citizens and experts, helped draw the best, least selfish, least compromised advice from its advisors, Vallentyne said. This "permits experts to work for defined times and purposes without organizational inhibitions that would otherwise frustrate consensus approaches to planning and problem-solving," he wrote. If political systems globally adopted similar working rules of openness and sharing, "it would pave the way for a shift from an egocentric to a person-planet perspective."[54]

My favorite memories are those days when the waves were high. The sheer power of the lake took on a new meaning as we would venture in—holding hands with each other. . . . and screaming or squealing when we saw the next wave coming. Sometimes we would try to body surf them in; other times we'd test our bravery, often times chickening out and diving down as the wave crashed above us.

I can also remember that feeling of exhaustion on the way home, and the feeling of water mist in your lungs as you took each deep breath, falling asleep in no time.

There is one winter scene which is etched in my mind. The lake had frozen over like glass near the shore. We found chunks of flat ice and then, running as fast as we could with these chunks in front of us, we would finally use them like bobsleds and glide a great distance.

—Deb Meadows Steketee

Losing the Lakes?

Even before the politically vexing issue of banning chemicals widely used in commerce arose in the early 1990s, governments were reluctant to make choices that would cost industry considerable money, even if it would protect the Great Lakes from an even bigger long-term threat. The zebra mussel had proven that.

What many in the Great Lakes region did not know after the mussel hitchhiked to the region was that the governments had had a full and fair warning of the danger that contaminated ballast water posed to the biological integrity of the lakes—but they had failed to act. In a 1981 document submitted to Environment Canada, Bio-environmental Services Limited reported sampling the ballast water of fifty-five ships entering the Great Lakes–St. Lawrence River system from ten regions of the world. Almost every ballast tank sampled contained aquatic organisms "in a viable state," totaling more than one hundred fifty distinct genera and species of phytoplankton and fifty-six aquatic invertebrates. The company concluded:

> There are numerous examples of innocuous organisms in their native habitat becoming serious pests in a new habitat. The absence of natural enemies and other environmental controls permit the introduced species to proliferate and develop into serious problem organisms. . . . A number of nonendemic aquatic organisms found in the ballast water samples and capable of establishing themselves in the Great Lakes are in this category.[1]

The company specifically mentioned the still-distant zebra mussel, whose scientific name is *Dreissenia polymorphus.* Although the mussel was not found in ballast water during the study, the report warned, "in some ports of Europe, it still occurs in estuarine conditions. This situation, coupled with the occurrence of its veliger larvae in the plankton for up to 3 months, greatly enhances its potential for introduction to the Great Lakes in ship ballast water. If introduced, Dreissenia could establish itself in North America."

Joseph Schormann, a senior program engineer with Environment Canada convinced of the threat posed to the Great Lakes by organisms in ballast water, commissioned the study. After his retirement, Schormann expressed regret about the failure of both Canadian and U.S. agencies to close the door before the zebra mussel entered the ecosystem. "After it came out," Schormann said of the study, "it was reviewed by a lot of people from both coast guards. The opinion was 50-50 whether it was worthwhile to pursue it and do something or do nothing. Much to my regret, the do-nothing vote won the day, and it was shelved."[2] University of Windsor aquatic biologist Paul Hebert said more tartly, "I think it was a very, very expensive mistake. There's just no question there will be a multi-million dollar cost to the Canadian population forever. I think it's just unacceptable that when this report was in, no action was taken upon it. It didn't take someone with a crystal ball to recognize this problem."[3]

In fact, as numerous commentators pointed out, the arrival of exotic species could easily have been foreseen once the St. Lawrence Seaway opened in 1958. For the first time, ships could enter the upper Great Lakes after originating their journeys in other freshwater or estuarine waters containing species foreign to the lakes. Some four hundred to six hundred ships each year, on average, began penetrating the Great Lakes ecosystem as far as Chicago or Duluth. This commerce presented a known, substantial threat to the health of the lakes—but its beneficiaries also constituted a formidable political lobby able to defend its interests before governments.

Like other such interests, the Great Lakes navigation and port lobbies formed a close relationship with the government agencies that regulated them—in this case, the U.S. and Canadian Coast Guards. Although nominally charged with regulating navigation, both Coast Guards also developed close ties with shippers. By necessity more aware of the practical difficulties of coping with regulation amid other multiple pressures, individual Coast Guard personnel also naturally developed close working relationships with vessel captains and companies. As the Coast Guard bureaucracy grew into the lakes to assist with control of the new oceangoing traffic, it began to recognize the reciprocal value of the ships. To a degree, stable or growing budgets and staff in the Coast Guards depended on the maintenance and growth of the navigation industry in the lakes. Tough controls on ballast water during the 1980s, in advance of a proven invasion by organisms in ballast water, threatened to increase costs of Great Lakes shipping out of proportion to the benefits, perhaps undermining the industry. Such controls also threatened to displease both the shipping and port lobbies and the members of the Canadian Parliament and U.S. Congress, who, with the Coast Guard, formed the three sides of the "iron triangle" defending Great Lakes navigation.

Once established in the system, however, the zebra mussel—like the problems of overfishing, pollution, and habitat destruction that had preceded it in the Great Lakes—got all the government attention it had failed to attract before.

The mussel became the potential villain for the decline of numerous species. In 2001 researchers suggested that the zebra mussel had led to a "virtual collapse" of the tiny crustacean known as *diporeia,* a food for whitefish, smelt, alewives, and chubs. "We're not just talking about a decrease in numbers," said Thomas Nalepa, a biologist at the U.S. Great Lakes Environmental Research Laboratory in Ann Arbor, Michigan. "We're talking about a wipe-out of the population."[4] Although the link between the mussel and the disappearance of *diporeia* was unclear, researchers said the mollusks might be filtering tiny plankton out of the water before the mud-dwelling *diporeia* could consume them. Nalepa expressed worry also because researchers had discovered mussels not only attaching themselves to structures and rocks, but also to each other on the sandy bottom of Lakes Michigan and Huron. The sport and remaining commercial fisheries of the lakes, most agreed, were at risk.

Yet even with such grave danger threatened, governments were slow in bringing about effective controls on the mussel and other invaders. The Canadian Coast Guard in 1989 promulgated voluntary guidelines for the exchange of ballast water prior to entry in Great Lakes waters. Made a part of U.S. domestic law in 1990 under the Non-indigenous Aquatic Nuisance Prevention and Control Act (NANPCA) and subsequently adopted as regulation by Canada, the guidelines called for ships entering the St. Lawrence Seaway each year to exchange ballast water between the European and North American continental shelves in waters at least two thousand meters deep and achieve a salinity in the ballast of at least thirty parts per thousand. The idea was to dump alien freshwater species into open ocean waters. Any marine organisms introduced to the ballast with the exchange would, it was assumed, fail to flourish if allowed to escape into the Great Lakes. A seemingly strong response with an estimated 89 percent compliance rate, the guidelines had two major flaws—even one noncomplying vessel could introduce an exotic species, and the rules contained a major loophole.

That loophole arose from the remaining "slop" in the ballast tanks of many vessels that reported they had no ballast on board (NOBOB) after pumping. At first assumed to be an inhospitable environment for the survival of organisms, the slop, researchers found, was capable of harboring them for the cross-ocean voyage.[5] Depending on the year and the study, somewhere between 20 and 80 percent of vessels in the 1990s were NOBOBs, and under the U.S. law, not subject to inspections and controls.

The NOBOB exemption, one former Coast Guard commander suggested, was widened and deepened by the agency charged with administering it. "NOBOBs should never have been exempt from the Great Lakes regime," wrote Eric Reeves, pointing out that both the 1990 U.S. law and the 1996 law that amended it defined ballast water as "any water and associated sediments used to manipulate the trim and stability of the vessel." But, Reeves said, "the U.S. Coast Guard officers who had drafted the original regulations, along with their technical advisor, had never envisioned applying the regulations to the NOBOBs entering with unpumpable slop. As a matter of administrative practice and practical politics, they were simply ignored."[6]

The reluctance of politicians and bureaucrats to legislate and enforce tough rules to exclude exotic species significantly weakened the effectiveness of the new standards, Reeves alleged. "In the nine years before [the 1989 voluntary Canadian guidelines], there were six new invasions documented. In the nine years since, 1989–1998, there were also six new invasions documented, exactly the same number."[7]

Despite this experience, the governmental response continued to be sluggish. Amendments enacted by the U.S. Congress in 1996, while extending the ballast water policy nationwide, also left it voluntary except in the Great Lakes and provided numerous hurdles before the national rules could become mandatory. One such hurdle was the requirement that the Coast Guard draw up rules for public comment that would toughen the ballast water exchange requirements. When the agency did so, releasing a draft in April 1998 that would have required a 90 percent exchange of ballast water and a goal of complete exchange or treatment before discharge, industry groups blasted the proposal and the Coast Guard withdrew it the following year. A safety exemption in the 1996 law, which left to the vessel masters of ships entering U.S. waters other than the Great Lakes the decision of whether to exchange ballast water in unsafe conditions at sea, effectively applied to lakes shipping as well, Reeves argued. "Even though there may be legal authority to force retrofitting design changes on the vessels entering the Great Lakes through the Seaway, it will remain a political impossibility to do so as long as any such action discriminates against the Seaway trade."[8]

The failure of the region's institutions to come to terms effectively with aquatic nuisance species and other risks was a symptom of a deeper problem. The author of the classic

Symbolic Uses of Politics, political scientist Murray Edelman, observed, "it is one of the demonstrable functions of symbolization that it induces a feeling of well-being: the resolution of tension. Not only is this a major function of widely publicized regulatory statutes, but it is also a major function of their administration. Some of the most widely publicized administrative activities can most confidently be expected to convey a misleading sense of well-being to the onlooker because they suggest vigorous activity while in fact signifying inactivity or protection of the 'regulated.'"[9]

Beginning in the 1980s politicians repeatedly and successfully crafted new laws and programs that sounded reassuring but failed to protect the lakes. On closer examination, most of these initiatives proved to be riddled with exemptions, gaping with loopholes, and either unenforceable or not intended to be fully implemented. Yet their enactment or proclamation would, for a time, satisfy a concerned public that something meaningful had been done. Applying the notion of symbolic politics to the zebra mussel, Reeves argued, "A great deal of legislation on the books at the federal, state and provincial levels exists, but the authority is largely ambiguous and avoids any clear mandate for action."[10] This, it might be added, is a result of an intention to quiet public concern as much as it is a result of a balancing of the interests of commerce and the environment.

Lake Superior was another subject of symbolic politics. Meeting at the International Joint Commission's 1991 biennial meeting on Great Lakes water quality, representatives of both national governments and of Ontario, Minnesota, Wisconsin, and Michigan felt compelled to respond to the commission's 1990 challenge that they designate Lake Superior as a "demonstration zone" for the concept of reducing to zero the direct discharge of persistent, bioaccumulative toxic chemicals.

The movement to protect Lake Superior had gained momentum in the late 1980s. Before the IJC recommendation, controversy had erupted in the Upper Peninsula of Michigan over a proposed $1.5 billion paper mill near Arnheim. Dividing area residents between those who wanted the fifteen hundred permanent jobs the mill might create versus those who feared the increased logging, air pollution, and discharge of dioxins to the lake, the proposal inspired the formation of a group calling itself Friends of the Land of Keweenaw, or FOLK. Rather than simply opposing the project, FOLK prepared an alternative strategy for the area's economic development that called for smaller-scale manufacturing of hardwood flooring and other value-added forest products and a reliance on less consumptive industries such as tourism that would not degrade air and water.

In the fall of 1991 citizens groups were clamoring for a response by the governments to the IJC. The National Wildlife Federation's Lake Superior project was promoting an agreement to clean up and protect Superior, its centerpiece a "toxics freeze" that would commit governments to an immediate cap on the discharge of toxins to lake waters. The environmental group Greenpeace had spent much of the preceding summer publicizing its Zero Discharge Tour of the lakes, using a vessel, the *Moby Dick,* to promote the cause in forty cities with extensive press coverage. "The IJC has warned the U.S. and Canadian governments that persistent toxic pollutants are poisoning the Great Lakes and the life which lives in and around the lakes, including humans," said Jack Weinberg, coordinator for the Greenpeace Great Lakes project. "But the governments are attempting to lower concerns. Great Lakes citizens are angry about that."[11]

Rejecting the IJC's proposal and the demands of citizens out of hand risked a dramatic, unpleasant confrontation at an event that would attract over one thousand participants and dozens of reporters. But industrial groups and supporters of economic development in the Lake Superior Basin were expressing worry about the effect of a zero discharge demonstration on industrial recruitment and retention. Caught between the competing demands of interest groups, the governments huddled to hammer out an agreement with environmentalists. Signed by the six governments, the "Bi-national Program to Restore and Protect the Lake Superior Basin" declared: "The challenge to designate Lake Superior as a 'demonstration area where no point source discharge of persistent toxic substances will be permitted,' is accepted. Following the process described in this document, the governments will use existing authorities, and seek expanded authorities, to pursue the goal of zero discharge."[12]

A close inspection of the document reveals that it did not set a final deadline for attaining the goal of zero discharge, although it committed the signatory agencies to a series of interim deadlines to convene working groups, issue reports, and research problems. In several cases, the actions committed were simply restatements of programs already underway; the U.S. EPA, for example, said it would "seek voluntary reduction of the release and off-site transfer of toxic materials from major corporations" through its 33:50 program—an initiative announced the year before by Administrator William Reilly to achieve a nationwide 33 percent reduction in toxic discharges within two years and a 50 percent reduction in five years.

Nonetheless, the governments hailed the agreement as a breakthrough and a demonstration of commitment. "The Lake Superior demonstration program will be an important part of Canada's over-all efforts towards virtual elimination of persistent toxic substances from the environment," said Environment Canada minister Jean Charest. "Lake Superior is the most pristine of the Great Lakes and it is up to the federal, state and provincial governments of Canada and the United States to keep it that way," Reilly declared.[13]

The document's failure to represent any vision of a finite date by which the governments would assure attainment of the zero discharge goal should have awakened suspicions. But it was not until time had passed and the agreement had begun to unravel that environmental advocates began to pose questions. By the summer of 1992 the National Wildlife Federation's Mark Van Putten and Gayle Coyer, while still heralding some features of the agreement, pointed out that the commitment in the pact that the states bordering Lake Superior would require the best technology in process and treatment to reduce toxic discharges "was so vague as to be meaningless."[14] Worse, they noted the program's advisory committee, designed to accept comments from citizen and industrial groups, was "floundering." Progress continued to be marginal at best. In urging a renewed commitment to the lake and the agreement in 1995, the *Detroit Free Press* observed:

> You've heard this all before: homage to Lake Superior goes with the territory in Michigan. Politicians and writers rhapsodize over it. Government commissions speak earnestly of the need to protect it. When you look at what actually has been done to preserve the greatest of the Great Lakes, though, the answer is: not enough. Four years ago, Canada and the United States pledged to make Lake Superior a zero-discharge area for persistent toxic chemicals. Nothing concrete has been done to fulfill that promise.[15]

A defining issue in the debate over implementation of the agreement was the commitment by the states in the 1991 agreement to "designate all U.S. Lake Superior basin waters as a special resource."[16] To the National Wildlife Federation (NWF), that meant invoking a rarely used clause of the U.S. Clean Water Act to prevent any new or increased discharge of toxins from a factory or municipal sewage point. Under the "outstanding national resource water" designation, the limit would apply to any of nine toxic chemicals, and the NWF sought to expand the list to fifty-five substances. "An Outstanding National Resource Water has some exceptional ecological, recreation or environmental significance," said the federation's Lisa Yee.[17] But Minnesota and Wisconsin officials sharply opposed the designation—while offering up a new terminology of their own, the "outstanding international resource water," a term not mentioned in the Clean Water Act. The Minnesota Pollution Control Agency, saying that fifty-two businesses and municipalities within its borders would be affected by the rules, argued that its approach was more reasonable. While not permitting an increase in the concentration of persistent toxic pollutants from a sewage plant or factory, the total amount could increase if the plants expanded and the volume of their discharge increased—even though this would move the lake away from the zero discharge goal. "If the technology would bankrupt the company, for example, that's not feasible or prudent and wouldn't be required," said the agency's David Maschwitz. "PCA officials say declaring the lake an Outstanding National Resource Water, as the National Wildlife Federation wants, would virtually ban any new development anywhere in the Lake Superior basin," the *Duluth News Tribune* reported.[18] Michigan and Minnesota ultimately adopted the weakened "outstanding international resource waters" rule, while Wisconsin set its proposed rule aside.

Ontario officials were similarly reluctant to move ahead toward zero discharge, in Lake Superior or elsewhere. When a new Conservative government came to power in 1995, it quickly targeted environmental regulations for review in order to spur a flagging provincial economy. In the summer of 1996, the Ministry of the Environment announced it would revoke a rule requiring pulp mills to halt the discharge of chlorine-related compounds by 2002 and a related requirement that the mills explain how they would reach a zero discharge goal. The announcement was a direct answer to a request made by the Ontario Forest Industries Association the previous February. "We feel that the zero goal is not environmentally justifiable and would like to see the reference to the goal, along with requirements for elimination reports, removed from the regulation," the association had said. Hearing of the ministry's decision, the president of the association said, "This is news to me but we're delighted."[19]

On the tenth anniversary of the 1991 agreement, a citizens group, the Lake Superior Alliance, took stock of its successes and limitations. The review was mixed. On the one hand, citizens noted a reduction in the release of some toxins to Lake Superior such as mercury and PCBs, although they were unsure whether this was a result of the binational agreement or larger economic and environmental forces. The alliance suggested that many of the gains were a result of local initiatives—for example, an effort by the Lake Superior Sanitary District in Duluth to reduce releases of mercury from the breakage of thermometers and fluorescent bulbs. Meanwhile, the International Joint Commission observed that the biggest decreases in releases of persistent toxins to the lake might have occurred when an iron sintering plant in Wawa, Ontario, and a copper mine in White Pine, Michigan, closed in the mid and late 1990s. But the vast amount of citizen time claimed by the binational program was undeniable:

> The stack of documents produced by the Lake Superior Binational program has grown to nearly a foot tall for

> those fortunate enough to have the paper version of the stage 3 Lakewide Management Plan, called LaMP 2000. While there is no denying their usefulness as a repository of information, there have been other suggested uses, including improving traction in older, rear-wheel-drive pickup trucks. The Lake Superior Binational Forum has met six times each year for a total of 60 meetings. And this does not include meetings held by the planners and managers, the Task Force and the Work Group.[20]

The alliance gave the binational program an "A" grade for "documents, policies, meetings and conferences."[21] It gave the program a grade of "D" for zero discharge demonstration.

The zebra mussel and Lake Superior cleanup cases were hardly alone in illustrating both the allure and the danger of symbolic politics. In case after case, a reluctance by politicians to break ranks with industrial interests defending the status quo combined with a desire by the same politicians to demonstrate concern for the Great Lakes, resulting in agreements, publicity, and little forward movement.

No episode better illustrated the unwillingness of elected protectors of the Great Lakes to defend their waters than the comical 1993 dispute over a Michigan irrigation project. Under the 1985 Great Lakes Charter, each state had agreed to notify and seek comments from all seven other Great Lakes states about proposed major water uses. A separate, 1986 federal statute gave any of the eight Great Lakes state governors the power to veto a proposed diversion of Great Lakes water. In 1992 Michigan governor John Engler surprised Indiana by casting a veto against a proposed diversion of 1.7 million gallons per day of Lake Michigan waters to supply the town of Lowell, which had sought drinking water to replace a groundwater supply contaminated with fluoride. "While we recognize the difficulties that Lowell, Indiana, faces in reducing high fluoride levels in its public water supply system, it is the first responsibility and obligation of the Great Lakes states and provinces to ensure continued protection of this valuable resource," Engler said.[22]

When, the following year, Michigan proposed permitting a federally funded irrigation project for eighteen hundred acres of farmland in the Thumb region of the Lower Peninsula, a withdrawal of up to 14.4 million gallons a day from Lake Huron, the state observed the charter provisions and submitted the project to review by the other states and Ontario. Three governors and Ontario premier Robert Rae objected to the project, but Engler's staff did not release the letters to the decision-making body, the Michigan Natural Resources Commission, until after it had approved the project by a five-to-one vote. Apprised a few weeks later that the other chief executives had opposed the project, commission member David Holli lamented, "We were assured that we had all the appropriate information at hand and it turned out we didn't."[23] Governor Evan Bayh of Indiana objected the most strongly to the project:

> In your May 8, 1992 letter disapproving the Lowell proposal, you stated that before approving diversion proposals there should be a showing that there is imminent danger to the public health, safety and welfare, and that there is no prudent or feasible alternative water supply. You also stated that any such proposal should contain plans to implement meaningful conservation measures. The Mud Creek proposal does not satisfy these conditions. In addition, the Mud Creek proposal appears to benefit 10 to 15 individuals primarily in the form of enhanced revenues related to the irrigation of their crops. The utilization of Great Lakes water for the economic benefit of such a small number of individuals does not represent a prudent water management philosophy for

> the Great Lakes. . . . the Lowell diversion proposal would reap far more public benefit with less negative impact on the Great Lakes than the Mud Creek proposal.[24]

Brushing aside the objections after they were belatedly revealed, members of Engler's staff said the arguments would not have changed their point of view on the project and should not have affected the views of the commissioners. They pointed to a technicality in the federal law giving governors veto power over the diversions of other states. Since the Mud Creek water would be returned to Lake Huron, they said, it would not constitute a diversion and could not be blocked by a veto. But hydrologic experts calculating water losses caused by evaporation from irrigation projects assume a loss of 50 percent or more of the water. In the case of Mud Creek, much of the irrigated water, they assumed, would evaporate and fall as precipitation outside the Great Lakes Basin, representing a net loss to the lakes. A Minnesota agency official suggested Michigan was being hypocritical in authorizing the Mud Creek project. But from another view, the state was being consistent—signing agreements and proclaiming a commitment to the Great Lakes but deciding against the interests of the ecosystem when in-state politics tilted the cost-benefit equation toward exploitation. Engler, endorsed by the Michigan Farm Bureau in his state legislative campaigns and his 1990 bid to become governor, was responding to the urging of a prime constituency to decree "that Michigan will operate under one standard while applying different standards for others."[25] While the damage done to the lakes from the Mud Creek withdrawal was minimal, the precedent—allowing a consumptive use of Great Lakes water to support an in-basin project of narrow economic benefit—had grave potential to undermine the region's case against long-range exports for decades to come.

Although the use of symbolism to define Great Lakes protection was nothing new in the 1990s, the basin's political leadership was new. Conservative politicians succeeded moderates as governor in Wisconsin in 1987; in Michigan, Ohio, and Illinois in 1991; and in Minnesota and New York in 1995. Replacing the New Democratic Party government of Premier Robert Rae, Conservative Michael Harris took control of the Ontario government in 1995. For the most part, these men took a dim view of the increase in power of the administrative state that had accompanied the rise of environmental regulation and sought to roll this authority back. But they could not do so overtly. Laws such as the U.S. Clean Water Act remained popular because the public associated them with the visible improvement in the environment over the preceding twenty-five years. Other means of shrinking the regulatory state were available, however. As political scientist Edelman observed of economic statutes, "The laws may be repealed in effect by administrative policy, budgetary starvation, or other little publicized means; but the laws as symbols must stand because they satisfy interests that are very strong indeed: interests that politicians fear will be expressed actively if a large number of voters are led to believe that their shield against a threat has been removed."[26]

The experience of the Ontario Ministry of the Environment after Harris took office as premier in 1995 demonstrates the point. Elected on the promise of reducing the size of government and freeing the private sector from burdensome rules, Harris over six years reduced the budget of the environment ministry by more than 40 percent while slashing the agency's staff by a third. Cuts of similar size were made in the Ontario Ministry of Natural Resources (OMNR), the management agency for approximately 80 percent of the province's lands and waters. Douglas Dodge, a longtime fisheries biologist with the OMNR, said that based on his actions, it appeared Harris "hated the environment's guts. . . . There was a double purpose to the cuts. One purpose was to cut budgets, but the other was to stop dealing with difficult problems."[27] A Hamilton columnist wrote that under the Harris government, "Monitoring and enforcement of [environmental] violations have been lax. Dozens of pollution incident reports were said to merit 'no further response.' . . . Bad news stories about environmental travesties abound."[28] By the time of his retirement as premier in October 2001, Harris had earned the nickname "Chainsaw Mike" from a "chaotic first term of changes."[29]

While the budget cuts and reduced tax burdens on Great Lakes Basin voters—and the government economies that continued to thwart fulfillment of long-established pledges to monitor pollution—were popular with many, they did not come without environmental consequences. People paid for these policies with their lives.

In April 1993 a protozoan known as cryptosporidium, a tiny one-celled organism, invaded the public drinking water supply for the city of Milwaukee. Often found in rivers, lakes, and streams contaminated with animal feces or that receive wastewater from sewage treatment plants, the Milwaukee cryptosporidium was believed to have washed into the city's harbor from upstream animal operations and been collected by a city drinking water intake. More than one hundred users of the drinking water system, mostly those with compromised immune systems such as AIDS sufferers and the elderly, died, and four hundred three thousand were sickened with flulike symptoms.[30] The tragedy prompted the U.S. Congress to toughen the Safe Drinking Water Act in 1996.

Seven years after the Milwaukee incident, seven residents of Walkerton, Ontario, died in a similar drinking water disaster. In May 2000 pathogens in animal manure applied to a farmer's field washed by heavy rains entered a municipal well and contaminated the community's water supply, sickening approximately twenty-three hundred. An inquiry attributed the disaster to poor operating practices by the supply operator and the Harris government's policies. Dennis O'Connor, a senior Ontario judge appointed to investigate the case, concluded that the "provincial government's budget reductions led to the discontinuation of government laboratory testing services in 1996. In implementing this decision, the government should have enacted a regulation mandating that testing laboratories immediately and directly notify both the [Ministry of Environment] and the Medical Officer of Health of adverse results. Had the government done this, the boil water advisory would have been issued by May 19 at the latest, preventing hundreds of illnesses."[31]

True to pattern, the provincial government worked after the disaster to assure upset constituents that it had a plan in place to protect them. The plan called for $500 million in spending over two years to increase the number of drinking water supply inspectors and to assist communities in upgrading sewage and water systems. "We are committed to ensuring that Ontario has the toughest policies in the world for safe, clean drinking water and will dedicate whatever resources are required to accomplish that goal," Finance Minister Janet Ecker said. Opposition leader Dalton McGuinty complained, "so we got more promises today. Big deal."[32] McGuinty pointed out that some of the $500 million was money being restored from the regime's own cuts in the environment ministry.

The neglect that killed Milwaukee and Walkerton residents was born of a perception of government as a meddler rather than a defender. The most vulnerable suffered. Other state and provincial policies condemned specific vulnerable groups, repudiating any responsibility for public intervention on behalf of people of color and those with low incomes.

Michigan's refusal to reinstate a health advisory regarding the consumption of PCB-contaminated sport fish in 1996 and 1997 prompted a scolding from the U.S. Environmental Protection Agency, which said the state's policy subjected women and children to an unacceptable risk of impairment of the reproductive, neurobehavioral, immunological, and endocrine systems.[33] The state had pulled the advisory in order to crow about the lowered pollution levels in the lakes. Its governor, Engler, bristled at the EPA's position, saying he would not "be bullied into positions based on politics, instead of science."[34] But when the EPA issued a tough health advisory of its own, Engler backed down and the state advisory resumed in 1998, an election year.

Ontario's Conservative government was similarly dismissive of a population it considered politically irrelevant, its First Nations peoples. The most spectacular example occurred in 1995 after members of the Kettle and Stoney Point band of Chippewas attempted to reclaim ancestral lands that included a burial ground in Ipperwash Provincial Park, on Lake Huron. Seized by the government for military purposes in 1942, the twenty-two hundred acres were supposed to be returned to the natives after the war, but the promise was broken. "While our people were giving their lives in Europe, the government here in Canada was taking their land away from them and putting us on post-stamp reserves," said Thomas M. Bressette, the tribe's chief.[35]

The 1995 tribal occupation generated international headlines and a confrontation between the natives and the provincial government of Harris. Four days after the standoff began, provincial police attempted to rout the natives. In the melee, they shot and killed tribal member Anthony Dudley George. Seven years later, evidence emerged that top aides to Harris ordered the police to use force to remove the protesters, and that Harris himself might have ordered the storming of the natives' stronghold.[36] But the premier left office in 2001 without acknowledging responsibility.

Those examining the fine print of plans repeatedly brandished as proof of the environmental commitment of governments were scornful. Henry Regier, a veteran scholar and champion of the lakes, offered a withering review of a 2001 draft of a Canada-Ontario Agreement (COA) to protect the Great Lakes. Such agreements had governed the federal-provincial relationship in meeting the terms of the Great Lakes Water Quality Agreement since the 1970s.

> Did the handlers of the premier and prime minister let the bureaucrats know in no uncertain terms that the main purpose of any new COA was to serve political greenwashing purposes? That the COA should contain few particulars about benchmarks? That it should imply no increased funding? That it should imply nothing about any shortage of seasoned, competent experts now that many of these experts have retired early? That it should make a virtue of not getting involved in local issues so as not to get in the way of eager volunteers?[37]

Other publicized efforts to defend the Great Lakes and its tributary waters amounted to even less. The region's U.S. politicians reacted with trumpet blasts of outrage when Senator Patrick Leahy in 1998 tucked an amendment into a congressional appropriations bill designating Lake Champlain on the Vermont–New York border as a Great Lake, for purposes of eligibility for some environmental research and education funds. Michigan governor John Engler, criticized at home for failing to do enough to protect the lakes, issued a press release praising bills introduced by U.S. representative Fred Upton and U.S. senator Spencer Abraham to right the injustice. "I am appalled that political opportunism has defeated common sense through the attempt to redefine the Great Lakes to include Lake Champlain," Engler told Upton and Abraham.[38] Upton huffed that four-hundred-thirty-five-square-mile Lake Champlain was a mere "pencil line on the map." Wisconsin U.S. representative Steve LaTourette called Champlain "a good lake but not a Great Lake." After attracting international media attention, Leahy backed down, agreeing to the repeal of his creative addition to the Great Lakes in exchange for a separate provision making institutions in his home state eligible for the Sea Grant funds. But for all the fury, nothing had been done to further protection of the lakes themselves.

Diverting the public's attention to the supposed outrage of contaminating the reputation of the Great Lakes with the addition of Champlain had a serious purpose: generating headlines on an easy-to-understand issue that would strengthen the identification of politicians with popular water concerns. But by 2002 the similarly motivated announcement of major new Great Lakes strategies had become so customary that the reflexive response from many reporters, editorialists, and environmentalists was skepticism. The symbolism had worn thin. In April 2002, for example, U.S. Environmental Protection Agency administrator Christine Todd Whitman traveled to Muskegon, Michigan, to draw attention to a new lakes cleanup plan. Crafted by the federal government's Great Lakes U.S. Policy Committee, the strategy called for reducing PCB concentrations in lake trout and walleye 25 percent by 2007, "sharply" cutting the rate of further introductions of invasive aquatic species, cleaning up thirty-one polluted hot spots, mostly in harbors, and cleaning up the lakes' six hundred U.S. beaches so that 90 percent would be open for 95 percent of the summer season by 2010. In comments typical of those made by officials of Republican, Democratic, Conservative, federal, state, and provincial governments for nearly twenty years, Whitman said, "Everyone who enjoys the Great Lakes can appreciate the goals the partnership has set to ensure that the Great Lakes basin is a healthy, natural environment for wildlife and people."[39]

This time, commentators questioned the seriousness of the government commitment. "Christie Whitman stood in Muskegon the other day and announced a great plan for the Great Lakes. Unfortunately, she didn't put any lousy money behind it," groused the *Detroit Free Press*.[40] A year after the EPA strategy was released, the U.S. General Accounting Office (GAO) critiqued it—and the whole U.S. government approach to Great Lakes protection—as completely inadequate. The GAO identified thirty-three federal Great Lakes programs and seventeen among the states, said the 2002 strategy and others like it was not resulting in "significant restoration," and faulted the governments for lacking even a reliable set of environmental indicators to determine whether the lakes were getting healthier or unhealthier.[41]

The true measure of government's failure was beginning to show up in the renewed struggle of Lake Erie—once again the most troubled Great Lake. The retrenchment in government spending on Great Lakes programs during the 1990s made the puzzle more complicated.

In the early 1990s Lake Erie was celebrated as a success story for the ages. Thanks to sharp restrictions imposed by government mandate and improved sewage treatment, phosphorus levels in the lake had fallen over 80 percent, eliminating most of the ugly algae that had served as a filthy green banner of pollution in the 1960s. Lake Erie had risen from the grave, headlines reported.[42] Determined to bray about the cleanup, governments went beyond what the scientists told them, proclaiming the job done. "Getting Better All the Time" was the title of a document on the lake's progress put out by Ohio state officials in the early 1990s.

Indeed, the success of thirty years of work to reduce phosphorus pollution of Lake Erie seemed excessive to some. In 1999 a group representing conservationists, the Ontario Federation of Anglers and Hunters, shocked the scientific and policy community by proposing that phosphorus be intentionally reintroduced to the lake in order to stimulate Erie's productivity and increase the food supply for fish. Controls on phosphorus had gone too far, they argued, making the lake cleaner than it had been before the arrival of Europeans. Joe Koonce, a professor of biology at Case Western Reserve University in Cleveland, saw beneath the newly clear waters of the lake. "An ecosystem careening around, showing this kind of instability, can't be healthy," he said. "I am not optimistic. We have taken our eye off the ball."[43] Koonce was proven correct three years later. In July 2002 news media surrounding Lake Erie once again pronounced it a water body in "crisis."

The symptoms of the sickly patient began with a slow and worsening suffocation. The central basin of the lake, also the site of anoxia in the 1950s and 1960s, was nearly devoid of oxygen. The "dead zone," as many reporters called it, was alarming in part because it was inexplicable. Scientists had multiple hypotheses. A warming climate, including a series of winters in which little or no ice blanketed Erie, might be depriving the central basin of oxygen. Algae that normally produce oxygen might, for some reason, no longer be doing so. Decaying wastes, including sewage and algae, might be consuming oxygen. A so-called cousin to the zebra mussel, the quagga mussel, also introduced to the Great Lakes system through ballast water, might be the problem, said an Ohio State University professor. Releasing far more phosphorus as waste than the zebra mussel, the quagga might be fueling algae growth, and the decomposition of the algae might in turn be gobbling up critical oxygen.[44]

The lake's deterioration had been noted as early as 1999, when researchers discovered a form of botulism not seen before in the lake had killed birds and fish whose corpses were scattered over the shores of Erie. In 2000 an aquatic salamander called the mud puppy had died off in large numbers, littering Ontario shores. Later the same summer, more dead fish and birds began washing up on U.S. beaches. Bill Culligan, head of the New York Department of Conservation's Lake Erie fisheries unit, estimated that tens of thousands of sheepshead, rock bass, and smallmouth bass had been killed by mysterious causes in 2001 and 2002. "It's amazing what's going on," said Phil Ryan, manager for the Port Dover, Ontario, Ministry of Natural Resources fisheries station. "It's a big research mystery."[45] Another mystery was the flourishing of a large bloom of toxic microsystis algae, achieving an unfortunate new abundance in 2002. Blamed on a hot summer and pollution by fertilizers and wastes containing phosphorus, ammonia, and other nutrients, the toxic algae were another worrisome indicator of trouble.[46]

Clues to the mysteries would have been more plentiful if complacent governments around the Lake Erie Basin had not declared a victory in the war against phosphorus pollution and pulled out their troops. One of the heralded Great Lakes strategies, the 1987 renegotiation of the Great Lakes Water Quality Agreement, facilitated the premature retreat. Shifting the responsibility of collating phosphorus pollution statistics from the International Joint Commission to the U.S. and Canadian governments, the 1987 "annex" to the agreement inadvertently put politicians in charge of deciding what data should be collected and reported. In 1994, with the Lake Erie phosphorus goals of the early 1970s achieved, both nations discontinued monitoring of phosphorus dumping, or loadings, to the lake. "By not having the loading data, we cannot tell exactly what is happening these days in Lake Erie," said Ohio State University researcher and Great Lakes Fishery Commission member Roy Stein.[47]

Governments, communities, industries, and citizens that had devoted enormous amounts of funding and effort for more than three decades to rehabilitating Lake Erie were now operating in the shadows as the lake faced a potentially significant new era of decline. "We thought that we had the problem licked, that we were in good shape and headed in the right direction," said Paul Bertram, a scientist with the U.S. EPA's Great Lakes National Program office. The agency announced its intention to devote $2 million over two years to deploy twenty researchers to test the various hypotheses of Lake Erie's new woes.[48]

Great Lakes citizen defender Lee Botts had long suggested that the problems of the Great Lakes were an "early warning to the world," signaling trends and scientific discoveries that would soon trouble water bodies on most continents. But Lake Erie had always been the early warning to the Great Lakes. Shallowest of the five large lakes, its U.S. shoreline heavily developed, quicker to respond to both pollution and cleanup than the other lakes, it was "the canary in the coal mine," said Great Lakes United executive director Margaret Wooster—the most vulnerable Great Lake.

On 10 September 1813 Commodore Oliver Hazard Perry triumphed over a British fleet in the Battle of Lake Erie, effectively ending two hundred years of power strife over the control of the largest freshwater system in the world. Approximately one hundred fifty years later, public agitation over the appalling decline of the lake drove Canada and the United States to launch a new fight. This time they worked together to restore the health of the lake—and set an example for the world of cooperation across international boundaries. But the war, initially successful, was never finished or won. Thirty years into the second Battle of Lake Erie, governments more concerned with satisfying influential business lobbies than with their responsibilities to the public trust curtailed their commitment. Lake

Erie was once again in trouble. What did this say about the future of the Great Lakes as an ecosystem and of the human society that surrounded it?

The Blobs That Girdled the Great Lakes

When a Jello-like substance drops from outer space and begins consuming the residents of a small American town in the 1958 movie *The Blob,* not even the film's characters seem convincingly terrified by the invader. Starring Steve McQueen, the film's working title had at one point been "The Blob That Girdled the Globe," six words more likely to amuse than frighten an audience.

In their mock horror, the movie's characters resemble nothing so much as corporate and government officials who professed to be shocked when, in 1985, a spill of chemical contaminants soon dubbed "the toxic blob" by the news media was discovered in the St. Clair River, at and downstream from Sarnia, Ontario.

The St. Clair River blob became known when Dow Chemical Limited of Sarnia accidentally discharged twenty-five hundred gallons of the solvent perchloroethylene, widely used by commercial dry cleaning businesses. But the publicity led reporters to dig deeper and to find that the Ontario Ministry of the Environment had known since 1975 of approximately eighteen toxic chemicals located on a patch of the riverbed about forty-five meters by forty-five meters wide that started at the Dow docks. Further, it was discovered, Dow had had eleven accidental chemical discharges in

1985, and other companies in Ontario's "chemical valley" in and south of Sarnia had racked up two hundred seventy-five in the previous decade.

While terming the spills unfortunate, a district officer for the ministry said, "There's no evidence of the material being released into the environment."[49] The statement failed to reassure some community residents, since the riverbed is the environment, by most definitions. And the river has been a drinking water source for dozens of communities on both the Canadian and U.S. sides. Prodded by the publicity, Dow spent $1 million to vacuum the PCE blob from the riverbed and claimed it spent $12 million to improve pollution controls at the Sarnia plant. But provincial court judge Louis Eddy fined the company a mere $16,000 for negligence it admitted in a plea-bargain arrangement with the Ontario government. "At Dow they're probably laughing up their sleeves," said Joyce McLean of the environmental group Greenpeace.[50]

The blob had performed a useful public service. Like the cinematic blob, thought by some to be an allusion to the menace of creeping Communist ideology in the United States of the late 1950s, the PCE spill turned the attention of governments to the condition of the St. Clair River, and the attention of independent observers to the behavior of the chemical industry both there and elsewhere in the Great Lakes Basin.

In 1987 a team of staff from federal agencies on both sides of the border and from Michigan and Ontario agencies began technical studies of the St. Clair's problems and needs. A year later, the governments appointed a binational public advisory council to provide a citizen viewpoint on cleanup plans. In 1991 the cleanup team published a remedial action plan, or RAP, identifying the causes of the river's problems, and in 1995, a second document outlining solutions to the problems. Some dealt with bloblike issues by calling for pollution prevention by industries and governments; others addressed the degraded habitat of the river, calling for wetland restoration.

By 1990, according to the governments, the river was showing improvement. A "severely degraded zone" near Sarnia was gone, and "degraded or impaired" river stretches had shrunk from about twelve kilometers to six kilometers.[51]

But by 2001 new worries arose. The recovery of small so-called benthic organisms on the bottom of the river was resurrecting old contaminants. Bug larvae living in the top ten centimeters of the river bottom were consuming chemical wastes deposited in the river as early as the 1950s and passing them up the food chain. Mercury, formerly dumped by Dow into the river at Sarnia, was persisting long after the discharges were stopped, contaminating fish and threatening the health of recreational anglers and their families.[52]

The blob raised bigger issues. Were the companies of Canada's chemical valley threatening creatures on land as well?

Like the Dow Chemical complex not far away in Midland, Michigan, Ontario's dozen or so petrochemical, glass, and plastics factories in and near Sarnia were capitalizing on a fortunate combination of raw materials, particularly brine and oil in underground formations deposited by ancient seas, and convenient access to Great Lakes shipping. And like Dow of Midland, they were frequently challenged, but never really cornered, by citizens and some government investigators upset about what they regarded as neglect of the environment and human health.

A ten-minute Shell Oil refinery malfunction at Corunna, Ontario on 16 March 2000 shut off a stack venting and burning noxious gases and spread gases that included hydrogen sulfide over nearby residences. Thirty-nine people went to Sarnia's hospital for treatment of breathing problems and nausea.

Remembering the sight of workers being ushered out of the Shell facility as the malfunction began, onlooker Deb Fournier said, "Then I was very sick to my stomach. I was dizzy, I couldn't breathe. . . . It was really bad. It was a very frightening day." Fournier was among those hospitalized. A spokesperson for Shell Oil apologized by saying, "Operating a refinery is a very complex operation and at times equipment will fail and things can happen. It was very unusual and very unfortunate and Shell is very sorry about that."[53]

The accident was again part of a larger pattern. There were twenty-two accidental releases of chemicals in chemical valley that year, thirteen in 1999, and twenty-one in 1998. Industry defenders called that almost inevitable, considering that 40 percent of all the chemicals produced in Canada passed through the area's plant pipelines. But Sarnia mayor Mike Bradley was unusually outspoken. "This isn't a public relations problem, it's an environmental problem," he said. "I'm not anti-business or industry, I'm pro-health." Bradley called for more aggressive work by companies to stop the air releases.[54]

Like other remedial action plans at more than forty "areas of concern" around the lakes, the St. Clair River cleanup and restoration crept along in the late 1990s and early in the twenty-first century. Citing lack of funds, agencies on both sides of the border apologized for the lack of progress. Meanwhile, more blobs began to show up in Great Lakes media accounts.

An angler stepped into a "toffee-thick" coal tar blob in the Thames River at London, Ontario, in 1999. [55] It turned out to be the remnant of a bigger blob that resulted from a coal gasification plant that operated on the banks of the river from 1853 to the 1930s. A $1.2 million (Canadian) 1990 cleanup had failed to catch the slug, which contained a group of more than one hundred toxic chemicals known as polycyclic aromatic hydrocarbons, or PAHs, some of them thought to cause cancer.

Another toxic blob showed up in media reports about the problems in Ontario's Thunder Bay in the mid 1990s. This blob was a fourteen-hectare patch of harbor bottom contaminated with solvents, wood preservatives, metals, and other toxic substances. The responsible companies and the Ontario provincial government inked a $9.3 million (Canadian) agreement to seal off and treat the blob.[56]

Stelco Incorporated responded to a report of a coal tar blob in Hamilton Harbor in 2001. Lake Ontario keeper Mark Mattson, accompanied by a TV crew, found patches of the oily matter floating on the water's surface by the Stelco plant. The company, in turn, hypothesized that the coal tar was the result of someone else's work.

The fact that all of the blobs were in Canadian waters was not proof that they're only found there. Instead, they signaled that Canadian news media had adopted the blob terminology after the pioneering use of the term to describe the 1985 Dow spill. On the U.S. side, such discoveries were generally characterized by the term "contaminated sediments."

While some blobs have been almost completely addressed—such as those lurking on the harbor bottom of Waukegan, Illinois, and some in Hamilton Harbor as late as the 1980s—blobs persist in dozens of locations throughout the Great Lakes. Some are likely to linger into the twenty-second century. Their staying power is a reminder that while the Communist revolution feared by 1950s movie characters is no longer a blob of great consequence, the industrial revolution's by-products are blobs that continue to girdle the Great Lakes.

Because Pelee sticks out so far into Lake Erie, it's the first landfall migrating birds come to after their flight across the lake. It helps that there is a refuge at Crane Creek on the Ohio shore, and a string of islands, from the Bass Islands on the United States side to Pelee Island in Canadian waters, leading like stepping stones across the lake. The birds need a green place to come down in, and they like to have the reassurance of a greenbelt below them as they travel. Many species migrate at night. So they come down on Pelee exhausted and hungry and at the first light of morning, the birders arrive to scout them out.

I was in my late 30s when I discovered birding and went over to Pelee first with Detroit Audubon, later on my own or with a friend. To catch a wave of warblers in those first years was incredible, like standing there in some sort of mythic rain of riches. The trees were alive with warblers, trembling with warblers. It was like walking into a jewel box, or an Aladdin's cave. There'd be dozens of them, Blackburnians, redstarts, yellows, Cape Mays, myrtles, orange-crowned, Nashvilles, parulas, magnolias, black-throated blues, black-throated greens, yellow-throated, Wilson's, Canadas. . . . It was glorious. You'd feel your heart lift from the beauty of it.

—Barbara Stanton

A Future in Peril

The one constant in the evolution of the Great Lakes since the arrival of Europeans is surprise. No government and few individuals foresaw the collapse of fish stocks, the invasion of the sea lamprey, thousands of deaths from typhoid and cholera, the sudden fall of Lake Erie. And while individuals successfully pressed governments to undo these disasters, there was always a great cost. In the twenty-first century, the greatest cost may result from failing to act in advance of disaster.

Many more people will inhabit the Great Lakes region. The U.S. Census Bureau predicts an increase in population in the Great Lakes states of approximately 12 percent between 2000 and 2025, rising to over 73.5 million. Ontario's population will expand at a faster clip. Its "fairly robust growth" will amount to an estimated rise of 31.5 percent, or 3.7 million, between 1999 and 2028, climbing to over 15.6 million.[1] Population will continue to translate to dramatic environmental impact, particularly if individual consumption patterns persist. Much of the environmental gain accomplished by the strong pollution laws passed on both sides of the international border since the 1960s has been nullified in recent years. Automobiles have cleaner exhaust, but there are more automobiles, and therefore amounts of the pollution they produce are stable or increasing. Sewage systems treat pollution before it is discharged, but more people are pouring their wastes into each system, and the combination of increased loadings and aging, decaying sewage plants is contributing to local and perhaps even generalized water pollution problems in the basin, such as the mystifying anoxia in Lake Erie. Since most communities still tolerate or even sanction the spread of impervious surfaces and the destruction of woodlands and wetlands that once restrained floods and treated runoff, habitats are disappearing. The Nature Conservancy in the mid 1990s identified one hundred thirty-one globally significant biological diversity features in the Great Lakes Basin that are critically imperiled, imperiled, or rare on a global scale. Twenty-two of these are considered critically imperiled on a global scale, including three community types and nineteen plant and animal species. Without abrupt and significant changes in the policies of Great Lakes governments, this list will only grow larger.

Some of the old problems, such as the use of chemical pesticides and fertilizers, have yet to be addressed—and, in fact, have worsened in some ways. A 1997 report estimated that fifty-seven million pounds of pesticides are used annually in Great Lakes Basin agriculture, 74 percent of the total on the U.S. side. The five most intensively used chemicals were metolachlor, atrazine, alachlor, oil, and EPTC. While the volume by weight of the top twenty-five most heavily used pesticides in Ontario fell 18.7 percent between 1988 and 1993, the volume of the top twenty-five in Michigan rose

5.7 percent between 1987 and 1992, and the number of acres to which the pesticides were applied rose 40.7 percent. The report said Great Lakes agriculture was "generally moving in the right direction at a slow pace."[2] But most governments in the basin are not actively promoting or mandating pesticide and fertilizer reduction nor adequately promoting organic agriculture, despite growing consumer interest and demand. The lakes, their aquatic life, and those who enjoy eating sport fish will continue to suffer unknown but significant risks as long as these policies persist.

Fed by humankind's reliance on petroleum and coal as fuel sources and the consequent release of greenhouse gases, the huge sweep of climate change will not spare the Great Lakes. The planet's two warmest years on record occurred in 1998 and 2001, shrinking if not silencing the caucus of disbelievers who disputed the existence of any human-influenced climate change. But acceptance of the reality of climate change is only one step on the road toward action.

The exact effects of climate change on the lakes are almost unknowable today, but they will be noticeable. The most comprehensive analysis of the basin's potential futures suggests a warming at first moderate, then dramatic. Average summer daily minimum temperatures are projected to rise by 1.8° to 3.6°F (1° to 2°C) across the region while daily highs will increase 0° to 1.8°F (0° to 1°C) by the end of the twenty-first century. Winter daily minimum temperatures could rise between 7.2° to 10.8°F (4° to 6°C), with maximums from 3.6° to 5.4°F (2° to 3°C).[3] Warmer winters will mean significantly less ice—a Union of Concerned Scientists study projects anywhere from thirty-three to eighty-eight more ice-free days on Lakes Superior and Erie by 2090.[4] Such changes are likely to alter ecosystems that evolved over centuries in response to conditions that changed much less rapidly.

The levels of the lakes, whose natural fluctuations have forced significant human adjustments and created fierce political controversies for over a century, will respond to the warming. A study commissioned by the U.S. government reported in 2000 that Great Lakes levels would drop "significantly" under most of the scenarios tested, with declines as great as two to five feet on Lakes Michigan and Huron by 2090:

> A one-meter average drop in Lake Michigan would disable the Chicago diversion. Beaches would be broad, but access to marinas and docks would be severely limited. Great Lakes commercial navigation would be crippled. Electricity generation from hydropower would decline as dramatically as the lake levels. Political discussions over costly and environmentally hazardous dredging projects would abound. Thousands of municipal water intakes and wells would have to be moved or extended. The nature of the fishery would be completely altered due to a lack of spawning ground and warmer water. Native American and Native Canadian populations that depend on the fishery or marshland for their livelihood would be impacted. Locks would have to be re-engineered and channel walls stabilized.[5]

But the report also cautioned, like the Ghost of Christmas Future in Dickens's *A Christmas Carol,* that a dramatic decline in lake levels is only what might come to pass, not what will. One of the models forecasts a relatively cool and damp effect of climate change in the region, resulting in an increase in the levels of the lakes. The single model might be enough for political interests opposed to changes in current industrial or institutional practices to resist mandates or incentives to reduce energy consumption, air pollution, and water use. Or a more generalized public worry about the fragility of the lakes under most of the scenarios could inspire the region to lead the way in creative response to the challenge of preventing such harm. Sensible preventive steps could provide a net increase in jobs.

A series of drought years and mild winters in the 1990s and early in the twenty-first century among the lakes stirred anglers, boaters, environmentalists, and some businesses to fret about a dark future. "There was a time in Michigan when there were certain things you could count on—such as ice in January," wrote Lynn Henning of the *Detroit News* in early 2002. "These days, old-fashioned harsh winters seem to have gone the way of the Model T. Ice fishing remained a hit-and-miss venture in many areas of Michigan heading into the weekend."[6] For the first time in its one hundred twenty-five years of existence, unhampered by ice, the Arnold Transit Company was able to ferry passengers between St. Ignace, Michigan, and Mackinac Island throughout the winter of 2001–2002. "Usually, we stop running in January," said Bill Porter, the firm's marketing director. "This has been a strange winter."[7] In Toronto there was also perplexity during the same month. "Record high temperatures lured thousands of Greater Toronto residents out of their homes to throng sidewalk patios, parks and lakeside promenades yesterday. But the very same conditions only increased worries for grape growers and farmers, as well as shippers who depend on normal Great Lakes water levels."[8]

Looking ahead to the year 2050, the *Buffalo News* tried to interpret the possible new local reality for the grandchildren of its 2002 readership:

> It's hot the way summers used to be hot in the Maryland panhandle, before it got hotter there, too. Broad sandy beaches line Lake Erie. Bathers enjoy this new weather extreme as if it were an antidote to Buffalo's other new weather extreme: a big increase in precipitation, sometimes in the form of blizzards, but mostly rain. One thing is missing from this lakeside scene: the ships. They

disappeared as the beaches appeared, driven out of business by the new low water levels.[9]

The *Erie Times News* looked at it this way for Pennsylvania lovers of Lake Erie: "Many recreational marinas would no longer be usable. . . . The lower lake levels and warming of the water would also concentrate pollutants, increase the likelihood of bacteriological contamination and cause an overall reduction in water quality, according to the assessments."[10]

For the regimes of most of the Great Lakes states and Ontario during the 1990s and first years of the twenty-first century, the prospect of dramatic but far-off dangers was no test at all. Few of the lake states were even acknowledging that emissions of greenhouse gases were a problem, let alone implementing measures to demonstrate stewardship that would help retard warming. Observing that "a remarkably diverse array of states have begun to move forward well ahead of the federal government" in attacking climate change, the University of Michigan's Barry Rabe noted only one significant innovation among the Great Lakes states, Wisconsin's mandatory reporting of significant greenhouse gas emissions.[11] A survey by the Michigan Environmental Council found that only two of the eight states had a requirement that electric utilities supply even a small fraction of their power from clean, renewable sources, and only three had politically painless programs to reward consumers for buying more energy-efficient appliances.[12] Ontario took a slightly different tack. On 27 June 2002 the provincial minister of environment and energy, Chris Stockwell, endorsed the phaseout of Ontario Power Generation's five coal-fired power plants, major contributors to the buildup of carbon in the atmosphere. The Ontario Clean Air Alliance, a citizens organization, expressed some skepticism, calling for a firm timetable for the shutdown of the plants.

If the idea of ecosystem integrity had been an operating principle for the governments of the Great Lakes region, climate change policies would have been far different. Like nation-states scattered over hundreds of Pacific Ocean atolls, Great Lakes governments should have been eager observers of, or participants in, United Nations discussions on restraining climate change in the last years of the old century or the first years of the new one. Representatives of the fifty-four thousand citizens of the Marshall Islands attended the Kyoto climate change talks in December 1997 "because they can already see the rising ocean eating at their young country."[13] Just as climate change could drown the nations of the atolls and force massive human relocation, it could shrink and harmfully transform the Great Lakes, and they deserved similar official advocates. Instead, most of the region's governments ignored or even denied the existence of the problem. Particularly after the ascension to power in the United States of the George W. Bush administration, which rejected the Kyoto climate change treaty and promoted research over action, inaction by the Great Lakes states was an unwise gamble at best.

But if Great Lakes governments were reluctant to consider climate change a threat worth addressing, they had a harder time ducking a threat of similar proportions: an urgent and worsening scarcity of fresh, clean water in the world. By 2025 up to three billion people in fifty-two countries are expected to have insufficient water to meet basic domestic and sanitation needs—a doubling from the year 2002.[14] After listening to a presentation on looming water problems worldwide, International Joint Commission Canadian section chair Herb Gray said the talk "scared the hell out of me."[15]

These forecasts point to a grim future. The practices contributing to North American water scarcity are rooted in consumption patterns and freedoms held dear by U.S. and Canadian citizens. The remorseless tapping of groundwater resources to support agriculture and industry is drying up aquifers alarmingly fast. The Worldwatch Institute estimated in 1999 that one hundred sixty billion cubic meters of water were drained from groundwater each year, with the United States among the top five consumers of the resource.[16] The problem is as monumental as it is simple:

> The trouble with water—and there is trouble with water—is that they're not making any more of it. . . . There is the same amount of water on the planet now as there was in prehistoric times. People, however, they're making more of—many more, far more than is ecologically sensible—and all those people are utterly dependent on water for their lives (humans consist mostly of water), for their livelihoods, their food, and, increasingly, their industry. Humans can live for a month without food but will die in less than a week without water. Humans consume water, discard it, poison it, waste it, and restlessly change the hydrological cycles, indifferent to the consequences: too many people, too little water, water in the wrong places and in the wrong amounts. The human population is burgeoning, but water demand is increasing twice as fast.[17]

Another demand on water is growing exponentially. Sales of the U.S. bottled water industry nearly tripled in the 1990s, reaching $6.5 billion in 2001. Per capita bottled water consumption in the nation rose from nine to twenty gallons per year. Initially stimulated by concern over the safety of public water supplies—a fear reinforced by the Milwaukee cryptosporidium tragedy in 1993—the use of bottled water soon became a matter of consumer convenience and a triumph of marketing. The plastic bottle of water has become as much a personal companion as a CD player, coffee mug, or cell phone—a necessary attendant to the fashionable "lifestyle" of the new century. In the late 1990s major water bottlers coveted the groundwater of the Great Lakes region, challenging governments and citizens to decide how far they were willing to permit water to become a commodity for sale like any other.

Advocates of exploiting the lakes for commercial and humanitarian reasons are not hard to find. In a 1999 editorial about the "Great Lakes water farm," *U.S. Water News* deplored the talk by the basin's politicians about banning exports. The paper reasoned that the basin's "excess water now just flows out to sea, unused." Its vision of the future takes the agriculture analogy to the limit. "When precipitation is high and runoff is burgeoning and lake levels are up, a full water harvest could ensue. When times are drier and lake levels are lower . . . the yield from the lakes would not be as great and the harvest would be more limited."[18]

The looming demand of the United States and the world for fresh water caught the attention of Great Lakes leaders in the early 1980s, but talk has exceeded meaningful conservation action over the last two decades. The cause of concern as the 1980s began was the simultaneous depression of the Great Lakes economy, prompting the flight of many unemployed and underemployed workers to fast-growing regions in the South and West, and the specter of a water grab by the western United States. The U.S. Congress in 1976 authorized a study by the Army Corps of Engineers of water resources in the High Plains states. Worried about the rapid depletion of the Ogallala Aquifer, a groundwater resource underlying over 170,000 square miles of land from Texas to South Dakota and Wyoming to Kansas, politicians wanted the corps to evaluate methods of protecting the agriculture industry that consumed 95 percent of the aquifer's water. Although the corps concluded that interbasin transfers of water were so expensive they would require "massive government subsidies," the U.S. government had been plowing huge amounts of public money into western water projects for decades. Increased voting power in Congress for the swelling, so-called Sunbelt states signaled the region might be able to muscle public subsidies for water diversions past Great Lakes politicians. A 1981 proposal by a Montana company to build a 1,923-mile coal slurry pipeline from Wyoming to the Duluth-Superior harbor, using lake water to process the coal, only deepened concerns.[19]

In June 1982 Michigan chief executive William Milliken organized a meeting of Great Lakes governors and Premier William Davis of Ontario on Mackinac Island to discuss the issue. The conference resulted in no decisions but enabled Milliken to remind the public of the significance of the lakes and to refer to the fast-growing southern and western United States as the "parchbelt" rather than the Sunbelt. Milliken said water "can become a major component in our region's economic recovery" but warned of "a growing threat of diversion of Great Lakes waters outside our basin without our mutual consent."[20]

The image of Texas cowboys slurping up Great Lakes water from a one-thousand-mile-long pipeline was irresistible to the region's politicians. It helped promote relatively quick agreement by the governors of the eight Great Lakes states on the 1985 Great Lakes charter of principles designed to resist threats to the region's water quantity. At the February 1985 signing, Illinois governor James Thompson decried the common belief in the United States that "the Sun Belt has it all over us and they plan to snatch the final prize," the region's water.[21]

But a more immediate threat was the thirst of the basin states themselves. As a board reporting to the International Joint Commission had observed in 1981, consumptive uses by cities, power plants, agriculture, and manufacturing industries in the Great Lakes region could grow fivefold by the year 2035. Reducing water flow in the system 8 percent, the in-basin demand had the potential to lower water levels in Lakes Michigan, Huron, and Erie six inches, with dramatic ecological and economic effects.[22]

The charter was in part an effort to curb the water appetite of the signatory states and the provinces that later joined it. Calling for the enactment of water withdrawal regulation and better data collection and analysis of water uses, it offered the promise of a new stewardship ethic. The first severe drought after the signing of the charter put the ethic to the test, and Illinois failed.

Thompson, who only three years before had decried raids by others on the lakes, proposed tripling on a temporary basis the Chicago diversion to help increase flows on the Illinois and Mississippi Rivers and float barge traffic. The diversion works were designed for a flow of ten thousand cubic feet per second (cfs), and infrastructure remains in place for a diversion of as much as eighty-seven hundred cfs, compared to the Supreme Court–ordered limit of thirty-two hundred cfs.

Reaction was harshly negative. Canadian politicians worried about U.S. arrogance. One member of Parliament compared the idea of increasing the diversion without consulting Canada to a 1985 incident in which a U.S. Coast Guard icebreaker traversed the Northwest Passage without obtaining Canadian permission.[23] Environment Minister Thomas McMillan called Thompson's bid "insane."[24] Heeding similarly strong sentiments from constituents who could see the dramatic decline in lake levels in the preceding three years, the Great Lakes states rejected the proposal to increase the Chicago diversion, and the end of the drought soon terminated discussion of it.

An Ontario company, the Nova Group, received a permit in the spring of 1998 from the Ontario Ministry of Natural Resources to export the equivalent of up to fifty tankers per year—one hundred fifty-six million gallons—of Lake Superior water to anticipated customers in Asia. Despite Great Lakes charter commitments, the Ontario agency had failed to notify or consult with its neighboring states on the Nova permit, which became news only after it had been granted. Although the amount of water the company proposed to withdraw from Lake Superior was negligible when compared to the volume of the second largest lake in the world, the permit had the potential to set a precedent that Great Lakes water was a marketable product. Even bigger was the symbolism of Superior water traveling to Asia. "One idea we came up with was that on Canadian TV we see Third World Asian countries that are starving because there is no water to be found," Nova Group's John Febbraro told a reporter. "We're looking at this as a twofold answer: They need the water over there, and here in northern Ontario our unemployment is very high."[25]

Any humanitarian impulses of basin politicians were trumped by knowledge that overwhelming majorities of voters opposed such shipments. "This is Pandora's box," U.S. representative Bart Stupak of Michigan's Upper Peninsula complained. "We've always worried that somebody will try to divert Great Lakes water to arid regions. If we ship to Asia, what's to prevent shipping to the Southwest or Mexico? Where do you stop?"[26] Under pressure, the Nova Group surrendered its permit, but a point had been made. The Great Lakes states set about refashioning the 1985 charter and bringing it up to date to reflect both political and legal realities.

The Council of Great Lakes Governors commissioned an analysis of the legal issues involved in defending the Great Lakes from large-scale water withdrawals.[27] Submitted to the governors in the spring of 1999, the analysis echoed the concern of the governors and other experts about the potential harm to be caused by large-scale water withdrawals and observed, "the ability of any authority—state provincial, federal or binational—to impose outright prohibitions on water exports is constrained by U.S. and Canadian constitutional and trade law." The lawyers called for "a commonly applied, resource-wide decision making standard that ensures benefit to the waters and water-dependent resources of the Great Lakes Basin."[28]

The International Joint Commission also weighed in. While the rhetoric of governors and the news media concentrated on the potential for transfers of water to far-off places, water demand projections submitted to the IJC for the next twenty years suggested an entirely different scenario. The Great Lakes states themselves, according to the IJC–commissioned studies, would place an increasing demand on the resource. In the most likely scenario projected by the studies, water consumption in the U.S. section of the Great Lakes Basin was expected to rise 27.05 percent by the year 2025. Study authors explained that this is the likely result of increasing use of Great Lakes water in manufacturing and, to a lesser extent, to support municipal water supply.[29]

But the IJC had even more to say that challenged the conventional wisdom about the source of threats to the hydrologic integrity of the Great Lakes system. "In the short run, pressures for small removals via diversion or pipeline are most likely to come from growing communities in the United States just outside the Great Lakes Basin divide where there are shortages of water and available water is of poor quality. The cost of building the structures needed to support such diversions would be relatively small by comparison to the cost of building structures to move water vast distances. Population distribution suggests that several communities that straddle or are near the Great Lakes Basin divide, particularly communities in Ohio, Indiana, and Wisconsin, may look to the Great Lakes for a secure source of municipal and industrial water supplies in the future."[30] Within two years of the IJC report, in fact, suburbs of Milwaukee, growing communities near the Lake Erie divide in Ohio, and Indiana communities began pressing for access to Great Lakes water to support their expansion.

Representatives of the Great Lakes states began crafting revisions to the charter based on the legal analysis and the IJC report. The governors and premiers signed an addendum to the charter, called Annex 2001, in June of that year. The pact envisioned a new standard for the review of all water withdrawal proposals, whether they benefit in-basin or out-of-basin users. If implemented by all the states and Ontario, applicants would have to demonstrate that they would cause "no significant adverse individual or cumulative impacts to the quantity or quality of the waters and water dependent natural resources of the Great Lakes Basin."[31] In a genuinely revolutionary touch, the annex also called for inclusion in the new statutes of a requirement that applicants improve the water quality and natural resource qualities of the basin. Those charged with putting the proposed standard into law could find no comparable requirement anywhere on the globe.

But that was the rub. The requirement that a project improve the basin was so far-reaching it threatened to derail Annex 2001. In September 2002, as several of the governors who signed the agreement were preparing to leave office, a participant in the talks from Michigan observed in a briefing memo, "Current efforts under Annex 2001 to develop a new decision-making standard have been stalled. The main reason is that all Great Lakes states, except Michigan, are potential water diverters. These states realize that they may be significantly impacted by any agreement that requires additional regulation, mitigation and/or improvement. . . . If the states agree to the original concepts of Annex 2001 they will, in effect, be putting their own communities in a position of having additional water supply costs putting them at a competitive disadvantage for potential new industrial/commercial users."[32]

Michigan had its own problems with Annex 2001. For the first time in the state's history, the annex would require water users to abide by statutory rules and to practice water conservation. After so many years of running free—except for the occasional lawsuit by an adjacent user—Michigan businesses and municipalities could not accept the idea of short-term sacrifice to assure long-term protection of the Great Lakes. Echoing the lumber barons who said the timber of the Great Lakes states would last five hundred years—and then cut it down in less than fifty—a spokesperson for the Michigan Manufacturers Association said, "There's no groundwater withdrawal problem in Michigan. We're at the center of the Great Lakes."[33]

Like other bold-sounding Great Lakes agreements before it, Annex 2001 was colliding with domestic political realities. It is one thing to rally against Sunbelt water pirates when defending the Great Lakes. But it is another to learn a water conservation ethic regulating one's own use. Living among or in sight of the world's largest lakes, residents of the Great Lakes Basin had seen no reason to limit their water use or consumption, and their governments were reluctant to educate them about the need for it. But now they were entering a new age of grave uncertainty and coming to grips with the vulnerability of those vast waters. As the IJC noted in its 2000 report:

> The waters of the Great Lakes are, for the most part, a nonrenewable resource. They are composed of numerous aquifers (groundwater) that have filled with water over the centuries, waters that flow in the tributaries of the Great Lakes, and waters that fill the lakes themselves. Although the total volume in the lakes is vast, on average less than 1 percent of the waters of the Great Lakes is renewed annually by precipitation, surface water runoff, and inflow from groundwater sources.[34]

Despite containing over sixty-five quadrillion gallons of water, about 18 percent of the world's surface fresh water, the lakes are not limitless. They are a gift of the glacial age, vulnerable to being lowered not just by climate change but also by increasing use. Yet politicians running the region's governments, as always setting their sights on the next election, were finding it difficult to consider the next generation, let alone the generation after that. Another example of this was the movement to replumb the lakes.

In 2002 the U.S. Army Corps of Engineers emerged with another ambitious plan to enhance the competitiveness of Great Lakes navigation. Recalling an earlier day in which government agencies had frankly and without embarrassment talked about improving the lakes to benefit the economy, the corps' reconnaissance report on Great Lakes navigation studied five options, including one worth $10 billion that would open up the system to the largest oceangoing vessels. "That would cover the cost of making the seaway as deep as the Panama Canal, dredging more than a dozen ports in places like Hamilton and Cornwall, Ontario, and installing new locks throughout the system," reported the *Toronto Globe and Mail.*[35] The corps predicted that the project could increase shipments of goods to and from Duluth by more than 50 percent by the year 2060. "We would become a very important port. As would the rest of the ports on the Great Lakes," said Mike Doran, the Toronto Port Authority's director of operations.[36]

But environmental critics were fierce in their denunciation of the corps' request for $20 million to study the proposed alterations in detail over five years. They decried the cost to taxpayers, questioned optimistic assumptions made by the corps about economic benefits, and charged the project would increase the invasion of the system by aquatic species from oceangoing vessels, lower lake levels by deepening trenches in connecting channels, and repeat the damage done by the 1970s experiment in year-round navigation, undermining sensitive shoreline habitat for fish and wildlife and damaging coastal properties.

> If ever there was proof that the Corps of Engineers needs reform, the draft Reconnaissance Report of the Great Lakes Navigation System review is it. First, the report declares that the Corps' "basic responsibility . . . is to facilitate the movement of boats . . . by deepening, widening and straightening channels, by regulating water levels with dams, and providing associated locks." The [National Wildlife Federation] believes it is time for the Corps to broaden its definition of who its customers are and consider the interests of those that live, work, hunt, fish, boat, drink and eat by, in and on the Great Lakes and St. Lawrence River.[37]

Ironically, the controversy over the corps' request for public funding to study "unconstrained" shipping on the Great Lakes in detail peaked just as the region's governments responded with alarm to an invader threatening to use one of the earliest alterations of the lakes to find a new home. Identified as close as twenty-five miles to Lake Michigan in the Illinois and Chicago River system, three species of Asian carp were "putting the entire Great Lakes Basin ecosystem at highest risk of invasion."[38] The silver, bighead, and black carp were said to grow up to six feet in size and one hundred ten pounds in weight, conjuring up images of cinematic monsters.

Introduced to the southern United States to control algal blooms and snail populations in aquaculture facilities, the carp had escaped confinement during floods in the early 1990s and headed up the Mississippi River and tributaries—ultimately exploiting the canal created to link Lake Michigan and the Illinois River in 1848. News reports warned that the carp might already have arrived, portending another major disruption of the Great Lakes aquatic food web. "The carp have been known to jump some 10 feet out of the water and wallop boaters in the

Mississippi River," raising fears that the nonnative species may spread throughout the Great Lakes, reported the Associated Press.[39] Robert Wellington, an aquatic biologist with the Erie County, Pennsylvania, health department, reported spotting a massive fish between thirty and fifty pounds and five feet long surfacing in Presque Isle Bay. In the spring of 2003 an Asian carp was pulled from a landlocked lagoon in the city of Chicago, touching off new fears.

Although Congress swiftly appropriated funds to install a permanent electric barrier in the canal, few observers thought technology would completely halt the fish. Rather, the question was whether they would die out quickly in their new, unfamiliar open lake environment or flourish and drive other large natural predators into sudden retreat or extinction. The unintended consequences of a century and a half of lake manipulations were putting at risk a modern-day wonder, the sport fishery of the lakes. Still, the Army Corps of Engineers and port interests throughout the lakes insisted on moving ahead with a study on how to master the system again, bringing in more ships—and more exotics.

If the governments have proven themselves so unwilling to act in the long-term interest of the Great Lakes, perhaps something can be done about the governments.

Scholars across the Great Lakes region have been suggesting just that for thirty years. At one time, the discussion and debate were lively. Peaking just after the revolutionary 1978 Great Lakes Water Quality Agreement, embedded with the startling concept of "ecosystem integrity," the dialogue was rich in creativity. Ideas ranged from minor tinkering with the patchwork of existing institutions to the invention of institutions likely unseen before anywhere on the planet.

Perhaps the International Joint Commission, established in 1909 and regarded as the only honest voice on Great Lakes issues associated with governments, could be improved. Granted a monitoring and oversight role of the two nations' progress in meeting the goals of the water quality agreements of 1972 and 1978, the IJC had the added virtue of providing parity between Canada and the United States. Three commissioners represent each nation, and budgets for staff support are traditionally comparable. Further, by tradition, commissioners represent the institution, not the respective national interests of either nation, providing the IJC an unusual moral authority, if exercised.

From the 1970s until the mid 1990s the IJC was instrumental in moving the basin forward. Insisting in each biennial report that both nations and the states and Ontario could do far more to meet their commitments under the water quality agreement, the IJC also provided a sounding board for a growing number of citizens groups—and later, for industries—concerned about the lakes as a whole. No single state or province or federal agency or commission could say the same. "I think for a long time the IJC played a strong role in providing the forums that brought a sense of citizenship and of working together," said Great Lakes United board member John Jackson. "People were seeing the connection. 'Yeah, we're working on the same set of problems.' Whether they were from Duluth or Montreal."[40] But by the mid 1990s, irritated by the IJC's prodding for what the governments regarded as politically unrealistic notions of cleanup, they had learned to bypass it or ignore it. Threatened with reductions in congressional and parliamentary appropriations after its 1992 recommendation that chlorine should be phased out, the commission sought to lower the volume of public protest at its biennial meetings by scheduling smaller, lake-by-lake sessions. "I've seen a real sort of diminishment of that sense of community," Jackson said. A longtime environmental writer, Paul MacClennan of the *Buffalo News,* was more blunt: "It was its integrity that led the governments to assign [the IJC] the mission of monitoring restoration of the lakes. Bit by bit it is losing credibility in the eyes of the public."[41]

The Environmental Law Institute proposed several changes in IJC management to revive the commission's effectiveness.[42] It called for permitting the public to petition the IJC directly for action on boundary water issues, rather than reserving that right for the respective national governments. The control of "references" by the national governments inhibited the commission from independently looking out for the ecosystem, the institute said. Similarly, the institute recommended terms of fixed length for commissioners, staggered to prevent complete turnover with changes in the respective national governments. The change was "essential for the IJC to regain its credibility as a technically expert, non-partisan body," the institute said. "It would also reduce the temptation for the Parties to use IJC appointments as political rewards and would preserve the IJC's institutional continuity."[43] Not surprisingly, by 2002 the two nations had failed to act on the institute's proposals.

Other Great Lakes institutions wanted a piece of the action. The Great Lakes Commission, established by a U.S. interstate compact in 1955, sought to assume the mantle of the central Great Lakes institution. Hoping to fill the vacuum created by the slow decline in the IJC's influence, the commission invited representatives of Ontario and Quebec to sit as unofficial members and promoted the Ecosystem Charter of Principles, signed by a large number of institutions and organizations in 1994. It also organized the region's governments to seek a multibillion dollar U.S. federal funding commitment to protect, restore—and develop—the lakes.

But that last verb was pivotal. Established in part to promote the Great Lakes as the "fourth coast" of the United States through construction of the St. Lawrence Seaway, the commission had conflicting institutional impulses. On the one hand, its president and chief executive officer, Michael Donahue, promoted stewardship as a fundamental part of the commission's work. On the other hand, port and shipping interests regarded the commission as *their* panel and assured that protection of the lakes as an avenue for commercial navigation got equal billing with environmental concerns.[44] The commission supported public funding of a study to "optimize Great Lakes navigation system infrastructure"[45]—innocuous language for the army corps' review that could justify the latest in a long series of efforts to improve the lakes through engineering. The commission carried forward into the twenty-first century a notion of the lakes that had dictated their development for almost two hundred years and nearly wrecked them through gross pollution, the introduction of exotic species, and fiscally ruinous subsidies.

Alone among the established Great Lakes governmental institutions, the Great Lakes Fishery Commission had cultivated and sought consistently to put into practice a protective ecosystem policy. It had urged the two nations to shut off the invasion of exotic species as zebra mussels penetrated the lakes in the late 1980s and had begged them to restore the vital collection of phosphorus loading data in Lake Erie two years before the absence of it frustrated those seeking to understand the lake's decline in 2001 and 2002. But the Fishery Commission was inherently limited by its 1954 mandate to "make possible the maximum sustained productivity in Great Lakes fisheries of common concern."[46] Commissioners and staff extended the mandate as far as they could, using fish as the bellwether for the health of the lakes as a whole. They reviewed the impact of land use and pollution on fish stocks and promoted the restoration of native fish species, but could not exercise more than a hortatory role on some of these issues and could or would not touch such questions as the use and release of contaminating chemicals on the fisheries and the people who depended on them. The commission's strengths were its low-key, collaborative method of operation, winning it willing partners in and cooperative arrangements with sea lamprey eradication agencies in the national government bureaucracies and its ties with fisheries managers in each of the lakes states and Ontario. But few citizens attended its meetings, other than representatives of sport fishing groups that participated in annual lake committee sessions at which catch limits were devised.

Some of the strongest statements made by any governmental agencies were those of environmental commissioners within the Canadian provincial and federal governments. Acting in an ombudsman's role, free of political suppression and protected from the worst budget cuts, the Canadian commissioner of the environment and sustainable development sharply criticized her nation's commitment to Great Lakes conservation in an October 2001 report. Johanne Gelinas faulted the federal government for inadequate funding, slipshod environmental monitoring and research, and weak anticipation of future problems. "Unlike the past, though, ahead the trip is uncharted and we are quickly approaching whitewater rapids. The future of the basin is one of increasing pressures, threats, and complexities. And so, I am troubled by the global messages emerging from our work," said Gelinas.[47] The report of the Ontario environmental commissioner a year later was equally scathing. Referring to the Walkerton debacle that had cost seven people their lives in 2002 after drinking from a contaminated water supply, Gord Miller said, "Walkerton is a terrible reminder that degradation in background water quality has very serious consequences." Miller charged that the province's water problems might be even worse than before Walkerton.[48] There were no such prominent, critical governmental voices on environmental issues in U.S. governments. A new fear of retribution muzzled once-blunt U.S. public servants, leaving the traditionally civil Canadians to speak honestly about government shortcomings.

Even in Canada, it was unclear whether the brief publicity generated by the independent commissioners' reports would result in significant political repercussions and policy changes. But they raised issues that informed the public's discretion. That was a critical first step. The Canadian approach revives and extends the early-twentieth-century tradition of institutionalizing within government independent voices willing to speak what elected officials dare not. All Great Lakes states could benefit by creating permanent, independent fact-finding environmental commissioners with the ability to assess the effectiveness of existing programs, anticipate future problems, and sound the call for important changes.

These auditors and the public they serve require good data to evaluate the progress—or slippage—of the ecosystem. Like governments elsewhere, Great Lakes states and Ontario traditionally slash funding for environmental monitoring and data analysis during cyclical economic downturns. A cynic might suggest that elected officials even exploit budgetary problems to conceal adverse trends from the public. Complacency is another reason for reductions in data, as the too-soon elimination of Lake Erie phosphorus loading data in the mid 1990s demonstrates. In the 1980s Great Lakes governments took steps to prevent budget problems from harming the region's research capability, establishing a $100 million Great Lakes Protection Fund as an endowment to support scientific work related to the ecosystem. The precedent, then, exists for an endowed Great Lakes monitoring fund of $250 million U.S. to assure money always exists to measure air and water pollution and habitat degradation of the lakes.

Visionaries have had greater notions, and in the twenty-first century it may be time for their thoughts to escape the pages of conference proceedings and back-shelf books and reach a broader audience. In a 1988 paper on governance of the lakes, Lester W. Milbrath of the State University of New York argued, "The most eloquent evidence for the limitations of the present structure is the continuation of physical injuries and threats to the well-being of the Great Lakes system." In Milbrath's analysis, the primary deficiency of the existing Great Lakes governance institutions was their apparent inability, or weak ability, "to learn."[49] Remedying that deficiency, he argued, would require a Great Lakes futures review board:

> Past human actions around the Great Lakes, guided primarily or solely by individuals seeking to maximize their personal advantage in a market system, have resulted in the resource depletion and environmental degradation. . . . Each individual may only take a little water, or only dump a little waste, but the cumulative effects of these actions have begun to overwhelm the natural balance in the lakes. We are being forced to conclude that human activities that impact on the Great Lakes must be guided by the knowledge of the systemic relationships that bind elements into an ecosystem and by skilled interpretation of that knowledge to arrive at reasonably accurate estimates of the future consequences of contemplated actions.[50]

The board contemplated by Milbrath would consist of approximately ten members, appointed for staggered terms of seven years, with a professional staff. Its mission: to review all "major human initiatives that could significantly impact the Great Lakes ecosystem" for "their consequences for the ecosystem as well as their consequences for the social system." Milbrath envisioned the futures board as "a step toward programming government to learn by designating a special group to give full time to acquiring the best information, thinking about it integratively and systematically, and projecting the future consequences of proposed actions."[51]

Milbrath was right about the governments' inability to learn. In fact, they have recently buried their heads in the sand. Troubling new water pollutants and ecosystem disrupters are now on the scene. When the U.S. Geological Survey confirmed the presence of eighty-two pharmaceuticals, hormones, and other organic wastewater contaminants in a nationwide reconnaissance in 1982, no state in the Great Lakes region stepped forward to call for a systemic reconnaissance of the world's greatest freshwater system—even though one of the survey's sampling sites was in the Lake Michigan watershed. "For many substances, the potential effects on humans and aquatic ecosystems are not clearly understood," the study's authors pointed out.[52] Similarly, the discovery in Great Lakes fish of a family of fire retardants known as polybrominated diphenyl ethers—compared by many to the now-banned PCBs that ravaged the lakes in the 1960s and 1970s—spurred no organized response. "Based on limited studies, the Great Lakes appear to be among the most PBDE-contaminated bodies of water in the world, with Lake Michigan the worst," said one environmental newsletter.[53] These failures to anticipate the next generation of ecosystem challenges underscore the importance of a board capable of assessing the future of the lakes.

If Milbrath's board is ever to be created, it must include representatives of the most burdened and least considered populations in the basin, particularly native peoples and minorities. These peoples tend to rely more on contaminated Great Lakes fish for subsistence, and some populations breathe the foulest urban air in the basin. They may provide a voice for a genuine reclamation of ecosystem integrity—an achievement that would encompass the oldest cities as well as the most remote old-growth forests, the homes of generations for thousands of years past as well as the newest mansions of the privileged.

With the decline since the 1990s of the IJC as a moral authority in the Great Lakes region—its shine perhaps permanently tarnished through control exercised by national governments fearful that its proposals might run afoul of conventional economic development—the board proposed by Milbrath might renew Great Lakes progress. Chartered and initially funded by the region's private foundations, a regionwide, future-oriented Great

Lakes citizens commission could slip the bonds of politics. It could examine, analyze, and report on the effects of looming global and local changes and make credible, uncompromising recommendations about actions needed to protect and restore the ecosystem, including its human inhabitants. The modest funding needed to create such a board would be a small repayment for the good the Great Lakes have bestowed on those who live among them.

If politicians refuse to consider the future, perhaps the future should be asked to sit down among them. The region's legislative assemblies need voices for generations unborn and unable to participate in today's policy debates. It is unlikely that conventional politics is ready to embrace the idea of delegates explicitly charged with advocating for the future in their midst. But is it too much to ask legislators, at least once per year, to receive from a Great Lakes futures review board a report on the sobering risks and soaring potentials of these Great Lakes one hundred years out and more?

The immense size of the Great Lakes Basin may discourage citizens from physically traveling to a central location for meetings, but the creative use of the Internet to inform and engage citizens can make such travel less necessary. The Great Lakes Information Network, managed since 1993 by the Great Lakes Commission and providing a single online location for information on the region, is an example of such a system. Regional institutions—or the new Great Lakes Citizens Board—could establish a virtual Capitol that provides a central location that explains the role of the various governments in Great Lakes decisionmaking, provides updates on the actions of the many governments affecting Great Lakes ecosystem health, and provides for both formal and informal means of assessing public knowledge and attitudes about Basin-wide issues. Such a virtual Capitol could experiment with participatory processes, including voting, to help inform Basin policies.

A citizens Great Lakes commission could serve as a bridge to even greater reforms. In the early 1980s a former IJC member,

Charles Ross, proposed a Great Lakes citizens assembly. Twenty years later, the idea of convening thousands of citizens from a host of backgrounds not only to discuss but also to decide on management of the lakes still seems beyond the tolerance of elected officials. But if the Great Lakes are truly to be a model for the world, as those same officials have suggested, why should they not be a model of innovative governance as well?

A change in government approaches is especially important because Great Lakes officials have turned their sights on federal riches. Noting that the U.S. Congress approved a $7.8 billion restoration plan for the Florida Everglades in the year 2000, mayors, governors, members of Congress from the lakes states, and regional agencies began talking up the idea that the Great Lakes deserved an equal or greater share of the booty.

"It's time to think big, to raise our sights and our ambitions," said Great Lakes Commission chief Michael Donahue. "It's time to reassert the national and global stature of the Great Lakes and let Congress know that saving the Everglades and the Mississippi and the redwoods is only part of the equation. It's time for all Great Lakes advocates to join forces and support the big picture, and leave quibbling over the details for another time and place." In devising a target for U.S. federal aid to Great Lakes restoration, Donahue said advocates should add "one or two zeroes" to the $50 million proposed by the Clinton administration for the Great Lakes in the fiscal 2001 budget.[54] Officeholders and candidates sounded the same theme. "The time is certainly right for a large-scale restoration effort on the Great Lakes and significant federal funding to this effort," said U.S. senator Carl Levin of Michigan. "The Great Lakes are a national treasure, and their restoration should be a national priority," said Rahm Emanuel, a former advisor to President Bill Clinton, who won a U.S. House seat in 2002. "We must establish a Great Lakes Trust Fund that actualizes the federal commitment to their future."[55]

On 14 July 2003 U.S. Senator Michael DeWine (R-Ohio) and seven other senators introduced S. 1398, which would provide $6 billion over ten years in grants to states for Great Lakes restoration. The same day, Representative Rahm Emanuel (D-Chicago) and nineteen other representatives introduced H.R. 2720, which authorizes $4 billion over five years for the same purpose.

A large national funding commitment to the Great Lakes is undoubtedly one element critical to their future health. But the evidence of almost two hundred years shows us that government can misspend as well as spend wisely on the Great Lakes. So in the end, it is not government but the people who elect and support government who will decide the fate of the Great Lakes. What clues can we draw about the future of the ecosystem from them?

The Return of the Mayfly

THE DIMMING OF LIGHTS IN NORTHWESTERN OHIO IN June of 1996 actually illuminated an astonishing ecological recovery.

Attracted to a Toledo Edison Company substation in Oregon, Ohio, by its bright lights, thousands of mayflies—also known as fish flies—shorted the system, causing a brownout for customers in several of the region's counties. The city of Port Clinton, along Lake Erie and Sandusky Bay, turned lights off on city streets, ball fields, and other public sites so the mayflies wouldn't be attracted into town, where they had been dying and accumulating in piles as deep as eight inches on roadways. Snowplows helped remove them. Port Clinton ultimately removed thirty-seven dump truck loads of the flies. "Signs warning drivers about piles of mayflies causing slippery road conditions will remain up in town," reported the *Columbus Dispatch.* "They're just as much trouble dead as alive." [56]

But the real trouble began in the 1950s, when the annual flourishing of Lake Erie's mayflies suddenly stopped. The likely result of an oxygen decline caused by phosphorus pollution from sewage and fertilizers, the 1953 crash of the mayfly population was a warning that the lake's health was in jeopardy. In the 1960s masses of repulsive algae floated on the lake's surface, a sign of the stress that was also endangering many fish stocks. The dying algae contributed to a sediment layer on the bottom of the lake that contained no oxygen, choking off the nymphs. Mayfly populations on Lake St. Clair also declined dramatically.

Aggressive action by the U.S. and Canadian governments and by some U.S. states reduced the dumping of phosphorus, particularly into Lakes Michigan and Erie, beginning in the mid 1970s. A critical step was a ban on high-phosphate laundry detergents, enacted by Minnesota, Chicago, Michigan, and New York (and later by Ohio) over the objections of the Soap and Detergent Association. Phosphorus levels in Lake Erie plunged by the beginning of the 1980s. By 1994 Ohio fish biologists were reporting robust mayfly hatches in areas where they hadn't been seen in forty years.

While sometimes inconvenient to human beings, the hatching mayfly of Lake Erie, which belongs to the genus *Hexagenia,* is a critical part of the lake's ecosystem. Spending the bulk of their lives as nymphs—also known as wrigglers—mayflies live in the shallow bottom muds of the lake, Saginaw Bay, and Lake St. Clair. After several winters there, they rise to the water surface anytime from late May to early July to emerge as curved-body, clear-winged adults. Leaving their exoskeleton, or skin, behind, male and females rise into the air at darkness to mate. The females lay thousands of eggs on the water, seeding the lake with a new generation of nymphs, after which the adults soon die, many of them first swarming to shore. It usually takes no more than about three days from the time the nymph swims to the surface to the time the eggs are deposited.

The mayflies are a critical source of food for the fish of the lake and some inland waters. An Ohio fisheries biologist noted in 2001 that the bellies of the lake's yellow perch and internationally renowned walleye were full of mayflies. The plummeting population of Lake Erie perch in the 1950s was linked, in part, to the mayfly decline.

Buffalo, better known for its lake-effect snows, experienced lake-effect mayfly deposits in 2000. An administrative assistant with the Buffalo Bisons minor league baseball team said masses of the mayfly were stuck to the wall of the ballpark's club level. "They were just flying all over the place," said Donna Notto. "They stuck to the scoreboard, and they stick to your car when you get out of the game." [57]

So abundant are the rejuvenated mayflies that they now appear on a National Weather Service radar tracking Lake St. Clair and Lake Erie in the late spring. Looking vaguely like rain or snowstorms heading toward the lights of shore, clouds of mayflies appear as blue or green stains on the radar. One method of measuring mayfly populations is to count the number of them inside a hula hoop thirty minutes after it's placed on the ground. When Pennsylvania State University professor Dr. Edwin C. Masteller retrieved one hula hoop from a site at North East, Pennsylvania, in the summer of 1999, he found more than fifteen hundred of them.

The recovery is not yet complete, nor is it uncomplicated. Some areas of Lake Erie do not have mayfly populations comparable to those before the peak of water pollution in the 1950s and 1960s. The invasion of the exotic zebra mussel may also have contributed to the recovery of the mayflies. By filtering sediments and clarifying the water, the zebra mussels have enabled sunlight to penetrate deeper into lake waters and have helped revive the oxygen levels on which mayfly nymphs depend.

The return of the mayflies is a revived memory, not just for the ecosystem, but also for the older residents of the region. Millions if not billions of the mayflies poured into the city of Cleveland as late as the early 1950s, dying en masse near its bright lights. In 1997 a seventy-seven-year-old volunteer mayfly tracker living near Lorain, Ohio, recalled masses of mayflies that crawled inside bathing suits of those who swam at Lake Erie beaches. "I was sorry to see them go because of the reason they went, not because I missed them," said Bill Baumler. [58]

Like howling winter winds, long days of lake-effect cloudiness, and fluctuating water levels that conceal and then recede from beaches and shoreline residences, mayflies are nuisances to some humans. But their absence was a greater nuisance; it meant the heart of the Great Lakes ecosystem was in dismal health. Brownouts testify to the light that aggressive public action can bring to heal a damaged ecosystem.

"I can't tell you how encouraging the return of the mayflies is to the whole Lake Erie system," said Roger Knight, head of Ohio's Lake Erie Fisheries Unit in 1994. "Virtually everything feeds on mayflies, from young walleye to freshwater drum, and especially the yellow perch." [59]

Yet by the year 2000 patches of Lake Erie were suffering again. Oxygen was disappearing from much of its central basin, and botulism was killing fish and birds. The recovery was dramatic, but not permanent—not without further human intervention.

On a trip to the Porcupine Mountains I connected with Lake Superior for the first time. Following a long hike, in the heat of middle summer, we followed a river to its mouth on the Superior shore. Walking along the rubble beach, swimming in the shockingly cold water, I felt that I had been transported to the north country of my heart. I spent hours on the rocks, watching mayflies rise from a hatch, deer come to the shore to drink, and loons paddle by calling out in their haunting voice. As the sun set, spreading colors across the sky and Superior, listening to the water lap the rocks, I felt myself center again. I felt myself release to the wilderness and the water.

—Chris McCarthy

Year after year I journey to Superior. Her many moods beckon me to come visit and witness her ever-changing, never-changing beauty. It's always a voyage filled with anticipation. Her mood is so easily discerned by merely glancing at her endless waters and horizon. I have seen her waters, smooth as glass, shattered by the incredible force of waves gathering momentum as they journey to her southern shore. A radiant playful day of skipping sunlight evolves into an ethereal night not of this world. Her joyful blue eyes conceal any hint of her impulsive disposition. I never know whether my welcome will be amiable or intimidating. Invariably I will slip down to the water's edge sensing the sacred and reaffirming my belief that while God may visit our places of worship on weekends, He hangs out the rest of the time on Superior's shore.

—Michelle Hurd Riddick

Hope for Home

Perhaps the residents of the lakes region have a greater capacity for cultivating an ethic of stewardship than the politicians give them credit for. There is, in fact, evidence that a precautionary principle could become the cornerstone of public attitudes toward the lakes. But the evidence does not all point in one direction, and how public thinking and feeling evolves in the next decade or two may determine the fate of these Great Lakes.

Two Canadians take different but ultimately converging views of whether individuals have developed a protective ethic toward the lakes. Henry Regier, a retired University of Toronto professor, Great Lakes Fishery Commission member, and former member of the Science Advisory Board that advised the International Joint Commission, has traced a growing circle of awareness in the Great Lakes region. He has written hopefully of informal international cooperation among citizens. "Self-organizing social institutions have generally been evolving toward integrity in all the political jurisdictions at all levels in the basin," Regier said in 1998. "There may be no transnational bioregion which has progressed as far as the basin within these 'new realities.' "[1]

But is the activity of a relatively small community of interested citizens, scientists, and government officials sufficient, even as a start on a general ecosystem ethic? Pointing out that Ontarians' primary identification has historically been with the lakes of its north central "cottage country," Trent University environmental historian Stephen Bocking says a broad movement to protect individual Great Lakes has evolved in the province chiefly since the 1960s. And whether American or Canadian, he adds, it may be too much to expect citizens to envision the vast system of the lakes as a single unit. "There has been a persistent effort to define a Great Lakes identity," Bocking observes. "But I don't think you can expect people to be concerned about the Great Lakes as a unit. The only thing that is likely to take off is concern piece by piece. For a local beach, a bay, or a single lake."[2]

On the other hand, Bocking argues, the public has come to appreciate concepts that many policymakers believe are beyond their grasp. Citing the examples of stratospheric ozone depletion and the decline of Lake Erie in the 1960s, Bocking says, "That the environment is a complex system, that human actions can have unexpected consequences on it, these ideas are quite widespread in society."[3]

Two recent fights in Michigan make the case that a substantial, vocal body of citizens prefers not taking needless risks with the complexity of the lakes. In 2001 the Perrier Group proposed pumping more than two hundred ten million gallons of groundwater per year from the watershed of Michigan's Muskegon River, which feeds Lake Michigan, and bottling it under the Ice Mountain label for regional sale. Governor John Engler and other

Michigan officials hastened to help the company and brushed off citizen arguments that the project undermined the state's and region's future defense of the lakes. Despite cooperation from Wisconsin state government officials that led one critic to say the state's Department of Natural Resources was "part of Team Perrier" in a bid to build a water bottling plant there, citizen outrage over the specter of water exports had already sent Perrier packing.[4]

Michigan's government was an even more willing host. Incentives totaling a reputed $9.5 million helped entice the company to locate in the state and create 120 jobs over six years at its Mecosta County plant. Engler rejected an opinion by then–State Attorney General Jennifer Granholm that the pumping of groundwater for sale amounted to a "diversion or export of water" from the Great Lakes under a 1986 federal law, and thus was subject to a veto by any of the other seven lakes governors.[5]

Hundreds of citizens turned out for a hearing on the Michigan permit for Perrier during the spring of 2001, most strongly opposed to the project. "The bottom line is that Perrier only cares about its bottom line," said Lynn Denney. "They're thinking short-term gains. The ones who are going to lose are the people."[6] Perrier called "absurd" citizen concerns about the drying up of private wells by the company's pumping and argued there was nothing unique about its use and sale of water. Water was also an "integral" constituent of baby food, yogurt, soft drinks, epoxies, and cherries manufactured in nearby cities and sold outside the Great Lakes Basin, Perrier said. "In short, a bottle of beer is not a bottle of beer without its integral use of water; a can of paint or stain is not a can of paint or stain without its integral use of water . . . if [the federal Water Resources Development Act] were to be applied to shipments of Ice Mountain bottled water, one might well ask what would be the dividing line that would distinguish these from other products."[7] Jim Olson, an attorney for the project's opponents, retorted: "This ignores the simple fact that the Act's language refers to water and water only. It does not say 'products that contain water,' and no one has ever claimed that WRDA should apply to anyone diverting or exporting anything other than water."[8]

Scoffing at the public protests against Perrier, a Michigan attorney said, "I don't understand the difference" between bottled water and other uses. "It may have a different emotional appeal, but our laws are based on principles, not emotions." In fact, good laws and institutions are based on both—on the capacity of humankind to reason critically and feel strongly. Anyone who has ever crested the last dune or bluff and viewed the shocking blue expanse of a Great Lake understands at once that emotion is inevitable and invaluable in responding to it.

A key organizer in the fight against Perrier was Terry Swier, a former librarian who had retired along with her husband to a home passed down through generations of her family along the shores of Horsehead Lake, a few miles from the site of the bottling plant. "Our local officials can't see past the economic development," Swier said.[9] She added that one of the area's township supervisors who had supported the project defended her position by saying, "our children will have a place to work. They won't have to leave Mecosta County."[10] So why did Swier, her husband, Gary, and others organize a new grassroots not-for-profit organization called the Michigan Citizens for Water Conservation to oppose Perrier? As Swier put it, "this was the first time that many of us had gotten involved in something like this. It's a little intimidating. We found our local government officials don't have to listen to us if they don't want to. . . . But we had to do something. Thank goodness I don't have blinders. I care about the Great Lakes basin and beyond, not just my lake, my township, or my state."[11]

Despite the legal concerns and public sentiment, the state issued the necessary permits to Perrier in August 2001. Another Great Lakes government was fulfilling an industrial wish and putting the health of the Great Lakes ecosystem at risk. While shouting their opposition to "water pirates" outside their borders, government officials were all too eager to board the pirate ship when it sailed into their jurisdiction and handed the buccaneers the keys to the ecosystem. It was difficult to see what, if anything, governments had learned from one hundred fifty years of ruinous exploitation of the lakes for short-term economic benefit. But the citizen opponents fought on without the help of their government, their suit against Perrier (now subsumed by the Nestle Corporation) going to trial in the summer of 2003.

Michigan citizens prevailed in another battle over the Great Lakes, forcing government to respond. In 2000 and 2001 a fierce debate arose in Michigan over the question of permitting leasing of rights to exploit oil and gas reserves under the Great Lakes from on-shore wellheads. Publicity over a proposal by the Newstar Energy USA Company to recover oil from underneath Lake Michigan resulted in a state moratorium in 1997. A study by a science panel appointed by Governor John Engler determined that there would be minimal risk to the lake of oil leaking upward from the reserves or the directional borehole but a slightly greater risk of a spill at the on-shore wellhead. The panel concluded that the issue was really one of coastal land use preferences and suggested the state take measures to identify sensitive areas along the shore where drilling should not be permitted. It did not recommend a permanent ban.[12] After Engler's successful 1998 reelection campaign, his agencies began to move toward rescinding the moratorium and authorizing as many as thirty leases for directional drilling under both Lakes Michigan and Huron.

The public would have none of it. Organized by the Lake Michigan Federation, which decried "numerous risks to the lakes, its coastline and communities and little interest by the state of Michigan to address them satisfactorily," citizens spoke out loudly.[13] One of them was Paul Parks, a retired engineer whose family had maintained a home in the sand dunes of Grand Haven, along Lake Michigan. Outraged at the idea of a state-sanctioned intrusion on the lake, Parks persuaded the Grand Haven City Council to draft an ordinance sharply restricting any drilling. The local state senator, Leon Stille, reacted by threatening the city with the loss of grants from the state's natural resources trust fund, whose revenues are derived from oil and gas operations on state-owned lands. Like many other lawmakers closer to regulated industries than their constituents, Stille wrote the city to say that "I feel state-generated monies should be channeled to those communities that don't oppose a state-supported, state-managed, scientifically-proven program."[14] The city ignored him.

The state natural resources commission approved a new round of leases for directional drilling on 14 September 2001. But the commission, regarded for nearly seventy years as the guardian of the state's resources, had fallen under the tight control of Engler. It no longer represented or even provided a meaningful forum for the conservation concerns of the public. It was the legislature that responded to public wrath about the drilling proposals. Reading the editorials and aware of polls such as one conducted by the League of Conservation Voters, which showed voters opposed Great Lakes oil drilling by a two-to-one margin, lawmakers that had previously supported the industry's position did an about-face.[15] In October 2001 the same state senator Leon Stille who had frowned on the Grand Haven antidrilling ordinance told a newspaper that "slant drilling is dead in Michigan."[16] He cited overwhelming opposition from voters. In March 2002 the state legislature sent a lakes drilling ban to Engler, who refused to sign it, saying the ban "runs contrary to Michigan's tradition of managing its resources based on the best available science."[17] Under the state constitution, a bill not vetoed by the governor within fourteen days of receipt becomes law, and the ban took effect.

Critics of the action said the public's opposition to drilling was the result of ignorance and that the virtuous position was to follow the guidance of technical experts who considered drilling acceptable, under strict regulatory conditions. But the ban was in fact the opposite of the symbolic politics practiced by politicians for a century, politics that had endangered the environment by catering to the immediate needs of industries at the long-term expense of the public trust. It embraced a policy of doing no harm. Polls and public comments suggested that Michigan citizens were well aware that the risks to the lakes of directional drilling were limited—but intolerable nonetheless. Wary of assurances from experts that had been proven wrong in the past, they rejected the notion that they should overlook their feelings and follow the lead of a government-industry alliance. "There's nothing wrong with emotion and there's nothing wrong with an emotional connection to the Great Lakes," said Lana Pollack, president of the Michigan Environmental Council.[18]

What does a more systematic review of Great Lakes public opinion find? In 2002 a Washington, D.C., based communications firm convened six groups of Great Lakes residents and interviewed twenty-one policymakers.[19] The firm also polled fifteen hundred thirty-nine residents of the U.S. states in the Great Lakes Basin. The findings could be the source of hope or worry.

Development is the trump card for government policymakers. The twenty-one interviewed tended to express more awareness of and concern about the vulnerability of the lakes than did citizens, but they were also more reluctant to interfere with economically lucrative industrial uses of the lakes. "Policy-makers talk tough about defending the resources of their region and not sending Great Lakes water to other states. Yet, when the issue is framed as one of free enterprise and whether or not to allow a company to bottle Great Lakes water, these same policy-makers are reluctant to forbid such activity," the communications firm found.

The poll found that public understanding was greatest for the most visible threats to the lakes: the dumping of sewage and industrial wastes. But far fewer linked construction of homes, stores, and roads on land near the lakes or climate change as real or potential problems. Like the government officials, citizens respect the idea of development. By substituting the words "from new development" for "from pollution" as threats, pollsters were able to reduce the percentage of respondents agreeing that "we need to do more to protect Great Lakes habitats" from 78 percent to 53 percent.[20] In the United States, at least, development per se is a good, and its relationship to pollution is not yet widely understood.

There is substantial reason to believe that citizens understandably view environmental threats as those that are tangible and immediate, rather than long-term and speculative. "Many harmful activities that spell potential doom for the Lakes in years to come either go unnoticed or are viewed as only somewhat problematic because the public is occupied thinking about the present, not [the] future," the pollsters found.[21]

How should advocates communicate with the public about threats to the Great Lakes? By appealing to values, they are advised. "Residents are motivated most by thinking of the Lakes as important places of natural beauty (55% extremely important) that deserve protection because they are created by God (58%), they serve to maintain the balance of nature that sustains us (54%), they are part of our regional identity (52%), and because we have a responsibility to future generations (64%)," reported the firm.[22]

Scientific opinion sampling tells only part of the story, and it is particularly ill-suited for getting at the idiosyncratic, emotional connections that people feel to special places on this Earth. Protecting the Great Lakes in the end will depend not just on how people feel about them, but how strongly they feel, and how willing they are to fight for them.

The lakes have, in fact, become the object of fascination, enjoyment, and love for multiple communities totaling hundreds of thousands of the basin's residents.

There are the lighthouse lovers, who publish newsletters, collect photographs of their favorite lights, and travel to observe or climb inside them, adding to a life list almost the way that birders do. They visit Raspberry Island in the Apostle Islands National Lakeshore, which began operation in 1863 and is the site of a $1 million reconstruction project; the imperial tower on Cove Island, built in 1858 at the entrance to Ontario's Georgian Bay; and the Tawas Point Light, built in 1853 and marking the western entrance to Michigan's Saginaw Bay. "This is a special place for us. I know years from now, no matter what happens between us in the future, this lighthouse will always represent a special moment in my life and a moment that was very important for both of us," said Craig Cooper of Ludington, Michigan, remembering walks with his high school sweetheart on the concrete pier to the North Breakwater Lighthouse.[23]

There are the shipwreck lovers, who study, perform underwater dives to observe, and tell eerie tales of the hundreds of vessels that have plunged forever to the bottom of one of the lakes. Recognizing the devotion of these people, Wisconsin, Michigan, Ohio, and the Canadian national government have established underwater parks to attract tourism and ward off looters. "To actually go down and touch history that's been untouched—it's a big thrill," said Gerald C. Metzler, an Ohio science teacher. "A few of these wrecks, we were the first people to touch them since they went down."[24]

There are the beach lovers, who turn out in force during the short summers of the Great Lakes region to perfect their tans and immerse themselves in refreshing cool waters. Meeting warning signs of unsafe conditions due to *E. coli* bacteria in recent years, they have become a core constituency for cleanup. From Thunder Bay, Ontario, to Wilson-Tuscarora Beach in Niagara County, New York, elevated bacteria levels have shut down beaches repeatedly in the last decade. In July 2002 more than sixty people suffered "punishing bouts of diarrhea and nausea" after swimming in what were believed to be contaminated waters at Nicolet Bay in Wisconsin's Peninsula State Park. "I've been coming here 34 years, and it's always closed with bacteria now," said Shirley Dacox of the Sixty-third Street Beach in Chicago one summer day in 2001. "To dump all this raw sewage into the lake on top of this stagnant water, it makes no sense at all."[25]

There are the freighter lovers. Calling themselves "boat nerds," they drive up and down the Great Lakes shore, delighting in and logging the sightings of the passing vessels. "I listen to the scanner, and when I hear a security call I go to the docks, where I usually take pictures," said Todd Shorkey of Bay City, Michigan. "Each ship gives a security call, where they're going, calling the bridges and I track them that way. Working a 24-hour shift, I don't catch everything, but I get as much as I can."[26]

There are the sport anglers. Returning in the millions to the open Great Lakes since the introduction of salmon in the 1960s and the revival of walleye in the 1970s and 1980s and benefiting from the antipollution laws that enabled the fish to survive and thrive, men and women spend an estimated $4 billion U.S. each year in pursuit of their favorite catch. "Tom Arlington of North Bay Charters gave me a call on Wednesday and asked if I wanted to go for a little fishing out of Port Sanilac. He could not have asked at a better time. I was in serious need for a fix. We had a few chores to do and we were on our way," reported a Lake Huron angler in the spring of 2003. "The weather looked like it wanted to do something, but with a few rays of sun shining through, it gave hope that we could get a couple of good hours. We were running planer boards, riggers and body baits. No sooner did we get the baits in and one hit. A nice laker came in without a hitch."[27]

There are the boaters. Five of the top ten U.S. states in boat registrations are Great Lakes states; Michigan has approximately one million registered boats. "The moon was full that night, with moonbeams dancing in the water," one boater reported at anchorage after a day sailing the North Channel of Lake Huron. "There is no way to describe the euphoria on a boat that accompanies an exciting day, a tiring day, when, after cocktails and dinner, the approaching night is quiet and idyllic. Imagine the best circumstance you can imagine, and it is better."[28]

There are the surfers. The hardiest of them are the small band that takes to frigid Lake Superior even with water temperatures in the thirties, riding the powerful waves of the world's largest lake by surface area. "Little by little, we're dispelling the lie that you can't surf this lake," said Greg Isaacson of Duluth.[29] Asked to describe the biggest wave he'd ever ridden on the lakes, surfer Ben Rayner said, "I was up in St. Joe's about five years ago on a really cold north-west. On the south side of the pier the waves were just huge. . . . I mean thick and fat, even fatter than on the ocean. In the line-up the sky would completely disappear when the sets rolled through. I'd say the wave was only eight feet or so but it had so much power and length."[30] In 2002 surfer Rick Boss joined the board of the Lake Michigan Federation. "My life pretty much revolves around the lake, so I'm really looking forward to being involved," Boss said.[31]

More important than any of these groups, aboriginal peoples have an ancestral home in the Great Lakes region. Known as First Nations in Canada, and as Native Americans in the United States, they possess both a legal and a moral authority that will prove indispensable to the defense of the lakes. In the United States they are organized in several ways to promote conservation, through the Great Lakes Indian Fish and Wildlife Commission and the Chippewa-Ottawa Resource Authority. Under U.S. law tribes act as sovereigns and have legal standing to bring actions to defend their rights to enjoy traditional hunting and fishing rights in the Great Lakes region. On the Canadian side of the border, the Union of Ontario Indians seeks through negotiations with the national government to reestablish the authority of the Anishinabek people to do the same. These powers could be decisive in the future of the Great Lakes.

The First Nations and Native Americans are not interest groups, but autonomous peoples entitled to co-equal authority and respect in resource conservation. They have connections to the Great Lakes that span dozens of generations and many hundreds of years, a connection deeper than that of any other people. Their sense of this place has already done much to define that of the Europeans and other immigrants. But have we heard their most important story, their deep and abiding determination to live in harmony with the Great Lakes?

So millions of Great Lakes region inhabitants, in scores of communities of shared interest, love the lakes, each for a different trait. What are the odds that they might come together—their fishing, boating, diving, swimming, and folkways at risk—as citizens came together once before, in the 1960s and 1970s, when the public revolted against pollution that seemed about to kill the lakes?

Much has changed since that time of turnaround. Women, who provided much of the people power that successfully petitioned governments to clean up the lakes in that earlier time, pursue busy lives of career and family in numbers far higher today. All families enjoy less leisure time that can be devoted to civic activity. Many citizens who do care look to the well-established environmental movement to represent them. Many others do not believe in either government or advocates as representatives of the public interest, turning away from civic affairs in distaste at scandal and official snubbing of the public trust. The laws themselves have become increasingly complex, and the rules and procedures that implement them can shut out all but the most dedicated citizens willing to learn about the intricacies of the NPDES system and the COA.[32] Too, since the early 1990s, a generation of Great Lakes politicians who exalt private profit over public protection have deliberately reduced the environmental monitoring that enables citizens to know that problems exist, while eliminating many of the informal mechanisms that citizens have traditionally used to speak back to their government and seek redress of their grievances.

But none of these adverse trends excuses shunning the cause of the Great Lakes, and it is unlikely even all of them cumulatively can mute the voices of the Great Lakes communities.

What progress has been measured in recent decades is almost all built around local efforts. A piece-by-piece approach to restoring the lakes has shown considerable strength—but also a fundamental weakness.

In the 1980s the International Joint Commission hoped to prod governments and citizens to restore these degraded rivers and bays. They became a focus of a new, collaborative approach to environmental recovery. Rather than assuming the burden of cleaning up the hotspots themselves, governments assembled teams of citizens representing business, local government, and the general public to review pollution and habitat degradation and develop remedial action plans, or RAPs, aimed at "de-listing" the areas of concern. The crosscutting nature of the groups excited great hope.

> The Great Lakes RAP Program represents a pioneering effort in ecosystem-based management. It has set the stage for a new way of doing business in terms of environmental programmes. It seeks systematic, comprehensive planning for complex problems on a watershed basis. It is inclusive and seeks partnerships. It encourages collaboration and co-operation at all levels. It encourages flexibility and innovation. It promotes co-operative learning and celebrates success.[33]

The risk of the approach was that, by emphasizing a process, it might play into the hands of politicians unwilling to invest the cleanup funds or make the difficult choices to restore the contaminated areas. Generating meetings and reports and good feelings of cooperation, remedial action planning had the potential to become a way of postponing rather than making a governmental ecosystem commitment. In 2002 the U.S. General Accounting Office criticized the program, noting that none of the twenty-six areas of concern within the nation's Great Lakes waters had been fully restored. "What you are seeing is failure," said U.S. senator Mike DeWine of Ohio, who had requested the audit. Cynthia Price, chair of the public advisory committee for the Muskegon Lake area of concern in Michigan, said, "In the years I've been involved, I have worked with many wonderful people at the DEQ and U.S. EPA Region 5, but have also watched the commitment to this program continually diminish. It has been very discouraging, particularly as we in Muskegon are beginning to get a handle on the extent of our contaminated sediment problem with its astronomical cleanup costs."[34]

But the impulse behind RAPs was a laudable one. By coupling community coalitions with the monitoring of national and regional institutions, citizens have the power to bring about a new era of Great Lakes restoration. That may seem wishful thinking—but unthinkable events of other kinds have changed the world in recent years. Most fundamentally, the United States and Canada have awakened to the vulnerability of their peoples as well as their ecosystems. The terrorist attacks of 11 September 2001 have stripped the United States of its delusions of isolation from an age of turmoil and reminded its inhabitants of their safety and mortality. The international boundary slicing through the lakes has again become a frontier rather than a meeting place. Both the United States and Canada have tightened border crossing procedures and increased patrols on the lakes. But these new security barriers have not divided the lakes themselves or diminished the passions of those who seek to protect them.

So what might bring these peoples together? What might unite and strengthen many unconnected individual and community feelings and actions into a shared sense or urgency and a commitment to act in unison?

Perhaps it will be, as it so often is, an emergency or the awareness of looming disaster. Governments often respond to the pressure of voters insisting on action after catastrophes or near-catastrophes. The Great Lakes are really many places united by water. Should that water fall below and stay below record low levels—especially in the presence of unusually mild weather—citizens may be shocked into action and driven to make both personal and social changes to protect the water they love. The same may occur as exotic fish overwhelm the native or as a new breed of chemicals assaults ecological and human health.

In the meantime, these citizens can go about honing their relationship with the Great Lakes themselves. As they do so, they must not be deceived, as the pioneer generations were, by the apparent vastness of the Great Lakes. Even in their time—and more emphatically in ours—it is we who are vast, the lakes that are vulnerable.

A clue was laid in the path by the small but influential Great Lakes activist community of the restoration era of the 1970s and 1980s. That community, it now appears, was the first generation of Great Lakes futurists of European descent. Citizens, scientists, and concerned government officials worked together to dream of a better method of living among the lakes that would avoid repeating the costly mistakes that Great Lakes society was then cleaning up—the fouling of the water and sediments, the draining and filling of fish spawning grounds. In a paper that resulted from a March 1983 "ecosystem approach workshop" convening fifty-six participants from "a diverse spectrum of backgrounds," authors W. J. Christie and J. R. Vallentyne—respected Canadian government scientists—and Mimi Becker and J. W. Cowden of Great Lakes Tomorrow cataloged a sweeping array of policy proposals, most still far from implementation. But their most valuable contribution was a simple description of environmental reality and how it might quietly revolutionize our nature:

> The ecosystem concept recognizes that you are new, yet not new. The molecules in your body have been parts of other organisms and will travel to other destinations in the future. Right now, in your lungs, there is likely to be at least one molecule from the breath of every adult human being who has lived in the past 3,000 years; the air around you will be used tomorrow by deer, lake trout, mosquitoes, and maple trees. The same is true of water, sunshine, and minerals. Everything in the biosphere is shared. . . .
>
> There is a simple, yet profound difference between "environment" and "ecosystem." The notion of environment is like that of house—something external and detached. In contrast, ecosystem implies home—something

> that we feel part of and see ourselves in even when we are not there. A home has an added spiritual dimension that makes it qualitatively different from a house. It is a happier place because of the caring and sharing relationships among its inhabitants.[35]

In a vocabulary unusual for an academic journal, the authors stated the imperative of the new twenty-first century for the Great Lakes Basin's inhabitants. By considering themselves as part of the basin's breathtaking past and expansive future, the authors suggested, the watershed's inhabitants could find themselves anchored safely in time and place, find satisfaction and fulfill the most basic of human needs—for a home.

It was the defense of home that inspired Chicago civic leaders and Indiana women to work, determined, for the protection of the Indiana Dunes for half a century. It was the defense of home that inspired Ontarians to protect Niagara Falls in the 1880s and Rondeau Park in the 1890s. It was the defense of home that peopled public hearings with citizens outraged about the decline of Lakes Erie and Michigan in the 1960s, and that filled the halls of government with citizens indignant about the toxic blob in the St. Clair River in the 1980s.

Professional consultants typically tell politicians of the early twenty-first century that environmental issues are secondary, important to address through palliative platforms but not something to stress. "In both Canada and the United States," wrote David Israelson, "the environment has a paradoxical position in the political structure. It's more noticeable than in many other countries as a political issue, because there's so much talk about it, but it's less significant—the political results have neither been as dramatic as those in Europe nor as comprehensive as those in places like Japan. It may be that we need a complete overhaul of the system, and we may come to realize this the next time we have a big environmental disaster."[36] In effect, Great Lakes issues and the Great Lakes community comprise a sleeping giant. Will they awaken in the first quarter of this century in response to a likely shift, either sudden or subtle, in the health of the Great Lakes ecosystem?

For nearly two hundred years, governments have been failing the Great Lakes. For the first one hundred of those years, they promoted exploitation of the lakes with the tacit consent of the governed. But today, after two generations of consistent public support for their protection, shame-proof governments captured by exploitative industries often betray the lakes in quiet defiance of the public. While the inhabitants of the region have an ambivalence of their own—occasionally clinging to a notion of development that can no longer be sustained in a world of fragile ecosystems—their voices increasingly express a bedrock commitment to the lakes they call home.

There is no escaping the fact, no matter how modern generations might seek to evade it, that democratic governments are tools of the people, subject to the popular will if the people choose to exercise it. The last two centuries of ecosystem instability, caused by greed and folly as much as understandable human ignorance, have penalized the people with periodic economic hardship and a fouled home. But there are signs that the people, if not the governments, have the capacity to learn from this history and *have* learned from it. Now it is time for them to instruct their governments on how to do so. If they act, they can show the world.

Notes

Chapter 1

1. *Report of Commissioner, U.S. Fish and Fisheries, 1872–73* (Washington, D.C.: U.S. Government Printing Office, 1874), 26–32.
2. Susan R. Martin, "The State of Our Knowledge about Ancient Copper Mining in Michigan," *The Michigan Archaeologist* 41, no. 2–3 (1995): 120.
3. Charles E. Cleland, "The Inland Shore Fishery of the Northern Great Lakes: Its Development and Importance in Prehistory," *American Antiquity* 47, no. 4 (October 1982): 781.
4. Harlan Hatcher, *The Great Lakes* (London: Oxford University Press, 1944), 53. Another version of Champlain's arrival at Georgian Bay implies a greater sense of wonder. In this telling of the tale, he is said to have written in his now-vanished journal, "Because of its great size, I named it Freshwater Sea." See Phil Weller, *Fresh Water Seas: Saving the Great Lakes* (Toronto: Between the Lines, 1990), 31.
5. Jerrold Rodesch, "Jean Nicolet," in *Voyageur,* the historical review of Brown County and Northeast Wisconsin, spring 1984, http://www.uwgb.edu/wisfrench/library/articles/nicolet.htm, accessed May 2003.
6. John Parker, "The Great Lakes and the Great Rivers: Jonathan Carver's Dream of Empire," (Lansing, Mich.: Historical Society of Michigan, 1965), 5.
7. William Ashworth, *The Late, Great Lakes: An Environmental History* (New York: Alfred Knopf, 1986), 38.
8. Grace Lee Nute, *The Voyageur* (St. Paul: Minnesota Historical Society, 1995), vii.
9. Raymond Seitz, review of Alex Madsen, *John Jacob Astor: America's First Multimillionaire, [London] Sunday Telegraph,* 10 June 2001.
10. Arthur D. Howden Smith, *John Jacob Astor: Landlord of New York* (Philadelphia: J. B. Lippincott, 1929), 292.
11. Phil Weller, *Fresh Water Seas: Saving the Great Lakes* (Toronto: Between the Lines, 1990), 34.
12. Ohio and Michigan each approved "war budgets" of over $300,000 before the dispute was settled, but the only casualty was a stab wound inflicted in a bar brawl between an Ohio warrior and a Michigan sheriff.

13. Richard S. Lambert and Paul Pross, *Renewing Nature's Wealth: A Centennial History of the Public Management of Lands, Forests and Wildlife in Ontario, 1763–1976* (Toronto: Hunter Rose, 1967), 16.
14. U.S. Commissioner of Fish and Fisheries, *Report of Commissioner 1872–1873* (Washington, D.C.: Government Printing Office, 1874), 10.
15. Ibid, 72.
16. Sharon Hanshue, personal communication with author, 22 May 2002.
17. Eric Slater, "Have Spear, Will Wait in Wisconsin; In an Ice Hole in a Lake Lurks a Holy Grail of Anglers: Sturgeon," *Los Angeles Times,* 13 March 1999.
18. Sharon Hanshue, personal communication with author, 22 May 2002.
19. Eric Sharp, "Sturgeon Jumps into Boat, Stuns Anglers," *Detroit Free Press,* 30 August 2001.

Chapter 2

1. Louise Phelps Kellogg, ed., *Early Narratives of the Northwest 1634–1699* (New York: Charles Scribner's Sons, 1917), 207.
2. Charles Lanman, *A Summer in the Wilderness: Embracing a Canoe Voyage up the Mississippi and Around Lake Superior* (New York: D. Appleton and Company, 1847), 159.
3. State of Michigan, *First Report of the State Commissioners and Superintendent on State Fisheries for 1873–4* (Lansing: W. S. George and Co., 1875), appendix.
4. Margaret Beattie Bogue, *Fishing the Great Lakes: An Environmental History, 1783–1933* (Madison: University of Wisconsin Press, 2000), 175.
5. Lambert and Pross, *Renewing Nature's Wealth,* 151.
6. Samuel Wilmot, *Report of Samuel Wilmot, Esquire, on the Several Fish-Breeding Establishments and Fish-Culture in Canada, during the Season of 1877. Appendix No. 2: Report on Fish-Breeding in the Dominion of Canada 1877. Tenth Annual Report of the Department of Marine and Fisheries, Being for the Fiscal Year Ended 30th June, 1877* (Ottawa: MacLean, Roger and Company, 1878), 16.
7. A. B. McCullough, *The Commercial Fishery of the Canadian Great Lakes* (Ottawa: Environment Canada, 1989), 83.
8. Bogue, *Fishing the Great Lakes,* 189.
9. McCullough, *The Commercial Fishery of the Canadian Great Lakes,* 153.
10. Bogue, *Fishing the Great Lakes,* 180.
11. U.S. Commissioner of Fish and Fisheries, *Report of Commissioner, U.S. Fish and Fisheries, 1872–73* (Washington, D.C.: U.S. Government Printing Office, 1874), 14–16.

12. Bela Hubbard, *Memorials of a Half-Century in Michigan and the Lake Region* (New York: Putnam, 1888), 276–77.
13. Russell W. Brown, Mark Ebener, and Tom Gorenflo, *Great Lakes Fisheries Management: A Binational Perspective,* ed. William W. Taylor and C. Paola Ferreri (East Lansing: Michigan State University Press, 1999), 316.
14. Ibid., 314.
15. Bogue points out that the "big four" of Great Lakes fish—whitefish, trout, herring, and sturgeon—declined from 74 percent of the total catch in 1880 to 63 percent in 1903. Even bigger changes were coming (Bogue, *Fishing the Great Lakes,* 169–70).
16. Neil S. Forkey, "Maintaining a Great Lakes Fishery: The State, Science and the Case of Ontario's Bay of Quinte, 1870–1920," *Ontario History* 87, no. 1 (spring 1995): 45–64.
17. Marks, *The Great Lakes and the Fish Commissions,* abstract.
18. Henry A. Regier and W. I. Hartman, "Lake Erie's Fish Community 150 Years of Cultural Stresses," *Science* 180, no. 4092 (22 June 1973): 1251.
19. Marks, *The Great Lakes and the Fish Commissions*, 9.
20. Ibid.
21. The fish culturists sought to defend the increasingly unpopular carp. In 1897 the Michigan Board of Fish Commissioners challenged the "mistaken idea" that the carp "is a scavenger and uncleanly in habit. . . . With greater propriety might this criticism be applied to the hog, whose habit as to uncleanliness is proverbial, and yet pork is one of our chief articles of daily diet in some form or another." Michigan State Board of Fish Commissioners, *Twelfth Biennial Report* (Lansing: Robert Smith Printing, 1897), 18.
22. Regier and Hartman, "Lake Erie's Fish Community," 1251.
23. Ibid.
24. Anna Jameson, *Winter Studies and Summer Rambles in Canada,* vol. 1 (New York: n.d., 1837), 295, quoted in Lambert and Pross, *Renewing Nature's Wealth,* 1–2.
25. Donald J. Pisani, "Fish Culture and the Dawn of Concern over Water Pollution in the United States," *Environmental Review* 8, no. 2 (summer 1984): 121.
26. Bogue, *Fishing the Great Lakes,* 193.
27. Ibid., 244.
28. Vernon C. Applegate, "The Sea Lamprey in the Great Lakes," *Scientific Monthly* 72, no. 5 (May 1951): 276.
29. B. R. Smith and J. J. Tibbles, "Sea Lamprey in Lakes Huron, Michigan,

and Superior: History of Invasion and Control, 1936–78," *Canadian Journal of Fisheries and Aquatic Sciences* 37, n0.11 (November 1980): 1786–87.

30. "Convention on Great Lakes Fisheries between the United States of America and Canada," 10 September 1954, article IV (d), http://www.glfc.org/pubs/conv.htm, accessed 21 December 2003.
31. Carlos M. Fetterolf Jr., "Why a Great Lakes Fishery Commission and Why a Sea Lamprey International Symposium," *Canadian Journal of Fisheries and Aquatic Sciences* 37, no. 11 (November 1980): 1591.
32. U.S. Fish and Wildlife Service, *Recovery Plan for the Pitcher's Thistle (cirsium pitcheri),* prepared by the Pitcher's thistle recovery team for Region 3, U.S. Fish and Wildlife Service, Fort Snelling, Minnesota, 20 September 2002, 6.
33. Chris Shafer, personal communication with author, 17 September 2001.

Chapter 3

1. Martin R. Kaatz, "The Black Swamp: A Study in Historical Geography," *Annals of the Association of American Geographers* 45, no. 1 (March 1955): 17.
2. Ibid., 32.
3. Albert H. Tiplin, *Our Romantic Niagara: A Geological History of the River and the Falls* (Niagara Falls, Ont.: Niagara Parks Commission, 1990), 27–32.
4. Margaret Fuller, "Summer on the Lakes, in 1843: Chapter 1, Niagara," *Organization and Environment* 13, no. 3 (September 2000): 329.
5. Alfred Runte, "Beyond the Spectacular: The Niagara Falls Preservation Campaign," *New York Historical Society Quarterly* 57 (January 1973): 35.
6. Gerald Killan, "Mowat and a Park Policy for Niagara Falls, 1873–1887," *Ontario History* 70, no. 2 (June 1978): 116.
7. The story of the creation of the Canadian park is well told by Gerald Killan in *Protected Places: A History of Ontario's Provincial Parks System* (Toronto: Dundurn Press, 1993), 2–5.
8. Reversing the position of his Republican predecessor, New York governor Grover Cleveland responded to the campaign to protect Niagara Falls by signing into law a bill authorizing a park on 30 April 1883, but it was not until 1885 that an appropriation to support the park was secured and the park opened on 15 July of that year.
9. Killian, "Mowat and a Park Policy for Niagara Falls," 130.
10. Ibid., 131.
11. Ibid., 132.

12. "Niagara Falls History of Power," http://www.iaw.com/~falls/power.html, accessed 16 January 2002.
13. Niagara Parks Commission, http://www.niagaraparks.com, accessed January 2002.
14. Patrick McGreevey, "Imagining the Future at Niagara Falls," *Annals of the Association of American Geographers* 77, no. 1 (1987): 52–53.
15. David Germain, "There's No Love Lost for Entrepreneur Who Envisioned Model City," *Los Angeles Times,* 16 May 1993.
16. "Genius at the Cutting Edge," *[London] Sunday Telegraph,* 6 May 2001.
17. "L.A. Then and Now: Home to Man on Cutting Edge of Shaving," *Los Angeles Times,* 31 March 2002.
18. Chatham-Kent Ontario, http://www.city.chatham-kent.on.ca.
19. Killan, "Mowat and a Park Policy for Niagara Falls," 17.
20. However, in petitions to both Canadian premier John Thompson and Ontario premier Oliver Mowat dated 26 January 1894, the Kent County Council did suggest public support for protecting Rondeau "in a state of primeval forests" and said the site should be preserved "in all its natural grandeur."
21. By 1996 the Ontario population had been reduced to no more than twenty birds, and the species jumped from being "vulnerable" to "endangered" in Canada. Efforts to restore the species in Canada began in 1997. In 1998 the adult population was estimated to consist of up to seventeen mated pairs. See http://www.bsc-eoc.org/prowmain.html.
22. Janet Foster, *Working for Wildlife: The Beginning of Preservation in Canada* (Toronto: University of Toronto Press, 1978), 194. Taverner, a Canadian citizen educated at the University of Michigan, became staff ornithologist at the National Museum of Canada and published books that became standard works in Canadian ornithology.
23. See http://parkscanada.pch.gc.ca/pn-np/on/pelee/natcul/natcu12_3_e.asp#, accessed 7 October 2003.
24. Janet Foster, *Working for Wildlife: The Beginning of Preservation in Canada.* (Toronto: University of Toronto Press, 1978), 81.
25. "Delicate Ecosystem, Heavy Industry," *Christian Science Monitor,* 14 March 1994: 11.
26. Samuel J. Taylor, "Michigan City in 1836," *Society in America* 1 (1837): 256–57, reproducing an account of stage travel by Harriet Martineau from Detroit to Chicago. Quoted in Alfred H. Meyer, "Circulation and Settlement Patterns of the Calumet Region of Northwest Indiana and Northeast Illinois," *Annals of the Association of American Geographers* 46, no. 3 (September 1956): 319.

27. Kay Franklin and Norma Schaeffer, *Duel for the Dunes: Land Use Conflict on the Shores of Lake Michigan* (Urbana and Chicago: University of Illinois Press, 1983), 12–14.
28. Ibid., 17.
29. Wille, Lois; *Forever Open, Clear, and Free: The Struggle for Chicago's Lakefront, 2d ed.* (Chicago: University of Chicago Press, 1991).
30. Ibid., 81.
31. Ibid., xv.
32. First expressed in his Ph.D. dissertation at the University of Chicago, "The Ecological Relations of the Vegetation on the Sand Dunes of Lake Michigan" (1898).
33. Stephen T. Mather, "Report on the Proposed Sand Dunes National Park Indiana, Including Transcript of Hearing Held October, 30 1916," (Washington, D.C.: Government Printing Office, 1917).
34. Franklin and Schaeffer, *Duel for the Dunes,* 41.
35. Earl H. Reed, *The Dune Country* (New York: John Lane Company, 1916), 17.
36. E. Stillman Bailey, *The Sand Dunes of Indiana: The Story of an American Wonderland Told by Camera and Pen* (Chicago: A. C. McClurg and Company, 1924), 15.
37. Stephen T. Mather, U.S. Department of the Interior, *Report on the Proposed Sand Dunes National Park Indiana,* (Washington, D.C.: Government Printing Office, 1917), 44.
38. Franklin and Schaeffer, *Duel for the Dunes,* 43.
39. Ibid., 42.
40. Franklin and Schaeffer, *Duel for the Dunes,* 93.
41. Ibid., 129.
42. Paul H. Douglas, *In the Fullness of Time: The Memoirs of Paul H. Douglas* (New York: Harcourt Brace Jovanovich, 1971), 537–38.
43. John B. Oakes, "Conservation: Indiana Dunes Imperiled," *The New York Times,* 1 June 1958.
44. Franklin and Schaeffer, *Duel for the Dunes,* 172–73.
45. "Dunes Owe Group a Debt of Gratitude," *Detroit Free Press,* 17 June 2002.
46. J. Ronald Engel, *Sacred Sands: The Struggle for Community in the Indiana Dunes* (Middletown, Conn.: Wesleyan University Press, 1983), 294.
47. Andrew Hurley, *Environmental Inequalities: Class, Race and Industrial Pollution in Gary, Indiana, 1945–1980* (Chapel Hill: University of North Carolina Press, 1995), 123.

48. "Congressman Urges Action to Save Shoreline for Public," (Associated Press), 9 September 2002, Lexis Nexis.
49. Michigan House of Representatives, *Report of the State Geologist,* 26 January 1838, H. Doc. 24.
50. Quoted in Vicki Urbanik, "Alice Gray, Woman of the Dunes," *Chesterton Tribune,* http://www.chestertontribune.com/Local%20History/alice_gray.htm.
51. David Hoppe, "Child of the Northwest Wind," *Traces of Indiana and Midwestern History: A Publication of the Indiana Historical Society* 9, no. 2 (spring 1997): 26.
52. Eugene W. Flack, "Six Foot, Two Inch Caveman Wins Dunes' Diana," *Chicago Herald-Examiner,* 27 June 1920.
53. "Death Takes 'Diana of the Dunes' From the Scenes She Loved and Cloaks Forever the Motive for Her Desire for Primal Life," *Gary Post Tribune,* 9 February 1925.
54. Hoppe, "Child of the Northwest Wind," 25.

Chapter 4

1. Martin V. Melosi, *The Sanitary City: Urban Infrastructure in America from Colonial Times to the Present* (Baltimore: Johns Hopkins University Press, 2000), 95.
2. Michigan State Board of Health, *Sixth Annual Report of the State Board of Heatlh of the State of Michigan* (Lansing, Mich.: W.S. George and Co., 1878), 10.
3. George A. Johnson, as quoted in ibid., 81.
4. Jennifer Read, "'A Sort of Destiny': The Multi-Jurisdictional Response to Sewage Pollution in the Great Lakes, 1900–1930," *Scientia Canadensis* 22–23, no. 52 (2002): 110.
5. International Joint Commission, *Final Report on the Pollution of Boundary Waters Reference* (Washington, D.C.: U.S. Government Printing Office, 1918), 21.
6. Ibid., 32.
7. Ibid., 43–44.
8. Ibid., 50.
9. In its 1918 report, the IJC also considered the question of industrial pollution of the boundary waters: "The immensity of the boundary waters, and their consequent capacity for dilution, will probably for some time to come prevent pollution from this source other than sawmill and pulp mill wastes becoming an international question" (ibid, 46.). However, the

commission's proposed treaty would have given it authority to investigate and set standards to control industrial wastes as well.

10. "Canal Purifies Water in Chicago River," *New York Times,* 14 January 1900.
11. Melosi, *The Sanitary City,* 147. "Toronto's Water Supply," http://www.lostrivers.ca/points/watersupply.htm, accessed 11 October 2003.
12. Case Western Reserve University and Western Reserve Historical Society, "Sanitation," *The Encyclopedia of Cleveland History,* http://ech.cwru.edu/, accessed 11 October 2003.
13. Tom Davey, *Recollections of Water Pollution Control in Ontario* (Aurora, Ont.: Pollution Control Association of Ontario, 1985), 14.
14. Read, "'A Sort of Destiny,'" 122.
15. Frank N. Egerton, *Overfishing or Pollution? Case History of a Controversy on the Great Lakes: Technical Report No. 41* (Ann Arbor, Mich.: Great Lakes Fishery Commission, 1985), 8.
16. Barry Boyer, "A Polluted River Comes Back," (Buffalo: New York Water Environment Association, 2002), 10.
17. Bay Area Restoration Council, *Hamilton Harbour Remedial Action Plan,* http://www.hamiltonharbour.ca/rap/rap_a1.html.
18. "7 Feared Dead in Big Wave," *Chicago Sunday Tribune,* 27 June 1954.
19. Gary Wisby, "Falling Lake Levels Giving Some a Lift," *Chicago Sun Times,* 2 July 2001.
20. Kathleen Kenna, "Record Great Lakes Levels a 'Time Bomb' Group Says," *Toronto Star,* 4 March 1986.
21. Lori Hall Steele, "Low Water Spurs Mucky Sand, Lament," *Traverse City Record Eagle,* 25 August 2002.
22. Michigan State University Extension, "Protecting Wetlands Along the Great Lakes Shoreline," *Extension Bulletin,* E-2751, April 2001.
23. Ibid.

Chapter 5

1. Ohio Department of Natural Resources, Division of Water, *Lake Erie Pollution Survey: Final Report* (Columbus, Ohio: Ohio Department of Natural Resources, 1953), 13.
2. See, for example, Alfred M. Beeton, *Limnological Survey of Lake Erie 1959 and 1960: Technical Report No. 6* (Great Lakes Fishery Commission, 1963) http://www.glfc.org/pubs/TechReports/Tr06.pdf, accessed 21 December 2003.
3. Alfred M. Beeton, "Eutrophication of the St. Lawrence Great Lakes," *Limnology and Oceanography* 10, no. 2 (April 1965): 244.

4. H. A. Regier and W. L. Hartman, "Lake Erie's Fish Community: 150 Years of Cultural Stresses," *Science* 180, no. 4092 (22 June 1973): 1248–55.
5. "War on Bacteria May Provide Safe Swimming Area in Lake," *Cleveland Press,* 12 May 1964.
6. Terence Kehoe, *Cleaning Up the Great Lakes: From Cooperation to Confrontation* (De Kalb: Northern Illinois Press, 1997): 61.
7. "David Blaushild, Concerned Citizen," *Clevelander* (summer 1970): 23.
8. Kehoe, *Cleaning Up the Great Lakes,* 62.
9. Betty Klaric, "Debris and Oil from Sewers Beach Boaters," *Cleveland Press,* 27 May 1965.
10. "Rhodes Snubs Blaushild's Anti-Pollution Petitions," *Cleveland Press,* 19 February 1965.
11. Betty Klaric, "Public Tells Officials: Act Now on Pollution," 5 August 1965.
12. "Funds Called Key to Lakes Cleanup," *Cleveland Plain Dealer,* 11 May 1965.
13. "Clean Lakes Authority Is Rhodes' Aim," *Cleveland Plain Dealer,* 11 May 1965.
14. Edith Chase, personal communication with the author, 25 September 2002.
15. "Clem and Pollution—A Curious Pair," *Cleveland Press,* 18 September 1964.
16. "Catalyst for a Cleaner Lake," *Cleveland Plain Dealer,* 3 August 1965.
17. The fire was cited by members of Congress, the public, and news media for the next three years, leading up to the enactment of the U.S. Clean Water Act in October 1972.
18. Ontario's Water Resources Commission, created in 1956, had already consolidated all aspects of water-resource management into one agency and did not undergo immediate change. But in 1972, with the OWRC under fire for failing to advocate strong actions to correct water pollution, it would be folded into the province's new Ministry of Natural Resources.
19. "U.S. Files Suit against U.S. Steel and DuPont in Indiana," U.S. EPA press release, 19 February 1971.
20. Henry S. Reuss, *When Government Was Good: Memories of a Life in Politics* (Madison: University of Wisconsin Press, 1999), 77.
21. Jennifer Read, "Let Us Heed the Voice of Youth: Laundry Detergents, Phosphates and the Emergence of the Environmental Movement in Ontario," *Journal of the Canadian Historical Association* 7 (1996): 245.

Read's research and analysis of the origins of the modern environmental movement in Ontario is superior.

22. Ibid., 250.
23. International Joint Commission, *Pollution of Lake Erie, Lake Ontario and the International Section of the St. Lawrence River* (Washington, D.C.; Ottawa, Ont.: International Joint Commission, 1970), 136, 143.
24. See, for example, "Down the Drain," *Cleveland Press,* 11 June 1964.
25. William McGucken, *Lake Erie Rehabilitated: Controlling Cultural Eutrophication, 1960s–1990s* (Akron, Ohio: University of Akron Press, 2000), 125.
26. Ohio did not enact a detergent phosphorus restriction until early 1988, facing determined opposition from the industry throughout even this late debate.
27. McGucken, *Lake Erie Rehabilitated,* 264–65.
28. "Average Guy Takes a Poke at Pollution—He's Winning," *Cleveland Press,* 23 September 1971.
29. Roger Brown, "1969 River Blaze Scarred Image," *Cleveland Plain Dealer,* 2 August 1989.
30. Roger Brown, "1969 River Blaze Scarred Image," *Cleveland Plain Dealer,* 18 June 1989.
31. Betty Klaric, "Stokes Promises to Lead Pollution Fight," *Cleveland Press,* 24 June 1969, D3.
32. "The Cities: The Price of Optimism," *Time,* 1 August 1969, 41.
33. Francis X. Clines, "Navigating the Renaissance of an Ohio River That Once Caught Fire," *The New York Times,* 23 January 2000.
34. Cleveland State University, "Cuyahoga River Online Exhibition," http://web.ulib.csuohio.edu/speccoll/croe.
35. "Cleveland as a Naval Depot: Report of Committee of Citizens," http://web.ulib.csuohio.edu/speccoll/croe/naval.html.
36. "The Cities: The Price of Optimism," 41.
37. Ibid.

Chapter 6

1. Ruins of the canal are still visible in Macomb County, Michigan.
2. See Ohio History Central, http://www.ohiohistorycentral.org/ohc/nature/geograph/using/lakes.shtml.
3. Canal Corridor Association, http://www.canalcor.org, accessed 11 October 2003.
4. Libby Hill, *The Chicago River: A Natural and Unnatural History,* (Chicago: Lake Claremont Press, 2000), 68.

5. The Welland Canal section of the St. Lawrence Seaway, http://www.greatlakes-seaway.com/en/pdf/welland.pdf.
6. U.S. Army Corps of Engineers, Detroit District, "The History of the Soo Locks," http://huron.lre.usace.army.mil/SOO/lockhist.html.
7. Irene D. Neu, "The Building of the Sault Canal, 1852–1855," *The Mississippi Historical Review* 40, no. 1 (June 1953): 44.
8. John H. Hayford, "The Best Use of the Waters of the Great Lakes," *Scientific Monthly* 19, no. 6 (December 1924): 588–97.
9. Philip W. Henry, "The Great Lakes–St. Lawrence Waterway," *Geographical Review* 17, no. 2 (April 1927): 276.
10. Great Lakes–St. Lawrence Seaway System, http://www.greatlakes-seaway.com/en/aboutus/seaway_history.html.
11. Ronald Reagan, "Year of the St. Lawrence Seaway and St. Lawrence Seaway Day, 1984, Proclamation 5221," *Federal Register* 49 (13 January 1984): 28537.
12. Cornell University Extension and Sea Grant, "The Lake Ontario Salmon Fishery," http://www.dnr.cornell.edu/ext/fish/salmon.htm.
13. William I. Aron and Stanford H. Smith, "Ship Canals and Aquatic Ecosystems," *Science* 174, no. 4004 (1 October 1971): 14.
14. Meg Jones, "Alewives a Bigger Stink Than Usual," *Milwaukee Journal Sentinel,* 29 June 1999.
15. Ben East, "The Risen Giant?" *Outdoor Life,* June 1969, 47.
16. Douglas Dodge, interview by author, 29 July 2002.
17. E. L. Mills, et al., "Exotic Species in the Great Lakes: A History of Biotic Crises and Anthropogenic Introductions," *Journal of Great Lakes Research* 19 (1993): 1–54.
18. "Marauding Mollusks Terrorize Great Lakes," *Newsweek,* 20 November 1989, 66.
19. "Alien Fish Species in Lakes Worry Environmentalists," *Journal of Commerce,* 6 July 1989.
20. "Lake Erie Pest May Be Trouble for Anglers, Fish," *Akron Beacon Journal,* 30 October 2001.
21. "Exotic Fish Species Discovered in Lake Superior," *Environmental News Network,* 19 October 2001.
22. Bernard J. Hansen, chairman, U.S. section, Great Lakes Fishery Commission, to U.S. representatives Sonny Callahan and Pete Visclosky, 19 June 2002.
23. "Canada Eyes a Pipeline of Sorts to Arid America," *Detroit Free Press,* 19 May 1985.
24. Richard M. Spencer, "Winter Navigation on the Great Lakes and St.

Lawrence Seaway: A Study in Congressional Decision Making" (master's thesis, Cornell University, 1992), 19–20.

25. Ibid., 47–48.
26. Ibid., 50–51.
27. Ibid., 79–80.
28. Wayne Schmidt, "Observations on Michigan's Environmental History," manuscript given to author, 3 January 2000.
29. Spencer, "Winter Navigation," 197.
30. Judith D. Soule, "Biodiversity of Michigan's Great Lakes Islands: Knowledge, Threats, and Protection," *Report for Land and Water Management Division, Michigan Department of Natural Resources,* 5 April 1993, iii.
31. "Lake Erie Water Snakes: An Endangered Species Designation May Be All That Saves Gray Reptile," *Cleveland Plain Dealer,* 25 August 1996, 6.
32. Karen E. Vigmostad, ed., *State of the Great Lakes Islands: Proceedings from the 1996 U.S.–Canada Great Lakes Workshop,* (East Lansing: Michigan State University Department of Resource Development, 1999), 113.
33. Ibid.

Chapter 7

1. Henry A. Regier, "Ecosystem Integrity in a Context of Ecostudies as Related to the Great Lakes Region," in *Perspectives on Ecological Integrity,* ed. L. Westra and J. Lemons (Netherlands: Kluwer Academic Publishers, 1995), 88–101.
2. Stephen Bocking, "Visions of Nature and Society," *Alternatives* 20, no. 3 (1994): 12.
3. Ibid., 15.
4. Rachel A. Carson, *Silent Spring* (Boston: Houghton Mifflin, 1962), 189.
5. "Joint Statement of Agreement by Lake Michigan Basin States: Illinois, Indiana, Michigan, and Wisconsin; Policy on Protection of the Lake Michigan Environment from Uncontrolled Use of Resistant Pesticides and Similar Economic Poisons," undated, State of Michigan Archives.
6. Statement by Ralph A. MacMullan, director, Michigan Department of Conservation, Public Hearing Concerning House Bill 3911, Lansing, Mich., 6 April 1968, document in author's collection.
7. Statement of the West Michigan Council on Environmental Action on House Bill 3911 to the House Committee on Conservation and Recreation, ibid.
8. Editorial, *Ann Arbor News,* 23 April 1969.
9. Lynton K. Caldwell, "The Ecosystem as a Criterion for Public Land Policy," *Natural Resources Journal* 10, no. 2 (April 1970): 206–7.

10. Terrance Kehoe, *Cleaning up the Great Lakes: From Cooperation to Confrontation* (DeKalb: Northern Illinois University Press, 1997), 94.
11. On page 101, Kehoe notes a nationwide U.S. poll showing that between 1965 and 1970, the proportion of respondents who believed water pollution was a very or somewhat serious problem increased from 35 to 74 percent.
12. "Stanley P. Spisiak, 80, Dies; Jeweler Was Devoted to Conservation Efforts," *Buffalo News,* 13 August 1996.
13. Paul Culhane, "LMF's Silver Anniversary," *Lake Michigan Monitor,* 1995, 4.
14. Ibid., 5.
15. "Earth Day Is No Longer a Street Scene," *Chemical Week,* 23 April 1975.
16. Thomas F. Bastow, *This Vast Pollution . . .* (Washington, D.C.: Green Field Books, 1986), 5.
17. Bastow, *This Vast Pollution . . .*, 8.
18. Ibid., 17–18.
19. Ibid., 28–29.
20. Ibid., 41.
21. David W. Hacker, "A Housewife Battles the Giants to Save a Great Lake's Beauty," *National Observer,* 18 December 1971.
22. "The Lady of Lake Superior," *Newsweek,* 29 October 1984.
23. Hacker, "A Housewife Battles the Giants . . ."
24. Bastow, *This Vast Pollution . . .*, 189.
25. Lois Marie Gibbs, "Learning from Love Canal: A 20th Anniversary Retrospective," 2003.
26. Ibid.
27. Most of this amount was recovered in a lawsuit against Occidental Chemical.
28. Rachel's Hazardous Waste News no. 186, "Niagara River Part 1: How Industry Survived Love Canal," 20 June 1990, http://www.ejnet.org/rachel/rhwn186.htm.
29. "An Ambitious Goal," *MacLean's,* 17 September 1990.
30. "Town's Protectors Don't Mind Being Called Cranks," *National Post,* 19 July 1999.
31. "In Fight against Pollution, the Great Lakes Get a New Lease on Life," *U.S. News and World Report,* 27 September 1976, 51.
32. International Joint Commission, Great Lakes Water Quality Agreement of 1978, http://www.ijc.org/agree/quality.html#agrm.
33. Great Lakes Research Advisory Board, "The Ecosystem Approach: Scope and Implications of an Ecosystem Approach to Transboundary Problems

in the Great Lakes Basin," special report to the International Joint Commission, Windsor, Ont., July 1978, document in author's collection.
34. Ibid.
35. *A Celebration of Great Lakes United, 1982–1992* (Buffalo, N.Y.: Great Lakes United, 1992), 3.
36. "Great Lakes Compact Aims to Protect Water: States, Canada Fear Thirsty Sun Belt," *Washington Post,* 12 February 1985.
37. "The Deteriorating Great Lakes," *MacLean's,* 26 August 1985.
38. Jennifer G. Read, "A Progressive Institution in the Environmental Era: The International Joint Commission and the Challenges of the 21st Century," undated, in author's collection.
39. Lee Botts and Paul Muldoon, "The Great Lakes Water Quality Agreement: Its Past Successes and Uncertain Future" (a project sponsored by the International Institute on Environmental Governance, Dartmouth College, 1996), 57–58, http://www.on.ec.gc.ca/glwqa/glreport-5-e.html.
40. Gordon K. Durnil, *The Making of a Conservative Environmentalist* (Bloomington: Indiana University Press, 1995), 125.
41. International Joint Commission, Sixth Biennial Report, http://www.ijc.org/comm/6bre.html#chap4.
42. "Their Goal: Restore Superior; Coalition Wants 'Zero Discharge' for Lake," *Wisconsin State Journal,* 18 December 1994.
43. "Great Lakes Agency Losing Headway Fast," *Toronto Star,* 15 November 1997.
44. J. R. Vallentyne, "Infusing Ecology into Politics," *Aquatic Ecosystem Health and Management* 2, n0.2 (June 1999): 83.
45. Ibid., 12.
46. Ibid., 13.
47. Ibid., 13.
48. Ibid., 13.
49. Rashne Baetz, "An Environmental Pioneer Fights On," *Hamilton Spectator,* 29 May 1996.
50. J. R. Vallentyne, "The Egosystem and the Ecosystem," lecture, Trent University, Peterborough (Ontario, Canada), 22 November 1994, http://www.trentu.ca/ers/sheperd/lecture3.html, accessed 21 December 2003.
51. Vallentyne, "Infusing Ecology into Politics," 20.
52. Ibid.
53. J. R. Vallentyne, "We Can't Grow on Like This," *Hamilton Spectator,* 10 November 1998.
54. Vallentyne, "Infusing Ecology into Politics," 21.

Chapter 8

1. Bio-environmental Services Limited, "The Presence and Implications of Foreign Organisms in Ship Ballast Waters Discharged into the Great Lakes," prepared for the Water Pollution Control Directorate, Environmental Protection Service, Environment Canada, (Georgetown, Ont.: March 1981), vii.
2. Darcy Henton, "Ottawa Ignored Zebra Mussel Warning, Scientist Says," *Toronto Star,* 2 October 1989.
3. Ibid.
4. "Zebra Mussels Kill Tiny Animal: Key Link in Food Chain Wiped Out, Study Says," *Detroit Free Press,* 19 October 2001.
5. "Alien Species Poised to Hit Lakes: Invasive Critters Found in Sludge at Bottom of Ships' Ballast Tanks," *St. Catherines Standard,* 15 March 2002. The article reported on research at the University of Windsor suggesting that tiny eggs of waterborne creatures could survive in the unpumpable sludge by remaining dormant until mixed with fresh water.
6. Eric Reeves, "Exotic Politics: An Analysis of the Law and Politics of Exotic Invasions of the Great Lakes," *Toledo Journal of Great Lakes Science and Policy* 2, no. 125 (spring 2000): 145. Reeves's analysis of the failure of the U.S. and Canadian governments to respond swiftly and decisively to the threat of exotic species invasions facilitated by ballast water should be a seminal document for study by all scholars of Great Lakes history and policy.
7. Ibid., 147. Citing Margaret Dochoda of the Great Lakes Fishery Commission, Reeves names the six post-1989 invaders as the tubenose goby, the round goby, the quagga mussel, the New Zealand mud snail, the amphipod *Echingoammarus ischnus,* and the cladoceran water flea.
8. Ibid., 158.
9. Murray Edelman, "Symbols and Political Quiescence," *American Political Science Review* 54, no. 3 (September 1960): 702.
10. Reeves, "Exotic Politics," 127.
11. "Zero Discharge Sought by Citizens at International Great Lakes Meeting," Greenpeace press release, *PR Newswire,* 23 September 1991.
12. U.S. Environmental Protection Agency and Environment Canada, "A Bi-National Program to Restore and Protect the Lake Superior Basin," September 1991.
13. "Bid Launched to Keep Lake Superior Pristine," *Toronto Star,* 1 October 1991.
14. Gayle Coyer and Mark Van Putten, "Saving Lake Superior," *Forum* (July/August 1992): 15.

15. Editorial, "Lake Superior: It Has Inspired Awe, But Not Enough Protective Efforts," *Detroit Free Press,* 27 November 1994.
16. "A Bi-National Program to Restore and Protect the Lake Superior Basin, September 1991, 4–5.
17. John Myers, "More Protective Designation Sought for Lake Superior," *Duluth News Tribune,* 17 September 1997.
18. Ibid.
19. "Ontario Out to Sink Pollution Law," *Toronto Star,* 26 July 1996.
20. Lake Superior Alliance, "10 Years of 0: The Lake Superior Alliance Reports on the First Decade of the Lake Superior Binational Program," October 2001, 9.
21. Ibid.
22. John Engler to Evan Bayh, Lansing, Mich., 3 April 1992.
23. "Word about Water Diversion Bottled Up by Engler Staff," *Grand Rapids Press,* 16 July 1993.
24. Evan Bayh to John Engler, 4 June 1993.
25. "Irrigation OK Hurts Engler," *Kalamazoo Gazette,* 18 July 1993.
26. Murray Edelman, *The Symbolic Uses of Politics* (Urbana: University of Illinois Press, 1967), 37.
27. Interview with author, 29 July 2002.
28. Joan Little, "Tories Earn Mixed Environment Reviews: Recent Announcements Hold Promise for Future," *Hamilton Spectator,* 8 April 1999.
29. "Ontario Premier Mike 'Chainsaw' Harris to Resign after Six Years in Office," *Canadian Press,* 17 October 2001.
30. Water Resources Research Institute, North Carolina State University, "Cryptosporidum: A Drinking Water Supply Problem," *Special Report No. 12,* November 1993, http://www.attorneygeneral.jus.gov.on.ca/english/about/pubs/walkerton/part1/WI_Title_pg_Contents.pdf, accessed 21 December 2003.
31. Dennis O'Connor, *Report of the Walkerton Inquiry: The Events of May 2000 and Related Issues. Part One: A Summary,* http://www.walkertoninquiry.com/report1/pdf/WI_Summary.pdf.
32. "A Boost for Safe Water: $500 Million to Be Spent over Two Years," Toronto Star, 18 June 2001.
33. U.S. EPA position paper on Great Lakes sport fish consumption advisory protocol, 29 February 1996.
34. John Engler to Robert Perciasepe, 5 February 1997.
35. "Chippewas Push Claim for Land in Canada," *New York Times,* 27 August 1995.

36. "Letter Suggests a Secret Agenda in Ipperwash Standoff," 4 September 2002, CBC News, http://www.cbc.ca/storyview/CBC/2002/09/04/ipperwash020904, accessed 13 October 2002.
37. Henry Regier, personal communication, "Comments on Draft New COA," 28 November 2001.
38. John Engler, "Governor Supports Upton and Abraham Bills to Restore True Great Lakes Definition," press release, 12 March 1998.
39. "Whitman Announces Environmental Plan for Great Lakes," (Associated Press), 2 April 2002, Lexis Nexis.
40. "Lakes Pollution: EPA Cleanup Plan Minus Money Equals Slim Results," *Detroit Free Press,* 6 April 2002.
41. U.S. General Accounting Office, *Great Lakes: An Overall Strategy and Indicators for Measuring Are Needed to Better Achieve Restoration Goals,* GAO-03–515, April 2003.
42. "A Great Lake Rises from Its Grave: Declared Officially Dead 25 Years Ago, Lake Erie Shows Real Progress toward a Partial Recovery, Thanks to Heroic Cleanup Measures," *Toronto Star,* 15 June 1991.
43. "The Shores of a Dilemma: Has Lake Erie Become Too Clean for Its Own Good?" *Citizen's Weekly,* 26 September 1999.
44. "Lake Erie's Health Again Facing Crisis," *Buffalo News,* 19 July 2002. "Low Erie Oxygen May Be from Clam," *Detroit News,* 8 August 2002.
45. "Lake Erie Fish Kill Puzzles Scientists," *Toronto Star,* 27 July 2002.
46. "Toxic Algae Thrive in Summer's Heat," *Toledo Blade,* 17 September 2002.
47. Roy Stein, e-mail to author, 15 August 2002.
48. "Scientists Question Health of Great Lakes in Wake of Lake Erie's Dead Zone," *Booth Newspapers,* 16 September 2002.
49. Kathleen Kenna, "Dioxin Has Been in River 10 Years, Official Says," *Toronto Star,* 4 November 1985.
50. "Pollution's Price," *Maclean's,* 3 March 1986, 13.
51. U.S. Environmental Protection Agency, "St. Clair River Area of Concern," http://www.epa.gov/glnpo/aoc/st-clair.html.
52. "Bug Larvae Draw Attention to Old Pollution," *Kalamazoo Gazette,* 16 December 2001.
53. Brian McAndrew and Richard Brennan, "Residents Ask: How Clean is the Valley?" *Toronto Star,* 24 February 2001.
54. McAndrew and Brennan, "How Clean is the Valley?" 1.
55. Deborah Van Burenk, "Toxic Blob Discovered in Themes," *London Free Press,* 29 September 1999, 56. David Flood, "Thunder Bay's Toxic Blob," *Superior Vision,* March 1997.

Chapter 9

1. Ontario Ministry of Finance, “Ontario Population Projections, 2001–2028,” July 2000, http://www.gov.on.ca/FIN/english/demographics/demog02e.htm#II2, accessed 13 October 2003.
2. Polly J. Hoppin, et al., *Reducing Reliance on Pesticides in Great Lakes Basin Agriculture* (World Wildlife Fund: Washington, D.C., 1997).
3. Peter J. Sousounis and George M. Albercook, “Potential Futures,” in *Preparing for Climate Change: The Potential Consequences of Climate Variability and Change, Great Lakes Overview,* a report of the Great Lakes Regional Assessment Group for the U.S. Global Change Research Program (Ann Arbor: University of Michigan, 2000), 19.
4. G. W. Kling et al., *Confronting Climate Change in the Great Lakes Region: Impacts on Our Communities and Ecosystems* (Cambridge, Mass.; Washington, D.C.: Union of Concerned Scientists and Ecological Society of America, 2003), 24.
5. Brent M. Lofgren et al., “Impacts, Challenges and Opportunities,” in *Preparing for Climate Change,* 34.
6. Lynn Henning, “Mild Winter Hinders Ice Anglers,” *Detroit News,* 13 January 2002.
7. Thomas Bevier, “Mackinac Winter Ferry Runs Made for the First Time,” *Detroit Free Press,* 26 March 2002.
8. “‘The Year They Cancelled Winter,’” *Toronto Star,* 28 January 2002.
9. “Chilling Results of Global Warming,” *Buffalo News,* 8 August 2002.
10. “EPA: Global Warming Will Heat Up Erie,” *Erie Times News,* 15 September 2002.
11. All facilities releasing more than one hundred thousand tons annually of carbon dioxide have been required to report their emissions since 1993, and legislation that became effective in 2000 broadens the reporting registry to include other greenhouse gases. See Barry Rabe, “Greenhouse and Statehouse: The Evolving State Role in Climate Change,” prepared for the Pew Center on Global Climate Change, September 2002.
12. Michigan Environmental Council, *Greening the Governments,* April 2002, http://www.mecprotects.org/greening.pdf.
13. “Rising Sea Levels Threaten Islands: Global Warming a Major Issue for Islanders Living on Pacific Atolls,” *Toronto Star,* 4 December 1997.
14. Stella Thomas, “Scarcity of Water Creates New Set of World Problems,” *Detroit News,* 4 June 2002.
15. “World Faces Crisis over Fresh Water,” *Hamilton Spectator,* 26 June 2002.
16. “Report Says Overpumping Keeps World Food Supply Stable,” September 1999.

17. Marq DeVilliers, *Water: The Fate of Our Most Precious Resource* (Boston: Houghton Mifflin, 2002), 12–13.
18. "It's Time to Consider Developing the Great Lakes Water Farm," *U.S. Water News,* April 1999.
19. "Water Wars Predicted in a Thirsty Nation," *American Bar Association Journal* 68, no. 1066 (September 1982).
20. William G. Milliken, governor of Michigan, *Addresses and Special Messages of Governor William G. Milliken, 1969–1982: Remarks at Great Lakes Water Resources Conference* (Lansing, Mich.: Office of the Governor, 1982), 137.
21. "Great Lakes Compact Aims to Protect Water; States, Canada Fear Thirsty Sun Belt," *Washington Post,* 11 February 1985.
22. International Great Lakes Diversions and Consumptive Uses Study Board, *Great Lakes Diversions and Consumptive Uses* (Burlington, Ont., and Chicago, Ill., 1981). Available from the International Joint Commission.
23. Arch MacKenzie, "Ottawa Says U.S. Can't Just Take Water," *Toronto Star,* 8 July 1988.
24. Ibid.
25. "Superior Is Ours, Legislator Protests," *Detroit Free Press,* 1 May 1998.
26. Ibid.
27. James S. Lochhead et al., *Report to the Council of Great Lakes Governors: Governing the Withdrawal of Water from the Great Lakes* (18 May 1999). Available from the Council of Great Lakes Governors.
28. Ibid.
29. Donald Tate and Geoff Harris for the International Joint Commission, *Water Demands in the United States Section of the Great Lakes Basin, 1985–2020,* March 2000, 50. Available from the International Joint Commission.
30. International Joint Commission, *Protection of the Waters of the Great Lakes: Final Report to the Governments of Canada and the United States, 22 February 2000* (Washington, D.C., and Ottawa, Ont.: International Joint Commission, 2000).
31. Council Of Great Lakes Governors, *The Great Lakes Charter Annex: A Supplementary Agreement to the Great Lakes Charter, June 18, 2001,* p. 2, http://www.cglg.org/1pdfs/annex2001.pdf, accessed 15 December 2003.
32. Memorandum, Office of the Great Lakes, Michigan Department of Environmental Quality, 13 September 2002), document in the author's collection.
33. Quoted in Michigan Land Use Institute, "State Senate Again Considers

Groundwater Protection," 12 March 2003, http://www.mlui.org/landwater/fullarticle.asp?fileid=16453, accessed 21 December 2003.

34. International Joint Commission, *Protection of the Waters of the Great Lakes,* 6.
35. "Seaway Idea Hits Wave of Resistance," *Toronto Globe and Mail,* 10 June 2002.
36. "Tossing a Life Preserver to a Great Lakes Industry," *Toronto Star,* 9 June 2002.
37. Statement by National Wildlife Federation before the St. Lawrence County Environmental Council (15 May 2002), document in author's collection.
38. Dennis Schornack and Herb Gray, International Joint Commission, to Colin Powell, U.S. secretary of state, and Bill Graham, Canadian minister of foreign affairs (5 July 2002), document in author's collection.
39. "Exotic Fish Pose Ecological Nightmare to Great Lakes," (Associated Press), 5 August 2002, Lexis Nexis.
40. Interview with author, 7 February 2002.
41. Paul MacClennan, "IJC Watchdog Turning into a Lapdog," *Buffalo News,* 29 September 1996.
42. Environmental Law Institute, *An Evaluation of the Effectiveness of the International Joint Commission* (Washington, D.C.: Environmental Law Institute, 1995).
43. Ibid., 60.
44. Great Lakes Commission, *The Great Lakes Program to Ensure Environmental and Economic Prosperity: Great Lakes Commission Priorities to "Restore the Greatness," 107th Congress, Second Session,* March 2002. See section on pages 7 and 8 entitled, "Enhancing the Commercial and Recreational Value of Our Waterways," http://www.glc.org/docs/GLprogram2002.pdf.
45. Ibid.
46. Convention on Great Lakes Fisheries between the United States of America and Canada, 10 September 1954, http://www.glfc.org/pubs/conv.htm.
47. Johanne Gelinas, *A Legacy Worth Protecting: Charting a Sustainable Course in the Great Lakes and St. Lawrence River Basin,* October 2001, http://www.oag-bvg.gc.ca/domino/reports.nsf/html/c101menu_e.html.
48. "Ecosystem Protection Ignored: Report," *National Post,* 26 September 2002.
49. Lester W. Milbrath, "A Governance Structure Designed to Learn Would Better Protect the Great Lakes Ecosystem," in *Perspectives on Ecosystem*

Management: A Reader, ed. Lynton K. Caldwell (Albany: State University of New York Press, 1988), 145.

50. Ibid., 47.
51. Ibid., 150.
52. Dana W. Kolpin et al., "Pharmaceuticals, Hormones and Other Organic Wastewater Contaminants in U.S. Streams, 1999–2000: A National Reconnaissance," *Environmental Science and Technology* 36 (2002): 1202.
53. "Here We Go Again: PBDEs," *Rachel's Environment and Health News*, 25 October 2001, http://www.rachel.org/bulletin/index.cfm?issue_ID =2109, accessed 17 December 2003.
54. Michael J. Donahue, "Commission Calls for New Advocacy Strategy for 107th Congress: Egrets, Alligators, Lake Trout and Eagles," Great Lakes Commission press release, 13 November 2000, http://www.glc.org/announce/00/11-00newstragtegy.html, accessed 13 October 2003.
55. Rahm Emanuel, "With No Cash, Great Lakes Plan a Washout," *Chicago Sun-Times*, 28 May 2002.
56. "Mayflies Make Driving a Hazard in Some Areas," *Columbus Dispatch*, 2 July 1996 and "It's Light's Out as Town Battles Mayfly Swarms," *Columbus Dispatch*, 7 July 1996.
57. Gene Warner, "WNY Bugged by Return of the Mayflies," *Buffalo News*, 6 July 2000.
58. Molly Kavanaugh, "Mayflies' Modest Comeback," *Cleveland Plain Dealer*, 11 July 1997.
59. D'Arcy Egan, "Entire Lake Erie System Welcomes Presence of Mayflies," *Cleveland Plain Dealer*, 23 June 1994.

Chapter 10

1. Henry A. Regier, "The Governance of the Shared Great Lakes Basin Ecosystem," in *Creating the Peaceable Kingdom and Other Essays on Canada*, ed. Victor Howard (East Lansing: Michigan State University Press, 1998), 125.
2. Interview with author, 27 June 2002.
3. Ibid.
4. Erik Ness, "Perrier Didn't Reckon on an Angry Citizenry When it Looked to Expand into the Midwest," *Grist Magazine*, 21 May 2000, http://www.gristmagazine.com/maindish/ness052101.asp.
5. Attorney General Jennifer Granholm to State Senator Christopher D. Dingell, State Representative Julie Dennis, and State Representative William O'Neil, Lansing, Mich., 13 September 2001.
6. "Bottled Water Fight Grows," *Detroit News*, 20 May 2001.

7. Great Spring Waters of America, "Memorandum to the Attorney General of Michigan Regarding the Issues Raised in the Letter Dated June 12, 2001 Directed to the Attorney General by Rep. Julie Dennis" (Greenwich, Conn., 9 July 2001).
8. James Olson, "Reply of Michigan Citizens for Water Conservation to GSWA/ Perrier's Memorandum to Attorney General Jennifer M. Granholm," 5.
9. Interview with author, 30 July 2002.
10. Ibid.
11. Ibid.
12. D. T. Long et al., "Evaluation of Directional Drilling under the Great Lakes, Michigan Environmental Science Board, Lansing, Michigan," http://www.michigan.gov/documents/dd-rpt_3722_7.pdf, accessed October 1997.
13. Lake Michigan Federation, *Lake Michigan Oil and Gas Drilling: Worth the Risk?* 2001. http://www.lakemichigan.org/conservation/oilreport.pdf, accessed October 13, 2003.
14. Chad D. Lerch, "Bill Would Punish City for Ban on Lake Drilling," *Muskegon Chronicle,* 11 June 2001.
15. "Michigan Citizens Agree: Oil and Water Don't Mix," League of Conservation Voters Education Fund press release, 28 August 2001.
16. John Charles Robbins, "State Senator: Slant Drilling 'Dead in Michigan,'" *Holland Sentinel,* 26 October 2001.
17. Governor John Engler, "Governor Will Not Sign Directional Drilling Ban," press release, 5 April 2002.
18. David Poulson, "NRC Approves Great Lakes Drilling," *Ann Arbor News,* 14 September 2001.
19. The firm of Belden, Russonello, and Stewart conducted the analysis of public opinion in the Great Lakes for the Biodiversity Project and the Joyce Foundation, releasing a final report in September 2002.
20. Belden, Russonello, and Stewart Research and Communications, "Protecting the Great Lakes: Responsibility to Awareness to Action, Summary Analysis of Public Opinion in Great Lakes States," (Washington, D.C.: September 2002). Conducted between 12 July 2002, and 28 July 2002, the poll sampled fifteen hundred thirty-nine adults living in the Great Lakes region.
21. Ibid.
22. Ibid.
23. "Guiding Lighthouses to a New Life: U.S. Handing 300 to Preservationists," *Chicago Tribune,* 6 July 2002.

24. "Call of the Deep: Love of Diving Has Led a Lakewood Science Teacher to Immerse Himself in Rescuing the History of the Great Lakes," *Cleveland Plain Dealer,* 2 August 1994.
25. "Beach Closings a Hot Issue: With Heat Wave to Hit, 3 Beaches Still Unavailable," *Chicago Tribune,* 6 August 2001.
26. "Linked to the Lakers: Boat Nerds Use Web Site to Display Their Passion for Great Lakes Freighters," *Bay City Times,* 25 May 2003.
27. Greatmich, "Great Lakes Fishing Report," http://www.greatmich.com/fishrep/report.htm, accessed 13 October 2003.
28. Great Lakes Cruising Club, founders award log, excerpts from "A Cruise to the North Channel of Lake Huron," by Peter F. Theis, http://www.glcclub.com.
29. "Surfing Superior: With the Nearest Ocean 1,500 Miles away, Intrepid Surfers Are Making Do on Lake Superior, Even Designing Boards Better Suited to the Fresh Water," *[Minneapolis] Pioneer Press,* 23 April 2002.
30. "On the Outside," interview with surfer Ben Rayner, http://www.lakesurf.com, accessed 21 December 2003.
31. "Surfer Named to Board of Lake Michigan Federation," *Holland Sentinel,* 24 September 2002.
32. National Pollution Discharge Elimination System (NPDES) of the U.S. Clean Water Act and Canada-Ontario Agreement (COA) to implement the Great Lakes Water Quality Agreement. For more information on the NPDES see the Michigan Department of Environmental Quality website at http://www.michigan.gov/deq/0,1607,7–135–3313_3682_3713–10197—,00.html, accessed 21 December 2003. See also: http://www.on.ec.gc.ca/laws/coa/agreement_e.html, accessed 21 December 2003.
33. Jan Abingdon, et al., "Implementing Ecosystem-Based Management: Lessons from the Great Lakes," *Journal of Environmental Planning and Management* 41, no. 1 (January 1998): 75.
34. Cynthia Price, personal communication with author, 15 August 2002.
35. W. J. Christie et al., "Managing the Great Lakes Basin as Home," *Journal of Great Lakes Research* 12, no. 1 (1986): 4.
36. David Israelson, *Silent Earth: The Politics of Our Survival* (Markham, Ontario: Viking, 1990), 215.

Index

Michigan State University Press is committed to preserving ancient forests and natural resources. We have elected to print this title on New Leaf EcoOffset 100, which is 100% recycled (100% post-consumer waste) and processed chlorine free (PCF). As a result of our paper choice, Michigan State University Press has saved the following natural resources*:

47	Trees (40 feet in height)
2,233	Pounds of Solid Waste
20,024	Gallons of Water
34	Million BTUs of Energy
4,401	Pounds of Greenhouse Gases
12	Pounds of Air Emissions (HAPs, VOCs, TRSs combined)
138	Pounds of Hazardous Effluent (BODs, TSSs, CODs, and AOXs combined)

We are a member of Green Press Initiative—a nonprofit program dedicated to supporting book publishers in maximizing their use of fiber that is not sourced from ancient or endangered forests. For more information about Green Press Initiative and the use of recycled paper in book publishing, please visit *www.greenpressinitiative.org.*

*Environmental benefits are calculated by New Leaf Paper based on research done by the Environmental Defense Fund and other members of the Paper Task Force who study the environmental impacts of the paper industry.